On the Ple

MW00699000

On the Pleasure Principle in Culture

Illusions Without Owners

Robert Pfaller

Translated by Lisa Rosenblatt,
with Charlotte Eckler and Camilla Nielsen

VERSO
London • New York

First published by Verso 2014
Translation © Lisa Rosenblatt 2014
First published as *Die Illusionen der anderen: Über das Lustprinzip in der Kultur*
© Suhrkamp Verlag 2002

1 3 5 7 9 10 8 6 4 2

Verso
UK: 6 Meard Street, London W1F 0EG
US: 20 Jay Street, Suite 1010, Brooklyn, NY 11201
www.versobooks.com

Verso is the imprint of New Left Books

ISBN-13: 978-1-78168-174-9 (PB)
ISBN-13: 978-1-78168-175-6 (HB)
eISBN-13: 978-1-78168-220-3 (US)
eISBN-13: 978-1-78168-643-0 (UK)

British Library Cataloguing in Publication Data
A catalogue record for this book is available from the British Library

Library of Congress Cataloging-in-Publication Data
A catalog record for this book is available from the Library of Congress

Typeset in Minion Pro by Hewer Text UK Ltd, Edinburgh, Scotland
Printed in the US by Maple Press

'Tis a vulgar Error to imagine Men live upon their own Wits, when generally it is upon others Follies . . . almost every Wind blows to Dover, *or* Holyhead *some fresh* Proprietor *amply qualified with sufficient* Stock.

Bernard Mandeville, *A Modest Defence of Publick Stews*

Contents

Introduction

Imagine you're sitting in a bar reading a newspaper, waiting for a friend. The friend arrives. He says hello, and then continues: 'Excuse me, can I have a quick look at your newspaper? I know it's silly, but I just have to know the score from yesterday's game.'

What we have here is a very special relationship between a subject and an illusion (in this case, the illusion that sports results really matter). The friend is in no way taken in by this illusion. On the contrary, he says that he knows quite well that it is silly, distancing himself from it. He does not claim allegiance to it, declare it as *his* illusion, or make any claim of ownership.

This is quite a different structure from the one we usually find. The ordinary relationship between an illusion and a subject is one in which the subject proudly attests to ownership – by professing, for example, a belief in God, or in human reason, or in self-regulation of the markets. Such subjects agree completely with their illusions and proudly claim ownership of them. They would never put themselves at a distance from these illusions, for instance, by saying things such as, 'I know it is quite foolish, but I have to go to church now,' or 'I know it is silly, but I believe in the self-regulation of markets.'

It thus appears that we are dealing with two different types of illusion: illusions with owners and illusions maintained by people who are not their owners; illusions with subjects and illusions without subjects. We are thus faced with a distinction based on a difference in the *forms* of illusion rather than a difference in their *content*: it is a distinction based on the relationship between subject and illusion, on the different ways in which people refer to these illusions (regardless of their contents).

In some cases, people identify with their illusions, which they often emphasize by adding the assertion, 'I believe (in) that, I really do.' On the contrary, in other cases, people 'know better'; they know that the illusion is 'nonsense' or 'something silly', and this knowledge seems to place an insurmountable gap between them and the illusion.

Whereas the first type is common and not difficult to detect, the second type of illusion, dismissed by knowing better, turns out to be

elusive – so much so that often it is difficult even to recognize its presence. The epistemological problem with regard to this form of illusion
initially rests on the fact that it is not easy to tell exactly who maintains such illusions. At first glance it might seem as if every illusion
must have at least one believer, as though those illusions that are not
one's own must necessarily belong to someone else. But might it be
possible that there are illusions that always belong to others, that are
never anyone's own illusions?[1]

This seems to be precisely the case for the illusion that sports
broadcasts, the horoscope and a number of other similar things are
actually important: they are obviously not *one's own illusions* (because
there is that better knowledge); thus, they are *those of others*. But
which others? Children? Ancestors? Fools? If not those in the know,
often we cannot really say who is meant to be their bearer. It is not
always possible to find those who aren't in the know. After all, who
actually says, 'I believe in the horoscope, and I am proud of it'? We are
dealing here with a form of illusion for which we are sometimes
unable to locate any believers at all. These illusions, which perhaps at
first seem to be the *others' illusions,* upon closer inspection prove to be
illusions without subjects.

A further difficulty in recognizing the presence of these illusions
without owners seems to stem from the assumption that knowledge
cancels them out. If someone has access to relevant knowledge, as a
result, they must be free of illusion. Perhaps they are aware of illusions
without owners; but does that really mean that those illusions have
power over them? Oddly enough, illusions without owners, without

---

1   Slavoj Žižek has formulated this type of thought most clearly: 'The
paradox . . . is such . . . that the shift is original and constitutive: there is no immediate,
self-present subjectivity that . . . belief can be attributed to and from which it was later
expropriated. There are several beliefs, and the most essential of them are "decentred"
right from the start: that is, they are the beliefs of others.' Slavoj Žižek 'Die Substitution
zwischen Interaktivität und Interpassivität', in Robert Pfaller, ed., *Interpassivität.
Studien über delegiertes Genießen* (Vienna/New York: Springer 2000), p. 14 ; English
translation, 'The Interpassive Subject', Centre Georges Pompidou, Traverses, 1998,
lacan.com/zizek-pompidou.htm. Some current philosophical advances seem to point
in a similar direction to this question of the possibility of illusions without subjects –
for example, those that search for the possibility of feelings without owners, or
experiences without subjects. See also Mario Perniola, *The Sex Appeal of the Inorganic*
(Athlone Contemporary European Thinkers), trans. Massimo Verdicchio (London:
Continuum, 2004), pp. 1ff, 127ff; Martin Jay, *Cultural Semantics: Keywords of Our Time*
(London: Athlone Press, 1998), pp. 46, 58–9.

subjects, are evident only in those who know better, precisely because they are always the illusions of others. Angry people slam their fist down on the table although everyone knows that the table is not guilty. Computer users know perfectly well that their machines are not equipped to respond to encouragement, yet they nonetheless talk persistently with their electronic darlings (which are, incidentally, sometimes given pet names) as if they could respond; and when a machine experiences a major mechanical breakdown, many users even resort to crude acts of violence, inflicting damage, hitting the machine, or even going so far as throwing it out of the window, as if the punished PC were actually capable of redeeming itself in response to the painful experience. When faced with the power of such illusions, people's knowledge does not seem to offer sufficient protection; quite the contrary, when considering the striking correlation between our knowing better and the illusions of others, we would even have to ask if knowing better does not somehow contribute to the power of these illusions. Is it possible that there are illusions that are not only not dismissed by knowing better, but are even first installed by it?

In addition to the problems of the bearer and the role of knowing better, the third difficulty is that of the compulsion that the illusions of others seem to exert. Although, due to their knowledge, bearers appear to be at a distance from these illusions, they are nonetheless obviously highly susceptible to them: 'I have to read the horoscope'; 'I have to see the ballgame on television right now.' Turning the key in the ignition of a car that doesn't immediately start, reasonable, civilized people, in particular, are often compelled to blurt out: 'Come on now, you can do it. Start!', and the like.[2] Those people, especially, who know that these types of reactions are childish, unimportant, and nonsensical are nonetheless unable to stop.[3] The others' illusions demand their immediate action. In comparison, some convinced believers appear more liberated with respect to their own beliefs: Catholics who miss mass can possibly visit a different one later in the day, whereas football fans have to see the game *live, in real time, on television*; strangely enough, they can

<hr />

2   A wonderful illustration is offered by the scene played by George Clooney in *Out of Sight* (dir. Steven Soderbergh, USA, 1998).

3   See also Gilles Deleuze and Félix Guattari, *Anti-Oedipus: Capitalism and Schizophrenia* (Minneapolis: University of Minnesota Press, 1983), p. 81: 'Oedipus is one of those things that becomes all the more dangerous the less people believe in it . . .'

never watch it later, from a recording. Why are the illusions of others more compelling than our own?

This compulsion is, by the way, often the only characteristic that allows us to recognize this form of illusion. The knowledge that produces a distance from such illusions is often so self-evident that it is not even worth mentioning (*à la*, 'I know perfectly well that the table is not at fault'). Based on the self-evidence of the knowledge, its object (the content of the illusion) often seems unthinkable, and is also never really thought. With illusions distanced by self-evident knowledge, we often do not even notice *that we are dealing with an illusion*. As Slavoj Žižek quite aptly remarks, not only do we not know how things really are, we do not even know how they appear to us. According to Žižek, if our boss is someone who we know is foolish and incompetent, we usually act with an odd respect. Despite our better knowledge, an appearance of respectability is called for.[4] This means, then, that we often do not even notice that something 'appears' to us. This realization adds a further challenge, formulating the problem of appearance in a new way. A strong philosophical tradition, embodied for example in the meditations of Descartes, examined the problem of appearance primarily in relation to one of its particular aspects – namely, that we see human beings but do not know whether they are mechanical figures; or, we see a city in the desert, and do not know whether it is a mirage. The content of such appearances would be manifest and evident; only their truth-value remains unknown. The illusions without owners, on the contrary, display exactly the opposite structure: we are entirely aware that they are not true; but the fact that we are nonetheless still defined by them, that we act on them, remains undetected. The problem does not concern a mere lifting of the veil of a manifest illusion for the benefit of a truth that lies hidden behind it. Instead, it concerns recognizing, at least, the additional presence of a veil where it seems as though nothing exists beyond self-evident, matter-of-fact knowledge of the truth.

The issue is not always one of having an image and not knowing whether or not it is a true image corresponding to reality. Often the problem consists, conversely, in having a thoroughly adequate picture of reality, and knowing that, but not knowing that, in addition, one also has another picture. We know exactly how things really are, and

---

4   See Žižek, 'Die Substitution', pp. 29–30.

perhaps believe that we don't believe in anything beyond that; and yet, without noticing, we are already wrapped up in an illusion without an owner – deeply and compulsively. Bang! That fist slams down on the table.

When it is not clear that we are dealing with an illusion, it is generally also difficult to recognize *the content of this illusion*. Why do people have to have music playing in a room, chew gum, doodle on paper while on the telephone, or drive around aimlessly? Where could there be an illusion in such seemingly simple, matter-of-fact, banal occurrences? For an illusion to take place, doesn't something at least have to be depicted, such as the deceptively realistic notepapers in *trompe-l'œil* painting,[5] which cast painted shadows on painted notice boards? Or can an illusion also be found in *non-representative* occurrences and products – such as in painting that comprises nothing but numbers or letters or lines on ruled paper?[6] The illusion without an owner, which has hitherto made itself noticeable only by the characteristic of compulsion, is quite often *an imagination without an image*.

Summarizing these first, rough observations, it is clear that we are dealing with illusions that (1) seem to have no bearer; (2) are not dismissed by knowing better, but instead even seem to be strengthened by it; (3) exert themselves in the form of a compulsion, albeit foreign and kept at a distance through knowledge; (4) often remain unnoticed; and (5) appear to be without content.

This form of illusion seems to contradict five seemingly plausible principles – namely, the assumptions that (1) there is a bearer for every illusion; (2) knowing better dismisses the corresponding illusion (or at least, if it does not dismiss it, does not strengthen it); (3) only our own, recognized illusions can be mandatory or compulsory for us; (4) when we imagine something, perhaps we do not know the truth but at least we know the illusion; and (5) we can immediately identify the content of every illusion.

If these characterizations are accurate, then the illusions without owners stir up a whole series of theoretical problems. Apart from those issues related to an explanation of their own paradoxical

---

5   See also, for example, C. N. Gijsbrechts, 'Trompe-l'oeil 1672' (illustration 128), and W. V. Nymegen, 'Trompe l'oeil mit der Bastille' (illustration 107), both in Patrick Mauriès, ed., *Le trompe l'oeil. De l'antiquité au XXe siècle* (Paris: Gallimard 1996).

6   See also, for example, the works by Roman Opalka, On Kawara and Hanne Darboven.

structure, they afford us the opportunity to ask more generally what it means to imagine something, or to be involved with illusions and the relationship of others' illusions to those illusions that we call our own, of which we are often quite proud and which we 'really believe in'. Taking this into consideration, acquiring a new, disturbingly uncanny nature is mainly the question of what 'enlightenment' might mean – that is, what it means to rid oneself of illusions through insight.

Research on this issue faces an extremely difficult situation. The problem of the illusion's *form* is seldom clearly posed. And even when it is posed, the attempt is usually made to solve the problem exclusively through information about the *content* of the illusion. Paul Veyne, for example, raised a number of very precise questions that touch upon our theme in his treatise *Did the Greeks Believe in Their Myths?* Veyne writes: 'How is it possible to half-believe, or to believe in contradictory things?'[7] He proposes the example of an Ethiopian tribe, the Dorzé, who believe that the leopard is a Christian animal and that it observes days of fast; nonetheless, they guard their live-stock on these days in order to protect them from leopards.[8] This is a good example of an illusion that is kept at a distance through knowing better: the religious myth seems to have been dismissed by an 'enlight-ened' practice. Veyne approaches the issue of ancient Greek 'theology' in a similar way. At first glance, the question arises of whether anyone could have ever seriously 'believed in' this theology – or at least the question is posed by those who have acquired their notion of religion from monotheistic religions. This is mainly because of the amazingly low moral standards among gods of the ancient world, rather than any possible contradictions (of which other theologies are no less at risk). Gods who exhibit behaviour that is frequently far less moral than that of people (or at least the more decent people) raise doubts about whether it was ever possible to believe in this type of mythol-ogy; or, at the very least, such deities bring up the question of what it actually means to believe in gods like these.[9]

Rather than following his own tracks and arriving at the conclu-sion that there must have been various historical forms constituting

---

7   Paul Veyne, *Did the Greeks Believe in Their Myths? An Essay on the Constitutive Imagination*, transl. Paula Wissing (Chicago: University of Chicago Press, 1988), p. xi.

8   Ibid., p. xi.

9   Ibid.

the meaning of 'belief', Veyne hastily resorts to the assumption 'that truth is the most variable of all measures', which he considers 'Nietzschean'.[10] Belief is always the same, but its contents change – according to the particular, historical transcendental conditions: one cultural construction allows one thing to appear plausible, another cultural construction, something else. Following Veyne, we must consequently answer 'yes' to the question of whether or not the Greeks believed in their myths.[11]

Veyne's theory surmises that belief occurs in the same way every time, but in one case it is belief in one thing, and in another, something else. And we only erroneously consider our own uncertain knowledge (about Tokyo's existence[12] or the truth of Einstein's theory[13]) as certain, and the assumptions of other epochs, on the contrary, as questionable or foolish. For this reason, things that were once self-evident to others seem peculiar to us. Without noticing, Veyne silences his own question with a series of relativistic platitudes, which might be true yet offer no answers to his own, very interesting question.

A remark from Friedrich Engels could have shown him the way out of this cul-de-sac. In his text from 1884, *The Origin of the Family, Private Property, and the State*, Engels maintained 'that Bachofen believe[d] at least as much as Aeschylus did in the Furies, Apollo, and Athena.'[14] According to Engels, the nineteenth-century scholar Bachofen had the same belief as Aeschylus. Consequently, there is not necessarily a difference in the content of the beliefs of two different epochs, as Veyne assumed, so that the one believes in one thing and the other in something else. Instead, in this case, members of different epochs in fact have the same content to their beliefs. The difference between them lies elsewhere: Bachofen, Engels states, believed 'at least as much' in the Greek myths as had the ancient poet. Does that mean that he might possibly have believed in them *even more* than

---

10   See ibid., pp. 117, 118.

11   See ibid., p. 129.

12   See ibid., p. 28.

13   See ibid, p. 117.

14   Friedrich Engels, *The Origin of the Family, Private Property and the State* (New York: Pathfinder Press, 1973), p. 14. For the translation used here, see Friedrich Engels, *Origins of the Family, Private Property, and the State*, preface to the fourth edition (1891), at marxists.org. See also Deleuze and Guattari, *Anti-Oedipus*, p. 107.

Aeschylus had? With this phrase, Engels allows us to imagine something quite striking: it is not at all the case that, due to their specific transcendental tenets from this historical epoch, Greek myths could appear plausible only to the Greeks and must seem absurd to all other cultures or epochs. On the contrary: they appeared perhaps even more plausible to the nineteenth-century scholars than they had to the Greeks themselves. The transcultural misunderstanding that Engels identifies here takes exactly the opposite form than Veyne assumed: the error is not made in considering one's own culture as justified and the other as absurd; instead, it involves granting the foreign culture more plausibility and showing it less scepticism than that culture itself would have done. The scholar pursues an exaggerated appropriation. He assigns the foreign culture a form of belief that is entirely foreign to it. He identifies with illusions that may have been mere illusions without owners for the culture that produced them. According to Engels, what Bachofen treated as though it were the equivalent of the Ten Commandments – that is, as a conviction in which one must believe – might have had the same status for Aeschylus as Santa Claus does for us.

That is to say, belief cannot always have meant the same thing. The same content can therefore be believed in, in one form (the ironic distance of antiquity) and then in another (the respectful appropriation of the nineteenth-century scholar). There is no correlation, as Veyne assumes, between the form and content of a belief, so that every epoch necessarily only believes in its own content. Some epochs do believe in other epochs' contents; and perhaps they believe in them just as strongly as in their own (or even more so) – and even more than the other epoch believed in its own content. Thus, what changes is not simply the content of the belief, which does not necessarily always change. Instead, sometimes it is only the form of belief associated with the content that changes.

It is not certain, however, that the ancient Greeks, for their part, had a culture in mind that filled the same role as theirs did for Bachofen. If the Greeks believed in their own content with reserve, then they did not necessarily have other contents in which they believed with any less reserve. Perhaps it was characteristic of this ancient Greek culture that they maintained beliefs *exclusively* in the distanced form of illusions without owners. What was special about this Greek culture was not that they believed in strange gods, but rather that their form of belief was one of divided, distanced belief – the form Veyne introduced so aptly with the example of the Ethiopian myth of the Christian leopards. What would separate Greek antiquity from some later epochs would be a historical break, in terms not of the content but more of the form of social illusion. Cultures with distanced beliefs are distinct from cultures that possess forms of appropriated beliefs and nurture illusions with which they proudly identify.

To insist on this break, and thereby on the appearance of something that had previously not existed, also seems more closely aligned with Nietzsche's position than with the relativism Veyne derives from it. Nietzsche says that all truths are illusions,[15] but also that not every epoch has thought that equally. Instead, at a certain point in history something new suddenly appears – namely, the illusion of possessing an illusion that is not an illusion. At some point in history, the sceptical, distanced illusion of the other lost its dominance as the sole form of social illusion. A new form – the form with which we are familiar, that of *our own illusions*, in which we believe with a true belief, with conviction – began to dominate over the illusion of the other, to produce truth-effects. When the bearers begin to believe truly in their illusions, rather than keeping them at a distance through knowing better, their illusions become their truths. Nietzsche's whole argument can be grasped as an attempt to mark the historical point at which this happened – to clarify the conditions that led to the development of *one's own illusion* as truth.

Truth as an illusion in which one truly believes is not an epistemological form on its own; it does not fulfil any additional, novel cognitive function with regard to prior knowledge. The cognitive function was already fulfilled quite well by the knowledge that was used to keep the illusion at a distance. Truth, on the contrary, is first and foremost something practical, a position: it is that which one believes. And we believe in the truth just as we believe in our morals. For Nietzsche, the historical development of truth (as one's own illusion) is thus a moral development;[16] its condition is the subject of a genealogy of morality.

---

15   See Veyne, *Did the Greeks Believe in Their Myths?*, p. xi.
16   See Friedrich Nietzsche, 'Beyond Good and Evil', in *Basic Writings of Nietzsche*, transl. and ed. Walter Kaufmann (New York: Modern Library, 2000), p. 187.

The problem that Veyne addresses – namely, whether anyone 'really' and 'truly' believes in something, or perhaps only 'halfway' – is not raised by truth as a cognitive achievement, but, rather, by truth tied to a moral. As we have seen, this problem does not emerge from the contradictions of Greek mythology, but is instead a result of the low moral standards of the Greek gods. Is it possible to believe in gods that deceive, rob, commit adultery, manipulate duels, and succumb to what are meant to be lowly emotions such as sexual desire, injured pride and vanity, jealousy, envy and anger? Can such characters seriously be called gods?[17] The problem of belief is not an intellectual one, but a moral one. The difficulty lies not in conceiving intellectually of the idea that raises the problem of credibility, but rather in the *ideal's lack of suitability for identification.*[18]

Any attempt to deal with this solely at an intellectual, epistemological level fails to address the problem. The issue is not 'historical transcendentalism', which granted the Greek gods more or less plausibility in certain epochs. Instead, it is the issue of whether all cultures need ideals with which to identify. Might it be possible that some cultures can survive without moral ideals, or without the necessity to identify with them? Cultures without morals? How might an ideological system function – particularly in a so-called high culture – if there are no gods, or if the gods are even lowlier than the people?

Veyne evades his own question and conceals its disturbing, uncanny nature under the more familiar problematic embodied in his answers. This appears *symptomatic* – not only in the sense of the '"symptomatic" reading' presented by Louis Althusser, which taught that a theory's answers should be compared with its questions;[19] but it

---

17   This problem already surfaces in ancient Greece. The 'monotheistic' pre-Socratic Xenophanes critically remarked: 'Homer and Hesiod have ascribed to the gods everything which is shame (*oneidea*) and blame (*psogos*) for human beings: stealing, committing adultery, and deceiving one another.' Xenophanes of Colophon, Sextus Empiricus, *Adversus Mathematicos* IX. 193, at csun.edu. See G. S. Kirk, J. E. Raven and M. Schofield, *The Presocratic Philosophers*, 2nd edn (Cambridge: CUP, 1994), p. 163; see also Karl Popper, 'Duldsamkeit und intellektuelle Verantwortung', in *Offene Gesellschaft – offenes Universum. Franz Kreuzer im Gespräch mit Karl Popper* (Vienna: Deuticke, 1983) pp. 103–17.

18   Veyne confirms that, when he describes the Christians' rejection of the pagan gods, 'they did not call the myths "vain fables" so much as . . . "unworthy ideas"' (*Did the Greeks Believe in Their Myths?*, p. 117).

19   See also Louis Althusser and Etienne Balibar, Reading Capital, trans. Ben Brewster (New York: Verso, 1997), p. 28.

also seems to be the typical and inevitable result of the crisis of a particular way of thinking nowadays – a postmodern perspective that no longer sees any difference in the face of so many differences. *Everyone believes their own thing* – this simple formula, characteristic of some postmodern theories, eliminates the question of whether it might be possible that *some believe the other's things*, and thus also eliminates the search for the differences in the *form* (and not only in the content) of belief. Here, relativism erects an epistemological obstacle.

Breaking through this epistemological obstacle seems important for two reasons: first, to avoid a crucial contemporary misunderstanding. Postmodern theory fancies itself a formation that – perhaps for the first time since the sceptical positions of classical antiquity – has achieved a distanced relationship to all 'great narratives'. All others, accordingly, believe strongly in one thing or another; only postmodernism believes in nothing, the theory exclaims, proudly – but not as cleverly as Madame de V*** in Sterne's *Sentimental Journey*,[20] who tells her guest in short, that she believed nothing. But at least postmodern theory believes – as we have seen – that belief has always been the same. It is thereby unable to recognize those historical as well as contemporary phenomena in which a distanced relationship to certain illusions was and is practised. And starting from this wrong assumption, postmodern theory fancies itself more sceptical than it actually is. But, most importantly, it does not notice that its form of alleged non-belief fulfils exactly the same affective conditions as every conviction in which one believes: postmodern scepticism, like every illusion of one's own, is a specific way of accommodating the libido that, instead of producing pleasure, first and foremost produces self-esteem. It creates the same ego-fixated enjoyment of those who believe in everything that they believe in, regardless of what it is, only in order to believe in themselves – including those who do not believe in anything else *but* themselves.

This libidinal function of postmodern scepticism, focused on the production of self-esteem, is the second reason why it seems necessary to break through the epistemological obstacle it erects. Not only does its sceptical *theoretical claim* seem dubious – so does its *promise*

---

20   Laurence Sterne, *A Sentimental Journey Through France and Italy: By Mr. Yorick*, (Basil: J. J. Tourneisen, 1796), p. 153.

of happiness. Thus, just as postmodern ideology claims to correspond with the scepticism of classical antiquity at the theoretical level, at the affective level it wants to be thought of as a return to the pleasure – lost to modernism – in games, myths, infantilism, irony and kitsch. On the contrary, I want to show that postmodernism, rather than being a thorough critique of Enlightenment-based modernism, is merely an extension of the same ascetic enterprise carried out by different, possibly more efficient means. One sign of this can be observed in the rampant self-pity present since the emergence of postmodern ideology. Whereas modernism produced an enthusiastic daring and a certain tolerance for frustration with its utopian promises, the disappearance of utopia from Western societies has mainly resulted in a certain passion for lamenting; a lust for airing grievances, which consumes all other pleasures; the yearning to be a victim.[21] These postmodern activities emerging from a tristful passion testify to an organization of affects that can be considered typical of ascetic ideologies.

The critique presented here, based on the concept of the illusion without an owner, thus applies equally to modern and postmodern ideologies. It sees the ascetic modern and the merely purportedly pleasure-friendly postmodern as accomplices – an 'epistemological pair' as defined by Gaston Bachelard.[22] Both obey the paradigm of *one's own illusion.* They create the same specific way of accommodating the libido, the desire for one's own self. This type of desire, as we would like to show, forms the substance of every ascetic, tristful passion that has advanced through Western society since the Enlightenment – and has been given even more strength by postmodernism. And this advancing march of tristful passions seems to be the main ideological cause of the amazing acceptance of, and weak resistance to, neoliberalism's economic policies in Western societies: Is it not obvious how the government is able to destroy the welfare state, limit the educational system to a few elites, and push major portions of the population to the borders of a so-called 'new poverty' without encountering enraged and organized revolt? Indeed, so-called

---

21   See also Robert Hughes, *Culture of Complaint: The Fraying of America* (New York: OUP, 1993), and Pascal Bruckner, *The Temptation of Innocence: Living in the Age of Entitlement* (New York: Algora, 2000).

22   See Gaston Bachelard, *Le Rationalisme appliqué* (Paris: PUF, 1949), p. 5.

'cutbacks' and the intensified dismantling of protective mechanisms are even greeted with pleasure. The form of *one's own illusion* creates – as I hope ultimately to show (on the basis of the work of Spinoza, Reich, and Deleuze/Guattari) – a desire for sacrifice, which makes people partial to so-called austerity measures – the destruction of public spheres and goods – as well as political oppression. To oppose that, I want to render *illusions of the others* visible, and make them conceivable as an alternative form of ideologically induced social cohesion. In doing so, we can counter the advance of ascetic tendencies by identifying them as such, even when they purport to be the advance of the opposite – for example, disguised as fun culture.

The main task of this study is thus an attempt to break through an epistemological obstacle, generating possible ways of thinking at a point that presently appears barred by massive theoretical blockages. These blockages have been penetrated by only very few theoretical advances, which are typically entirely unaware of one another. Such circumstances create a rather unusual 'research situation' and rather unusual methods. Whereas other questions – ideally, at least – can and must be resolved mostly through continuous, measured steps, this question seems to call for a leap. Whereas other problems can be solved through a quantitative gain in knowledge, this paradox of illusions without subjects seems to confront theory steadily with an 'all or nothing' approach.

The present work proceeds by tracking down the individual attempts made in this field, studying them, and bringing them together. It seems that often one theory has asked precisely the question for which another has produced the answer (possibly without ever having posed the question). Thus, just a few authors provide the pillars of this investigation: Mannoni, Huizinga, Žižek, Wittgenstein, Spinoza, Freud, Althusser, Pascal, and Alain. And even with these authors, sometimes it was necessary to search *in the gaps in their texts* for the questions they ask unknowingly, and in the unwitting answers they provide, rather than limit my search to the texts themselves, for information about the proposed problem.

This text does not expand its argument beyond the specified authors; expansion is not possible in this case, and any pretence of it would be deceptive. Although the discussion does not exclude the possibility of finding other foundations, an attempt is made to show how sceptical we should be in dealing with such expectations. The discoveries will not be readily available; they will not be found in close proximity to others; and lengthy infiltration is required to recognize discoveries as such, and to clarify their relevance to one another. Without making any claim to being exhaustive, this work does claim to provide an entry into the theme, and create the greatest possible clarity at those points where little evidence is available. When philosophy sets out to overcome epistemological obstacles, engaging with just a few theses from a few philosophers is a typical method – perhaps even the only possible one.

Precisely for these reasons, the fact that we are standing on the shoulders of others in making our discoveries, as Pascal put it, is more pertinent here than it is in less unusual research situations. We are looking for a way to move from shoulder to shoulder, so that we can look from different angles in order to continually improve our view over the wall.

CHAPTER ONE

Interpassivity: Fleeing from Enjoyment, and the Objective Illusion

The problem of illusions without owners becomes apparent through interpassivity – a different, equally paradoxical issue. When dealing with people who display the tendency to delegate their own enjoyment to other people or to an apparatus, we are here unsuspectingly confronted with the fact that people enact illusions dramatically, with great precision, without noticing in the slightest that they are doing so. It is obvious that they know better, but they behave contrary to this knowledge in compliance with illusions of which they are not even aware. They produce imaginations without any image. The method that interpassive subjects employ in their flight from enjoyment thereby leads us to the trail of imaginations without owners. In what follows, my aim is to reconstruct as succinctly as possible the opening that leads from the method of interpassivity to illusions without subjects, without delving into the complex and intricate questions posed by the motives for the interpassive subject's behaviour.[1] I therefore refrain from lending plausibility to all of the individual theses that further examples might possibly provide, and, at every tenet of the argument, focus only on the one key example leading directly to the subsequent theoretical assumption. This reconstruction appears useful not only because all cases of interpassivity are examples of illusions without owners, but also because the concept of interpassivity contains a useful analytical tool that can be applied in subsequent chapters with reference to other phenomena.

HOW TO AMUSE ONESELF *OBJECTIVELY*

At the beginning of the 1990s, when the art world was dominated by a seemingly omnipresent discourse about 'interactivity', Slavoj Žižek made an extremely astute comment that was a significant break from the discourse. He maintained that television sitcoms using 'canned

---

1 See also the many contributions concerned with this problem in Pfaller, *Interpassivität*.

laughter' are actually laughing at their own jokes and funny situations *on behalf of the viewers*. According to Žižek, viewers can be perfectly amused without having to follow the content of the sitcoms, and even without having to laugh:

> Why this laughter? The first possible answer – that it serves to remind us when to laugh – is interesting enough, because it simply implies that laughter is a matter of duty and not of some spontaneous feeling; but this answer is not sufficient because we do not usually laugh. The only correct answer would be that the Other – embodied in the television set – is relieving us even of our duty to laugh – is laughing instead of us.
>
> So even if, tired from a hard day's stupid work, all evening we did nothing but gaze drowsily into the television screen, we can say afterwards that, objectively, through the medium of the other, we had a really good time.[2]

Žižek here illustrates a Lacanian thesis about the role of the chorus in Greek tragedy. In a passage that has rarely been treated by commentators, Lacan developed a unique perspective:

> Next then in a tragedy, there is a Chorus. And what is a Chorus? You will be told that it's you yourselves. Or perhaps that it isn't you. But that's not the point. Means are involved here, emotional means. In my view, the Chorus is people who are moved.
>
> Therefore, look closely before telling yourself that emotions are engaged in this purification. They are engaged, along with others, when at the end they have to be pacified by some artifice or other. But that doesn't mean to say that they are directly engaged . . . Your emotions are taken charge of by the healthy order displayed on the stage. The Chorus takes care of them. The emotional commentary is done for you . . . Therefore, you don't have to worry; even if you don't feel anything, the Chorus will feel in your stead. Why after all can one not imagine that the effect on you may be achieved, at least a small dose of it, even if you didn't tremble that much? To be honest, I'm not sure if the spectator ever trembles that much.[3]

---

2   Slavoj Žižek, *The Sublime Object of Ideology* (London/New York: Verso, 1989), p. 35.

3   Jacques Lacan, *The Ethics of Psychoanalysis 1959–1960, Seminar VII* (New York: W.W. Norton & Co., 1992), p. 252.

From these seemingly paradoxical examples – canned laughter and the Greek chorus (in Lacan's interpretation) – Žižek drew the conclusion that our supposedly most intimate feelings can be transferred or delegated to others. Our feelings and convictions are therefore not internal, but rather can lead an external, 'objective' existence: a television sitcom can laugh for me; weepers can mourn in my place; a Tibetan prayer wheel can pray for me;[4] and a mythical being, such as the renowned 'ordinary man in the street', can take my place and be convinced of things that I cannot take seriously.[5] The respective attitude or conviction is realized through these external agents. As Žižek states,

> the wheel itself is praying for me, instead of me – or, more precisely, I myself am praying through the medium of the wheel. The beauty of it is that in my psychological interior I can think about whatever I want, I can yield to the most dirty and obscene fantasies, and it does not matter because – to use a good old Stalinist expression – whatever I am thinking, objectively I am praying.[6]

INTERPASSIVITY: DO-IT-ALL ARTWORKS THAT EVEN INCLUDE THEIR OWN RECEPTION

Žižek's contemplations on canned laughter and the Greek chorus make it possible to derive another conclusion relevant for art theory: apparently, there are artworks that already contain their own viewing and reception. And there are viewers who want it that way. It seems that they would prefer to be replaced than to feel their own laughter, their own fear, or their own sympathy. These are thus artworks and viewers who present us with exactly the opposite of what the theory of interactivity so persistently preaches. Whereas interactivity entails shifting a part of the artistic production ('activity') from the artwork to the viewer, here the opposite occurs: the viewing ('passivity') is shifted from the viewer to the artwork. I have decided to call this type of displacement 'interpassivity'.

Interactive art attempts to activate its viewers: in interactive art, viewers are not only required to view the artwork, but also to

---

4   For more on these examples, see Žižek, *Sublime Object of Ideology*, pp. 33–5.
5   See Žižek, 'Die Substitution', p. 14.
6   Žižek, *Sublime Object of Ideology*, p. 34.

participate in its production. For interpassive artworks, however, the opposite seems to be the case: viewers are not required to participate; moreover, they are not even required to view. The work is there, completely finished – not only completely produced, but completely consumed as well. Contained within such works is not simply the necessary activity, but also the requisite passivity. Interpassive art absolves viewers of any necessary activity whatsoever, and also of their passivity. They can now be even more passive than passive. Deprived even of their passivity, they end up in the uncanny hereafter of their couch-potato existence.

FROM ART'S SELF-VIEWING TO DELEGATED ENJOYMENT IN GENERAL

The discovery that the sitcom's canned laughter and the Greek trage-dy's chorus present examples of self-viewing artworks, and can therefore be understood as cases of interpassivity, allows us to draw a further conclusion. Here, what is delegated is the reception of art – including the enjoyment of art. *Interpassivity comprises delegated enjoyment.* Not only can laughing at a sitcom be left to others, but also the act of watching television: rather than watching our favourite shows, we can record them and never watch the recording. It is as though the recorder has already watched for us. This opens up an entire series of everyday interpassive phenomena: Is it mere coincidence that travellers immediately hold a camera up to their eyes for protection when looking at a monument? Might it even be possible to say that they go so far as to place their friends, to whom they will later show the snapshots of their vacation, between themselves and the pictures that the camera takes? Isn't the utterly common statement 'How interesting!' a downright negation in the Freudian sense? Doesn't it really mean: 'That doesn't interest me in the slightest!' And isn't there an entire genre of 'interesting' books (with titles such as 'The Etruscans') that show up in shops just before Christmas: books that no one ever reads, but everyone gets as gifts? And in electronic media, isn't there a steady stream of new forms of actors and avatars constantly turning up in place of people – for example, in chat rooms, on Facebook, Twitter, and other 'second lives'?[7]

---

7   See Mathias Fuchs, 'Disembodied Online' in Pfaller, *Interpassivität*, pp. 33–8.

In addition to the artistic aspect of the matter – delegated viewing – there is also a more general, economic aspect – namely, delegated consumption. Interpassivity can be understood as every movement that shifts the consumption of a product from the consumer to a delegated consumption agency. This type of consumption agency can be either already contained in the product (such as the canned laughter in the sitcom) or added to the product (such as a recording device in a television set). The role of this agency is embodied by persons, machines, animals, plants, and so on (which then function as *interpassive media*). Consumers who tend towards this delegation of their pleasure are identified as *interpassive subjects*.

The theory of interactivity has assumed a highly questionable conceptual classification, with artistic production and 'activity' on the one hand, and art reception and 'passivity' on the other. Yet, from the more general, economic perspective, it is now possible to speak on firmer ground of 'activity' and 'passivity': production is activity; consumption, however, is passivity. Whether a process is active or passive depends on whether something consumable is produced or consumed.

If we regard interpassivity as delegated enjoyment, then it is necessary to change the questions that are posed along Žižek's path of investigation – the inquiry into the possibility of delegating convictions, feelings, and so on. This change also enables a consideration of Žižek's examples from a new perspective: the delegation of convictions and feelings creates special cases of the general principle of delegated enjoyment that we have now been able to identify. The fact that Tibetan belief can be delegated to a prayer wheel, for example, is just as much an example of delegated or substituted consumption as the delegation of Christian belief to a burning candle representing a Catholic. The so-called 'comforts of religion' are the consumable elements. Worshippers consume them on a regular basis, thus the producers of religion must constantly produce them. The producers of Christian belief, for example, also conceive of this belief as just such a consumer item, and charge for its consumption in the form of a church tax or tithes. In the interpassive case, the prayer wheel and the candle consume the commodity of religion in place of the worshippers. What we are dealing with here is not merely substituted belief, feeling or thought, but, rather, substituted consumption or enjoyment.

Whereas Žižek's thesis states: *feelings and convictions can exist externally*, our double thesis states: *1. There are artworks that view themselves; and 2. there are consumers who want to be replaced by something that consumes in their place.* Fortunately, there is strong support in the art world for these apparently utterly paradoxical considerations. Not only in philosophy, but also in art, people have begun to discover the varieties of delegated consumption. A series of contemporary artistic works thematize common interpassive phenomena: artists engaged in so-called service art, for example, offer to take the viewer's place at a rendezvous, or trash their cars, or correspond with their acquaintances.[8]

Numerous artworks also include in their form the possibility of whether to avoid or engage with interpassive reception. Jenny Holzer's text installations, for example, seem to repeat the methods of the Tibetan prayer wheel. Holzer's aesthetic principle comprises creating such a strong presence for texts in a public space that it has become seemingly unnecessary to read them. The texts themselves, their 'truisms', also seem to correspond with that principle – they appear to be no one's 'truths', meant for no one in particular. For an audience that has grown weary of reading, they bring a pleasant moment of relief. Interpassivity thus builds a formal principle of contemporary art. It is the cause of its specific aesthetic effects.

From this perspective, it becomes possible to gain a general understanding of the massive emergence of texts within the fine arts in recent decades. Why are theoretical texts presented on the walls of exhibitions, in videos, installations or performances, and not in books?[9] Do the fine arts, with their love of theory, serve as the last aid for a culture that – as Marshall McLuhan concluded – has reached the final stages of its reading ability? (Similar to the way in which the prayer wheel stood at the beginning stages of literacy?)

---

8   See the artworks by Ruth Kaaserer, Astrid Benzer, Ronald Eckelt, Martin Kerschbaumsteiner, and San Keller; cf. for example, 'Kunstaktion "Arbeit" Teil1 – "ausgraben"', documentary of an artistic action in 1998, posted on YouTube by 'interpassiv' on Jan. 22, 2009, and 'Kunstaktion "Arbeit" Teil2 – "zuschuetten"', documentary of an artistic action in 1998, posted on YouTube by 'interpassiv' on Jan. 22, 2009; see also Pfaller, *Interpassivität*, pp. 53–4.

9   See also Arthur C. Danto, *The Philosophical Disenfranchisement of Art* (New York: Columbia University Press, 1986), pp. ixff.

The steady growth in the ranks of art curators also seems to be an example of interpassivity. Don't they in fact view the curated art, replacing traditional viewers who have recently become scarce (for example, because they have been re-educated by the interactive installations to become active artists)? And the numerous video installations in major exhibitions, whose length regularly surpasses (many times over) the time spent by even the most patient viewers – aren't they also self-viewing apparatuses, which in an interpassive way mediate to exhibition visitors the feeling of having seen something (and to non-visitors, the feeling of not having to see)?[10] Isn't there a peculiar conformity here, such that the viewers (who actually see only very little) perceive the situation *that there is a lot to see*, in such a way that it seems as though they have seen a lot?

THE FLIGHT FROM PLEASURE

The next question, then, is the following: Is it possible that interpassive subjects don't want their enjoyment? There is evidence for this assumption. Žižek's text, for example, reveals a mischievous pleasure derived from escaping, via canned laughter, the experience of being amused by television comedy.[11] The remark by Klaus Heinrich – that art collectors would most like to banish their collection to a safe, where they don't have to look at it – also points in this direction.[12] And doesn't the popularity of interactive art prove that the art viewer only wants to create art, but does not want to view any – or at least not anyone else's?

An initial 'soft-core' explanation of interpassivity hereby proves insufficient: the delegation of enjoyment is applied not only in

---

10   See also Wolfgang Kemp, 'Echtmensch im Kosmodrom', in *Die Zeit*, 31 May 2000, p. 46.

11   The Lacanian study of interpassivity repeatedly asks what happens to *jouissance* – enjoyment, in Lacan's sense – in cases of represented pleasure. Žižek's mischievous pleasure at the success of his delegated laughter seems to offer an answer to this question: the interpassive subject's joy at escaping enjoyment is *jouissance*. And is the expression 'mischievous pleasure' not a precise counterpart to the likewise slightly devious connotations of the French term 'jouissance'? See also Bruce Fink, *A Clinical Introduction to Lacanian Psychoanalysis: Theory and Technique* (Cambridge, MA/ London: Harvard University Press, 1997), p. 9: 'The term "jouissance" nicely captures the notion of getting off by any means necessary, however clean or dirty.'

12   See Klaus Heinrich, *anfangen mit freud* (Basel/Frankfurt am Main: Stroemfeld [Roter Stern], 1997), p. 55.

situations where direct and personal enjoyment is impossible. Inter-passivity is not just a method of 'extended', indirect consumption that increases one's (necessarily limited) direct consumerist capacities. Instead, we have to tackle a 'hard-core' explanation straight on: interpassive subjects are actually fleeing from their enjoyment. They even avoid it in those situations where personally experiencing it would be easy. Owners of recording devices, for example, watch less television once they have the recorder than they did when they owned only the television set.[13] And travellers, who are certainly capable of viewing scenic attractions themselves, hold a camera to their eyes as if by reflex.

This poses two fundamental questions. First, the *reason* for inter-passivity: Why don't people want to enjoy? And why do they choose the most complicated form of substitution instead of just leaving things be? Why are they so intent on someone else taking over the enjoyment that they don't want? Why do they undertake measures that work simultaneously for and against enjoyment?

And second, how does this delegation work? What *method* do interpassive subjects use? What gives the represented subjects the feeling (or, more precisely, the often unconscious certainty) of being represented? How is it possible that they treat the television's mechanical laughter as equivalent to their own laughter? What is the connection between that which is replaced and its replacement or delegate? Why don't we perceive the laughter of others as simply *their* laughter? And why is one's own not-laughing in no way understood as not-laughing, but instead as an effect of the successful delegation of laughter? It appears that these two fundamental issues are interdependent. The issue of methods seems to provide a key for understanding the reasons for interpassivity.

THE OBJECTIVE ILLUSION

In order to track down the riddle of why interpassive people do not want their own enjoyment, first we will investigate the methods they use for representation: What constitutes the interpassive subject's certainty that they are represented by something or someone else? In Žižek's examples – the Tibetan prayer wheel, canned laughter, the

---

13   See also Žižek, 'Die Substitution', p. 21.

Greek chorus, mourners, and so on – it soon becomes clear that one obvious answer can be eliminated: the certainty of delegation in no way has to do with a *subjective illusion* held by the person who delegates.

Both the effect and that way it is achieved are usually not conscious acts on the part of the actors. As a rule, actors don't believe in the possibility of delegation, and they are not aware – or, if so, only in a distorted way – of the relief effect achieved through delegation. When Tibetan prayer-wheel users imagine something, then it is the opposite: namely, *not* being perfectly represented by the rotating prayer wheel. Their illusion – to remain with Žižek's example – is that they were merely clinging to their obscene fantasies rather than praying. In truth, however, as Žižek remarks, they have prayed 'objectively'. Excessive video-recorder users, too, deceive themselves by falling back on 'general explanations' about the actual benefits they gain from the recording. They really believe that they will watch the programmes at a later date, and don't even notice that they have already 'objectively' seen them (and have already experienced complete relief at having done so).

Interpassive subjects neither imagine the possibility of having a vicarious experience of their enjoyment, nor entertain the illusion of the success of their actions through a delegate – even when such success is actually present. The illusion is not theirs; instead, the interpassive subjects seem to 'not get it' in a double sense: in full 'knowledge' of the alleged unsuitability of an interpassive process, the actors nonetheless carry it out, and then actually obtain successful results from it – yet once again conceal these results from themselves.

Thus, it is not the interpassive subjects who imagine the possibility of having a delegate – they often don't even think of it. This representation is, instead, something that can only be described by the paradoxical-seeming concept of an *objective illusion*. The illusion is objective for two reasons: (1) someone other than the practising actor has to believe in this illusion. Theory must therefore reconstruct this illusion and prove its effectiveness in the completed action against the ignorance and even amazed objection of the actors; and (2) this illusion of realized substitution – for example, of a person by a recording device – is not entirely untrue. In fact, video aficionados can realize a nearly television-free life on the basis of their recording activities. Even when they maintain the illusion of watching all of the recordings someday, this can easily be revealed as a subjective illusion. Ultimately, the recorder is permanently busy; the interpassive subjects, who in some cases have dedicated up to four machines per night to recording, never have a free machine available to watch what they have recorded. If they did watch, then they would be in danger of missing something in the current television schedule.

We therefore have a phenomenon similar to Spinoza's realization that we love something more when we hated it before. However, we can't intentionally increase our love by first hating something, because then we would never be able to emerge from our hatred.[14] The video aficionados seem to increase their love of television by having pre-recorded it. But now they never emerge from the recording process. For both of these reasons –because of the non-subjective bearer of an illusion and the truth-content of that illusion – it seems appropriate to speak of an objective illusion.

FROM OBJECTIVE LAUGHING TO TELEVISION IN EFFIGY

Who, then, is the 'subject' of this 'objectivity'? Who believes in what the actors themselves don't even think about – and, if confronted with, would consider senseless? A first, obvious answer equates the interpassive subjects and their actions with the audience at hand. If, for example, I pay mourners to weep at a memorial ceremony, which I also attend, then the other participants in the ceremony can view this as my wailing. My own (albeit non-wailing) presence at the wailing makes this wailing my own. In a similar situation, when person A is present while person B makes a statement and person A accepts it without protest, person A is also considered by the others present as party to the opinion expressed by person B. In this case, the audience at hand would be the 'subject' that is able to establish the 'objectivity' of my interpassive wailing, my praying with the help of a prayer wheel, or my amusement attained with the aid of canned laughter.

However, the example of the video recorder raises some pertinent issues related to this initial answer. Television viewers are apparently

---

14   See Benedictus de Spinoza, 'Ethics III', in *On the Improvement of the Understanding, The Ethics, Correspondence* (New York: Dover Publications, 1955), pp. 159–60.

not only capable of amusing themselves 'objectively' (with the help of canned laughter), but can also watch television 'in effigy', with the help of a video recorder. A video recorder is always humming somewhere far away from the interpassive video aficionado – but there is no longer an audience present to discern the connection between the interpassive subject and their means of representation. Interpassive subjects are not even present when their intermediaries consume television programmes for them, as substitutes. No one is able to view them side-by-side – the one apathetic, the other eagerly consuming.[15]

There is thus not only uncertainty in relation to a possible subject that could testify for the 'objective' television, but also difficulty in assigning what it replaces: For whom does a lonely, video-recording instrument watch television? For its owner? For whoever has programmed it? For the person who has given the order to have it programmed? For everyone who thought of it? Or even for all of those who are not there?

INTERPASSIVITY'S SUBSTITUTE ACTIONS

Not only does the question of *who* notices the replacement resurface, but also, emerging for the first time, is the question of exactly *what* the replacement consists of. The question about interpassivity's methods has intensified drastically; its solution seems to have once again slipped out of sight. At this impasse, the interpassive subject's treatment of books offers a way for the theory of interpassivity to move forward. Almost no other cultural practice is currently so strongly determined by interpassive usage as the handling of literature. People who find interesting books prefer to give them as gifts to their friends rather than read them themselves. Entire literary genres (mainly lavish, highly illustrated volumes) serve this widespread form of interpassivity.

Along with that, there is still another form of interpassive treatment of books: bibliomania. As Gustave Flaubert noticed, bibliomania,

---

15   The same also applies to the example mentioned by Žižek of the Tibetan prayer wheel, which is not turned by the Tibetan, but rather with the aid of a windmill. The Tibetan could already be far away while the wheel continues to pray (see Žižek, *Sublime Object of Ideology*, p. 34). Prayer flags, widespread in numerous cultures, correspond to the same principle.

similar to gift-giving,[16] consists of not reading the acquired books. Whereas, when books are given as gifts, the receivers of the books become interpassive media (even if they perhaps never read the books, but instead, for example, give them to someone else), it seems that in bibliomania, such a consumption medium is no longer present. Bibliomaniacs buy books and put them on shelves at home, or hide them in boxes (where they will possibly never find them again). For the bibliomaniac, the purchase of books seems to be the decisive act that provides the fugitive from reading the relief of not having to read the book. The comparatively brief act of purchasing a book replaces the tedious process of reading it. The methods of interpassivity thus consist in replacing certain actions with others and enacting *substitute* actions. This is what creates the connection between absent interpassive subjects and their lonely, humming video recorders: the recorder watches television for the absent subject because the subject has programmed it to do so (or has given someone else the order to do so).

The 'objectivity' of the method therefore refers to a *virtual* – not an actually attendant – audience. Interpassive substitute actions are commonly performed in shameful isolation. The interpassive subject does not perform the drama for an actual audience, but solely for an ideal audience. This ideal audience is the bearer of the objective illusion. Not the interpassive subjects themselves, but, rather, the ideal audience recognizes the representative significance of the respective substitute act and the success of substitution. In the eyes of this audience, the measure must prove itself – which is why the minor, carefully performed act of programming saves the video aficionado from a long night of watching television, just as the careful treatment of a doll saves voodoo practitioners from the need to perform the tedious task of murdering a distant enemy.

THE DISCRETE MAGIC OF THE CIVILIZED

The discovery of substitute behaviour as a method of interpassivity, as well as the surprisingly close analogy with magic practices of tribal cultures, leads us to a further, unexpected realization: interpassivity is an unobtrusive magic appearing in everyday civilized life. This

---

16   See Gustave Flaubert, *Bibliomania: A Tale*, trans. Theodore Wesley Koch (Evanston, IL: Northwestern University Press, 1929).

characterization also coincides with compulsive moments of inter-passivity (shown particularly clearly in bibliomania). As Freud pointed out, substitute behaviours are the result of a compulsion that arises from a conflict between impulses of desire and defence. Smaller, substitute acts thus take over the entire psychological value of substi-tuted, resisted acts. These acts attain the same urgency and must be carried out with the same necessity as the ones whose resistance they assure. However, in doing so, by appearing as a form of resistance, they also satisfy the impulse that is meant to be resisted.[17]

The same seems to be true of interpassive actions. For example, bibliomania, by giving the appearance of promoting reading, satis-fies mainly the impulse of simply not reading. The same is the case, as has been shown, in dealing with videos. Hiding under the appear-ance of a manifest 'pro' is a latent, and even stronger, 'contra'. The attempt to resist the anti-cultural impulse is precisely what always simultaneously realizes this impulse. Interpassivity is thereby the creation of a compromise between cultural interests and latent cultural aversion.

The fact that obsessional neurotic defence can be achieved with the help of little symbolic 'ceremonials' apparently already led Freud's analysands to the idea of equating the symptoms of obses-sional neuroses with those of religious life.[18] Freud discerned one of the few differences to be the private character of compulsive acts as opposed to the public character of 'religious practices'. Yet, if one compares compulsive acts with magic rather than religion, it seems that this difference, too, vanishes.[19] According to many anthropolo-gists, magic also has this private character.[20] Precisely the 'anonymous', technical-seeming nature of 'defensive' magic acts – rarely directed at an individual power, and always compelling rather

---

17   All quotations from Freud's work are taken from *The Standard Edition of the Complete Psychological Works of Sigmund Freud* (London: Hogarth Press, 1965–74), 24 vols, translated from the German and edited by, among others, James Strachey, Anna Freud, Alix Strachey and Alan Tyson (henceforward, 'SE'). See Sigmund Freud, 'Obsessive Actions and Religious Practices' (SE IX), pp. 124–5; and 'Totem and Taboo' (SE XIII), pp. 87–8.

18   See Freud, 'Obsessive Actions', pp. 119–20.

19   Freud made such a comparison in 'Totem and Taboo' (p. 87): 'The primary obsessive acts of these neurotics are of an entirely magical character.'

20   See Émile Durkheim, *The Elementary Forms of Religious Life*, trans. Carol Cosman (Oxford: OUP, 2008), pp. 42–3.

than requesting – seems to present an obvious analogy to similar 'non-theological' compulsive acts.[21]

If compulsive acts can be compared with magic, then it seems that so, too, can interpassivity's similarly compulsive substitute acts. Like compulsive acts, interpassive acts are substitutive and symbolic acts. They constitute attempts – using such symbols – to fend off what is substituted and symbolized. These attempts at influencing what is symbolized by fiddling with symbols also correspond to the most common descriptions of magic: with magic, it is typical that 'a symbol takes over the full functions of the thing it symbolizes'.[22]

This symbolic, figurative nature seems equally characteristic of magic acts, compulsive acts, and interpassive, substitute acts. In all three areas, this figurativeness is distorted beyond recognition in some cases, and can be clearly recognized in others. With regard to magic, unless it is already evident (in voodoo, for example), it has been pursued and described by European ethnologists in terms of homeopathy and contact.[23] In obsessional neurosis, Freud emphasized the figurative character of the substitute acts, which necessarily escapes from the actor's consciousness: for example, a constantly repeated and senseless order given to a maid to remove a presumed spot on a tablecloth is recognized as the complex re-staging of the events of a failed wedding night.[24]

With some interpassive acts, the figurative moment is still clearly recognizable. Intellectuals, for example, often photocopy hundreds of pages from books in the library and then go home with a feeling of deep satisfaction. In doing this, they often have never considered that the photocopier might have just 'read' the texts for them. Should they be aware of their satisfaction, they trace it back to the fact that they now own the texts and can read them whenever they like – even if they know that it is unlikely that they will ever do so. The satisfaction,

---

21   See also James George Frazer, *The Golden Bough*, originally published 1922, available at sacred-texts.com, p. 70; and Durkheim, *Elementary Forms*, p. 47.

22   Sigmund Freud, 'The Uncanny' (SE XVII), p. 244.

23   Homeopathic magic works by similarity – for example, doing something that looks like rain in order to provoke rain. Contagious magic, on the contrary, works with elements that have been in contact – for example, it tries to get power over an enemy by stealing and manipulating a piece of hair or clothing. See Frazer, *Golden Bough*, Chapter 3, Section 1; Freud, 'Totem and Taboo', pp. 79ff.

24   See Freud, 'Obsessive Actions', p. 121.

already present, is imagined (if at all) as something that will take place in the future; on the other hand, as a rule, the delegation of reading to the copier does not play a role. Yet through this they have delivered a very clear staging of reading: via a machine that runs through the book, page-for-page and in linear succession, offering every passage of text the spotlight of attention, as it were. They have acted out 'reading' for someone else, without even noticing it. The figurative nature of their little magic act equals that of voodoo, thus revealing a further, apparently paradoxical property of interpassive magic: so-called 'primitives' seem clear about what they are doing when they perform magic. On the contrary, through their interpassive acts, so-called 'civilized people' perform magic without even noticing.

UNPLEASURABLE AND PLEASURABLE
INTERPASSIVITY: NEUROSES AND PERVERSION

The actor remains unaware of both the symbolic character of inter-passive acts and the gain in pleasure associated with them, which seems to point to a causal connection. When the magical character of interpassivity goes unrecognized, its achievements, too, are not perceived as pleasurable. Just as they are incapable of recognizing that they have played a game of watching television with the help of the recorder, interpassive subjects are unaware of the fact that they have succeeded in satisfying themselves through this game of enact-ment. They thus continue to complain that they are never able to watch their videos.

On the basis of these two misjudgements, interpassivity reveals a similarity to obsessional neuroses. There, too, the inability to recog-nize the compulsive acts corresponds with the impossibility of experiencing them as pleasurable. Magic, on the contrary, does not seem necessarily to have these traits. So-called 'primitives' know *that* they are practising magic; they also know *what* they are conjuring up (the depictions are often extremely clear) – and the results do not seem uniformly bound up with *reluctant experiences*.

Whereas the majority of cases of interpassivity that I have noted show no pleasurable outcome, there does also seem to be a pleasura-ble variant. Žižek's example of the use of canned laughter presents a case of misjudgement-free interpassivity: these interpassive subjects know that they are 'objectively' amused by way of delegation, and they enjoy it. Like the neurosis, which according to Freud constitutes the 'negative' of the perversion,[25] the reluctant variant of interpassivity seems to be the 'negative' of a pleasurable, shrewd variant. Because the interpassive fans of canned laughter are aware of the figurative character of their substitute act, because they know that they are feigning amusement, they are also capable of drawing pleasure from their interpassivity.[26]

DOUBLE DELEGATION: ENJOYMENT AND BELIEF

The example of the photocopying intellectual clarifies a differentiation of two levels, which in Žižek's example of 'objective praying' (through the prayer wheel) might be easily confused or falsely identified with one another. There are always *two levels* of delegation – namely, the delegation of *enjoyment* and the delegation of *belief* (in the enacted performance of enjoyment). Interpassivity is always carried out simultaneously at both of these levels: on the one hand, consumption is delegated to a consumption medium – for example, reading to a photocopier; on the other hand, the belief in the equivalence between the consumers and their vicarious consumption media must also be delegated. The interpassive subject does not personally believe that he or she has read via the copy machine; this belief is transferred to the scene's virtual audience. Delegated enjoyment thus always entails feigning enjoyment for an observing agency with the help of a consumption medium, and simultaneously surrendering belief in this feigned fiction to the observing agency. In every act of delegated enjoyment, there is both delegated enjoyment and delegated illusion. The enjoyment is delegated to a consumption medium, the illusion to an observing agency.[27]

The same applies to Žižek's example of 'objective praying' or 'objective belief' through prayer wheels and the like. There is an initial, religious level – the content of the rotating text in the prayer wheel, or

25   See Sigmund Freud, 'Three Essays on the Theory of Sexuality' (SE VII), p. 165.

26   In what follows, this difference between neurotic reluctance and perverse pleasure will be treated in greater detail. See also Chapter 8.

27   The differentiation suggested by Žižek ('Die Substitution', p. 25) between delegated enjoyment and delegated belief, in my opinion, therefore does not describe two different classes of interpassive phenomena; instead, it is immanent in every case of interpassivity.

even, more generally, the entire bodies of religious belief of which these texts form a part. However, there is also a second level: namely, the idea that a rotating prayer wheel (even if it is not moved by a worshipper, but by the wind) is equivalent to an actually praying worshipper, or that a burning candle is the same as a praying Catholic.

Whereas the first level – that of the beliefs expressed by the rotating religious texts – necessarily belongs to religion (and is usually also contained within the ideas that a worshipper is accustomed to), this does not have to be the case at all for the second level. The thought of equivalence between a prayer wheel and a worshipper does not have to be an explicit idea within Tibetan theology; the concept does not have to be familiar to a Tibetan worshipper. (If it is, then this is more of an anomaly: religions that also have this second level as a conscious idea appear as interesting exceptions, as, in such cases, misrecognition as one of the dimensions necessary for most interpassive practices seems to be suspended.) Only the first delegation is *religious* in an 'orthodox' sense. The second, on the contrary, hardly seems religious, and instead appears to be more *magical*, in a way similar to the procedure of the interpassive video consumer. Perhaps this is why an animosity towards the worshippers' own rituals emerges in the history of many religions.

If 'praying' is feigned with the help of a prayer wheel, then there is first a religious (for example, Tibetan) belief, and second, a belief in the feigned fiction. The first belief is delegated to the prayer wheel; the second, to a virtual, observing agency. It is thus important to emphasize that delegated *enjoyment* (consumption) is realized with the help of the prayer wheel: the religious belief is enjoyed – i.e. consumed – by the ritual instrument rather than by the ritual participant. And the belief that it makes no difference whether the prayer wheel or the owner consumes religion is not held by the person who carries out the ritual act, but instead by the virtual audience.

In all interpassive occurrences, belief in the fiction of the equivalence between the interpassive person and their consumption medium is delegated to some kind of observing agency. 'Objective belief' at the second level is thereby a universal characteristic of all interpassive occurrences – and not only those in which the enjoyment of the commodity of religion is delegated to a consumption medium. 'Objective belief' is also present, for example, when a video aficionado lets the recorder watch television. Feigning for someone else's benefit also takes place here – in the pretence that it does not matter whether the film is watched by the recorder or the recorder's owner. Interpassivity is thus the process of delegated consumption, which always – and usually without the actor's knowledge – contains an occurrence of delegated belief. The interpassive actors 'believe objectively', even if they are not aware of it. The 'objective', delegated belief contained in interpassivity involves only the substitute acts' virtual audience. This belief thus appears as an illusion without a proper owner, as an illusion without a subject. The enjoyment, which the interpassive subject evades, is pulled off with the help of an illusion from which he or she likewise escapes.

The mischievous pleasure, which appears in some cases of interpassivity, such as that described by Žižek, seems to rest on the dual character of this withdrawal: having escaped both enjoying *and* the illusion of enjoyment, and having delegated both to someone else, seems to be enormous fun. First, one withdraws from the enjoyment, then from the illusion of it – and apparently that produces new, even greater enjoyment.

ILLUSIONS WITHOUT SUBJECTS: THE ISSUES RAISED BY THE DISCOVERY OF INTERPASSIVITY

The examination of interpassivity has brought us this far. Yet before we have been able to unravel its riddle completely, it has made a new, more general issue accessible, and at the same time unavoidable: *the question of the form in which illusions are able to exist in a society*. We have observed in the interpassive subject that there are people who, although they do not share certain illusions, are nonetheless occupied with these illusions. Although intellectually they seem to be beyond such illusions, they are almost affectionately bound to it. They do not believe in magic, and they do not notice that they practise magic, but nonetheless they do so, and even with a conspicuous compulsion: they *have to* photocopy, video record, and so on.

Starting from interpassivity's practices, we thereby hit upon illusions, which quite obviously are *no one's* illusions. It is not possible to discern an actual bearer: either these illusions are supposed to be those of a mythical 'someone else' (for example, those of the 'ordinary person on the street'), or perhaps they are not even manifest, and are only staged for a virtual audience, which for the time being remains enigmatic. They are always *the others' illusions*, incessantly displaced, illusions without a subject. This is even more surprising in that illusions, as psychoanalytical theory has recognized, work to form the subject.[28] Although it may indeed be true that without illusions there are no subjects, it nonetheless seems that there are, at least, illusions without subjects.

Knowing better seems to prevent people from considering themselves as bearers of such illusions. Discovering the discrete magic of interpassivity leads us to a theory of *illusions kept in limbo by knowing better*. It raises the question of the form in which illusions are able to exist in an enlightened society that considers itself beyond such illusions, and the role played by this feeling of intellectual superiority, this knowing better, in the unrecognized yet pervasive continuation of these illusions. At the same time, the discovery of interpassive magic suggests that we should pursue the issue of what 'objective' illusions are – which means finding out *who exactly the virtual audience is* that lends these illusions an independent existence in the assessment of real people, and even a true effectiveness (after all, they lead to actual experiences of gratification). Who then, is the subject of this 'objectivity'?

Furthermore, it seems worth examining in greater detail the *mischievous pleasure* that we notice in the interpassive subject's behaviour. It seems to be linked to the 'objective' illusions: to offer an illusion to an unspecified Other and withdraw from it oneself is obviously a considerable source of pleasure. This seems to be the key to the unanswered question of the reason for interpassive behaviour: why interpassive subjects prefer double delegation to simple enjoyment, and how they obtain their increased pleasure. But this perspective also poses a very general question about cultural pleasure: Might *all* forms of pleasure that culture is able to produce be associated with 'objective' illusions? Can we possibly prove that an illusion is always present when people experience pleasure (even when it is, perhaps, hidden from those who obtain pleasure)?

And finally, the phenomenon of 'civilized' magic seems to have raised a historical and epistemological problem: What prevents

28   See Jacques Lacan, 'The Mirror Stage as Formative of the I Function as Revealed in Psychoanalytic Experience', in *Écrits*, trans. Bruce Fink (London: Norton, 2007); Louis Althusser, 'Ideology and Ideological State Apparatuses', in *'Lenin and Philosophy' and Other Essays* (New York: Monthly Review Press, 1971), available at marxists.org.

'civilized people' – apparently in contrast to so-called 'primitives' – from recognizing that they are performing magic? What differentiates the social reality of a society that is aware of its magic from one that is (apparently of necessity) unaware of it? In what type of society is this misjudgement characteristic and necessary? Does the entire self-evidence of 'civilized' society rely solely on this characteristic? And why do 'civilized people' tend to have such false ideas about what it means *to believe something*? Does it mean that 'civilized people' also have equally erroneous ideas of what it means *to know something*?

There are two theories that seem particularly suitable for pursuing these questions posed by the theory of interpassivity, and for providing clues leading to a theory of illusions that are held in limbo by knowing better: Octave Mannoni's psychoanalytical contemplations on disavowal, and Johan Huizinga's cultural study of play. Since these two theories agree on the most important theses related to the status of illusions, and complement one another with regard to those points covered by only one of them, they will be brought together in the following chapters.

CHAPTER TWO

Belief: Octave Mannoni and the Two Forms of Conviction – *Croyance* and *Foi* ('Belief' and 'Faith')

If there has ever been a theory capable of systematically investigating the issue of the forms in which illusions exist, then it would have to be Octave Mannoni's theory of *disavowal*. In his two essays 'Je sais bien, mais quand même . . .'[1] and 'L'illusion comique',[2] in particular, Mannoni took up the Freudian concept of denial (disavowal) and clarified it through numerous baffling, yet entirely common, everyday examples.

The analysis of the concept that Mannoni develops in the two studies recognizes precisely those moments that are of interest to our inquiry: a specific type of illusion distinguished by the fact that it exists independently of those persons who might might be suspected of being its carrier; and a specific type of person who takes pleasure in dealing with an illusion, but has better knowledge allowing him or her to see through this illusion (so that he or she obviously does not come into question as its owner).

DISAVOWAL AND FETISHISM: MANNONI'S NOVEL REPOSITIONING OF THE PROBLEM

The first innovative move in Mannoni's studies on disavowal is his recognition of the concept of disavowal – which for Freud seemed bound mainly to the problem of (sexual) fetishism[3] – as a concept

---

1   Octave Mannoni, *Clefs pour l'Imaginaire ou l'Autre Scène* (Mayenne: Seuil, 1985), pp. 9–33. The essay originally appeared in *Les Temps Modernes* 212 (January 1964), pp. 1,262–86, as 'Je sais bien . . . mais quand même. La Croyance'. For an English version, see: Octave Mannoni, 'I Know well, But All the Same . . ', in *Perversion and the Social Relation*, eds Molly Anne Rothenberg, Dennis A. Foster and Slavoj Žižek (Durham, NC: Duke University Press, 2003) pp. 68–92.

2   Ibid., pp. 161–83.

3   See Sigmund Freud, 'Fetishism' (SE XXI), pp. 147–57; Jean Laplanche and Jean-Bertrand Pontalis, *The Language of Psychoanalysis*, trans. Donald Nicholson Smith (London: Karnac 1988), pp. 118–21.

with a more general structure. Although Jacques Lacan had already understood disavowal as the basic constitutive operation of all perversions (not only fetishism),[4] Mannoni's analysis goes beyond this diagnosis at two decisive points. First, according to Mannoni, disavowal is a general operation appearing not only in fetishisms and other perversions, but also in everyday phenomena, both pathological and normal. Accordingly, disavowal even presents the basic principle for a series of art forms and cultural institutions: the vaudeville show's magic tricks, theatrical illusions, familial *mises-en-scène* around Santa Claus, and so on.

Second, Mannoni states that, although disavowal produces fetishism, it is no longer manifest in fetishism. Thus, as he determines, Freud's entire fetishism essay from 1927 offers not clarity on fetishistic perversion, but instead analysis of a prerequisite for this perversion. The question that Freud's text answers is 'how a *croyance* [belief] can be simultaneously abandoned and retained'.[5] With this, Mannoni also facilitates psychoanalytic theory's approach to a phenomenon that was originally indicated by the term 'fetishism': those peculiar religions – or those peculiar colonial ideas about foreign religions – that shaped the beginnings of the fetishism discourse.[6]

Within psychoanalysis, the term 'fetishism' was used exclusively in relation to sexual theory, and remained reserved for the area of perversion, in contrast to this widespread religious-scientific, or theological, use of the term. From a psychoanalytical perspective, religious phenomena that others identify as 'fetishisms' (and even name as such) would, on the contrary, be examined from the perspective of obsessional neuroses.[7]

By opening up religious and mystical subjects for investigation through the psychoanalytical concept of disavowal, Mannoni thereby made it possible to reflect for the first time on religious fetishism,

---

4   See also Dylan Evans, *An Introductory Dictionary of Lacanian Psychoanalysis* (London/New York: Routledge, 1996), pp. 43–4.

5   See Mannoni, *Clefs pour l'Imaginaire*, p. 11.

6   See also Jean-Bertrand Pontalis, ed., 'Objets du fétichisme', *Nouvelle Revue de Psychanalyse* 2 (Autumn 1970), Alfonoso M. Iacono, *Le fétichisme. Histoire d'un concept* (Paris: PUF, 1992); Emily Apter and William Pietz, eds, *Fetishism as Cultural Discourse* (Ithaca/London: Cornell University Press, 1993); Hartmut Böhme, 'Das Fetischismus-Konzept von Marx und sein Kontext in Berliner Debatte', *INITIAL. Zeitschrift für sozialwissenschaftlichen Diskurs* 8: 1–2 (1997): pp. 8–33.

7   See also Freud, 'Obsessive Actions', pp. 115–27.

which from this perspective appeared as anything but primitive. Rather than considering it an incomprehensible fixation of religious passion on an inanimate object, religious fetishism, like its sexual counterpart, must now be viewed as a practice that operates, in principle, by presuming that others believe. Rather than worship of a primitive, *tangibly present god*, religious fetishism instead proves to be a complex event directed at an *absent true believer*. Psychoanalysis also understands religious fetishism, like sexual fetishism, as an event in which the illusion of the other is at work.

STARTING POINT FOR THE PROBLEM: *LES CROYANCES*

Via the term *croyance*, Mannoni opens up contemplation of questions such as 'how a belief [*croyance*] can be simultaneously abandoned and retained'. Not all languages have in store a word that is advantageous for the theory, as do French and English. The clear advantage of this word derives both from the fact that in French it takes an apparently neutral position between the expressions *foi* ('faith') and *superstition* ('superstition') and that it has a plural form. In German, for example, there is no corresponding word.

Perhaps that is also the reason why, as Mannoni noted, neither the term *croyance* nor any other equivalent term appears in the index of a Freud volume.[8] Freud's awareness of this problem and his encounter with the terminological difficulties is evident in a remark about the 'Rat Man': 'Thus he was at once superstitious and not superstitious; and there was a clear distinction between his attitude and the superstition of uneducated people who feel themselves at one with their belief.'[9] Here, Freud encountered the difficulty of finding an adequate term for the peculiar 'educated' form of superstition existing in his analysand. In contrast to the 'uneducated believers', his analysand appeared to have access to better knowledge, by virtue of which the superstitious belief appeared ludicrous to him. Unlike the 'uneducated believers', Freud's patient does not feel 'at one with [his] belief'. At the same time, however, he seems unable to free himself from these beliefs that are so separate from him.

---

8   See Mannoni, *Clefs pour l'Imaginaire*, pp. 9–10.
9   Sigmund Freud, 'Notes upon a Case of Obsessional Neurosis' (SE X), p. 229.

Precisely this peculiar, 'educated', 'provisional' form of belief that Freud discovers, which allows an uncertainty to arise about its carrier, is the form that Mannoni identifies by the term *croyance* – a word that initially leaves open whether the *croyance* is a belief or a superstition. For Mannoni's argument, the expression *croyance* has the advantage of being initially indefinite and fickle enough to allow an open presentation of the problem. For Mannoni, the problem that psycho-analytical theory faces consists in the difficulty of saying what a *croyance* (or even an *incroyance*) comprises, or once comprised – for example, in the sixteenth century with Rabelais; or (as Mannoni remarks), the equally difficult issue of our contemporaries who have a discordant attitude with regard to forms of superstition.[10] As Mannoni ascertained, there are forms of belief in which it is unclear who once believed them, or whether a given individual believes in them or not.

Mannoni says that ethnologists, for example, are often confronted with odd statements from their informants (with reference to a mask ritual) whereby they are told that people *once believed* in masks ('qu'on croyait aux masques *autrefois*'). However, as Mannoni detects, ethnology has not dealt sufficiently with the issue of what might possibly constitute the transformation implied in this statement between an earlier belief and a subsequent lack of belief – whether one can register this transformation as, for example, 'a type of enlightenment progress'.[11] On the contrary, he adds, it is more likely that a belief in masks had always been attributed to an earlier epoch. But this provokes the question (central for Mannoni) of why this occurs.[12]

Mannoni explains that the vaudeville show offers similar examples, where the audience to a magic trick plays the perfect incredulous viewer (*incrédule*), but nonetheless demands that the illusion be perfect – without ever having a clear idea of who it is now that should be deceived.[13] Theatre, too, offers the opportunity to observe such illusions that have been shifted to others – such as the commonly recurring myth of the naive spectator who was meant once to have thought the happenings on stage were real and, for example, tried to

---

10   See Mannoni, *Clefs pour l'Imaginaire*, p. 9.
11   Ibid., pp. 9, 163.
12   Ibid.
13   Ibid.

warn Julius Caesar at the last moment by calling out: 'Watch out! They're armed!'[14]

When an actor plays a dead person this structure is less obvious, but, as Mannoni detects, it has a similar effect. According to theatrical conventions, which in this particular case do not seem to allow much theatrical freedom (in contrast to other cases, where, for example, a tea towel is capable of indicating a castle), the actor has to lie there without moving. This alone seemed striking to Mannoni: 'If the actor doesn't lie still, would one say that it is obvious that he isn't dead? But everyone knows that anyway . . . nonetheless, everything proceeds as though this knowledge has to remain concealed. From whom?'[15] But if the actor were to get a bit of dust in his or her nose (which no stage convention can prevent), then the 'corpse' would have to sneeze. The tension maintained by theatrical convention would then suddenly collapse, as Mannoni suggests, and the audience would break into laughter.

As he says, just as in the case of the mask cult, in the case of theatre, too, it seems to be about an illusion that we are not the victims of, but for which we seem to require a victim who – for our satisfaction – is held in check by the illusion: 'Everything seems to be set up to produce the belief, but for someone else – as though we (the audience) were in cahoots with the actors.'[16] In all of these cases – both 'primitive' and 'civilized' – actors appear who have situated themselves quite close to an illusion, but repudiate belief in this illusion. Some identify other persons by name, in a more or less vague way ('earlier people'), as the carriers of this illusion; others are perhaps satisfied with clarifying that they themselves are not its carriers. And, finally, others say nothing, but do not appear to be the true carriers of such a belief – while simultaneously drawing their pleasure from precisely that.

MANNONI'S FORMULA FOR DECEPTION: 'I
KNOW QUITE WELL, BUT STILL . . .'

Echoing Freud's experience with his obsessional neurotic analysands, Mannoni confronts an element of 'education' in the cases he examines. They, too, have better knowledge available with which they can

---

14   Ibid., p. 163.
15   Ibid.
16   Ibid., pp. 163-4.

distance themselves from the illusion in question – although they cannot do so completely, since they simultaneously express a certain devotion to the illusion. Thus, in analysis one often hears expressions along the lines of 'I know quite well . . . but still . . .'[17] This formula makes the structure of disavowal explicit. According to Mannoni, its emergence is the indication that disavowal has taken place.[18] But this formula cannot always be expressed when disavowal occurs. The fetishist, for example, also disavows, but, as Mannoni notes, he is not able to formulate these words: 'Of course, the fetishist does not use a phrase of this sort to describe his perversion.'[19]

It is possible to derive this from Freud's own theses. Freud analyzed denial/disavowal in fetishism as follows: against the backdrop of an infantile sexual theory, according to which all people have a penis (as well as castration fantasies, possibly intensified through an authority figure's threats that masturbation will lead to castration), discovery of the female genitals shocks the young boy, as it appears to be the result of castration (which, accordingly, could also happen to others such as himself). The fetishist overcomes this 'reality' of 'castration' in a peculiar way: he acknowledges it as an 'attitude which fit[s] in with reality', yet at the same time maintains his 'attitude which fit[s] in with the wish'. In his fetish, he creates the evidence for female penis ownership.[20] The fetish's role as evidence is, however, unknown to the fetishist: it is Freud's reconstruction.

The fetishist *knows* quite well (that the woman has no phallus), but the other phrase, 'quand même . . .', remains silent – it constitutes, as Mannoni writes, the fetish itself.[21] The situation for neurotics is similar, even though the illusions that they deny (starting from the basic model of denial of the maternal phallus) have shifted to other issues.[22]

This difference between 'explicit' and 'silent' disavowal, which Mannoni dealt with only briefly, can possibly be explained as follows: there is disavowal in which the content of the illusion in question is

---

17   Ibid., p. 11.
18   Ibid., p. 13.
19   Mannoni 2003, p. 70.
20   See Freud, 'Fetishism', p. 156; and Juan-David Nasio, *Enseignement de 7 concepts cruciaux de la psychanalyse* (Paris: Editions Payot, 1992), pp. 7–19.
21   See Mannoni, *Clefs pour l'Imaginaire*, p. 12.
22   Ibid.

manifest. With a familial *mise-en-scène* of Santa Claus, the game being played is quite clear. Moreover, the children for whom the play is being enacted actually step into view as carriers of the illusion (which, however, may also be a fallacy). The situation is similar with mask cults where the ancestors are meant to have believed. With magic tricks, the content of the illusion is, at any rate, manifest, even if it does not seem possible to identify any likely carriers in this case. Conversely, with fetishism, as well as the obsessional neurotic's ceremonial acts, the actor is not aware that anything at all is being depicted in their – usually secretly enacted, seemingly 'senseless' – acts. The symbolic character, the figurativeness of the act, is lost to them, thus the depicted illusion is not manifest.

Yet both types of disavowal, manifest illusions as well as latent ones, exhibit a shared defining characteristic: knowing better, which prevents the actors from considering themselves as carriers of the illusion. If someone were to label them as the illusion's carrier, then they would reject it indignantly. (The fetishists and obsessional neurotics who operate with latent illusions would quite possibly also deny the symbolic character of their actions. That is, they would not only deny that they are the carriers of an illusion, but also that there is any type of illusion involved at all.)

Mannoni thus delivers a structural formula for sexual fetishism: there is knowledge and, at the same time, a libidinal fixation on a (desire-based) illusion. And there is also a specific, seemingly paradoxical connection between these two sides: *knowledge is the condition for devotion to the illusion.* Contrary to the assumption of ego psychology (as well as some elements of psychoanalytic theory), which considers it feasible to strengthen the 'better half' of the analysand against the other half, Mannoni emphasizes that both sides of the ego-split form a complex structure in which the 'knowing' side does not form the opposite to, but instead the backup for, the 'believing' side. As Mannoni emphasizes, 'the "but still" exists only because there is an "I know quite well." '[23] Without the knowledge that women do not have a phallus, there would be no fetish. In order to do away with the fetish, it does absolutely no good to confirm fetishists in their knowledge. (What would be 'useful' – although only in the sense of displacing the symptoms – would be to rattle the fetishist's knowledge).

---

23   Ibid., pp. 12–13.

Mannoni thus worked out the details of a striking, paradoxical quality of *croyance*. It is about illusions that are maintained only where there is better knowledge that suspends them. This discovery not only contradicts the common versions in which the illusion dissolves after knowledge of the truth is attained; it also goes beyond the already thoroughly disconcerting discovery by a few philosophers who recognized that there are illusions that remain alive even when they are falsified by acquired knowledge. Kant, for example, established in his 'Transcendental Dialectic' that the transcendental illusion remained and did not dissolve even after critique had rendered it entirely transparent as an illusion.[24] In a similar way, Spinoza defined the manner of functioning, resistant to all better knowledge, of 'knowledge of the first kind'.[25]

As we have seen, Mannoni's discovery goes even further. He detects that certain illusions not only are not destroyed by contradictory knowledge; in fact, they are only able to exist on the basis of such knowledge and in conjunction with it.[26] The difficulty in finding carriers of such illusions comes from the form in which these illusions exist – namely, a form that is tied to knowledge: it is not possible to find a carrier of the illusion, because it is impossible to find anyone

---

24   See Immanuel Kant, *Critique of Pure Reason*, trans. Norman Kemp Smith (New York: St Martin's Press, 1965), pp. 299–300.

25   See Benedictus de Spinoza, 'Ethics IV', in *On the Improvement of the Understanding, The Ethics, Correspondence* (New York: Dover Publications, 1955), pp. 191–2.

26   That also clarifies an issue with reference to which Mannoni himself remained characteristically undecided in his essay, 'Je sais bien, mais quand même' – namely, whether disavowal identifies a *process* or a *structure*: must we even believe in the illusions (such as the existence of Santa Claus) before we are able to deny them and accuse others of having them? Or, as Slavoj Žižek emphasizes, are they beliefs that, right from the beginning, have always been the convictions of others, without ever having been our own? (see Žižek, 'Die Substitution', p. 14). At least in the case of denial that is crucial for a fetish (the illusion of the maternal possession of a penis), Mannoni seems to grasp denial as a *real process* (which once again traces the story of the illusion of Santa Claus). The later, structural disavowal would then at least have had a real, procedural archetype. But even with the 'infantile sexual theory' claiming the universality of penis ownership, it does not seem clear that the children ever had to believe in it. See also Ludwig Wittgenstein, 'Remarks on Frazer's *Golden Bough*', in *Philosophical Occasions 1912–1951*, ed. James Klagge and Alfred Nordmann (Indianapolis/Cambridge: Hackett, 1993), p. 152. On the basis of other examples, Mannoni shows that children are certainly capable of operating with several illusions that they never believed in (see, for example, Mannoni, *Clefs pour l'Imaginaire*, p. 162).

who is not in the know. And even if someone were found who did not know, it would be doubtful that they could be considered the carrier of such an illusion. *Only those who know can be afflicted by such illusions* – with this thesis, Mannoni formulates an epistemological fact that appears no less paradoxical than the theological notion of a God who punishes only the pious.[27]

Mannoni's designation of *croyance*, which arises through disavowal, can be summarized as follows: *croyance* is an illusion

- that always coexists with better knowledge;
- that is assigned to others when it is consciously held;
- and that the subject is often unaware of (they think neither of the content of the illusion nor that they could possibly be its carrier).

Beyond that, Mannoni highlights a further trait: the apparent 'confirmations' of this illusion, for example, through chance events, can elicit *strong affective impacts*. He explains, for example, that if the horoscope says that a certain day on which he has long planned a move is 'particularly favourable for changes at home', he falls into a fit of laughter.[28] But he also admits that the tone of his laughter would be different if the horoscope had said that this day was particularly unfavourable for such a purpose. Mannoni shows that the formula 'I know perfectly well . . . but still . . .' can, in such a case, be completed as follows: 'I know perfectly well that these coincidences mean nothing at all; but still, I more or less take pleasure in them.'[29]

In some cases, the amusement and the triumph over such 'confirmed nonsense' are also confronted by a strong experience of

---

27   The clearest formulation of the same thought can be found in Freud's theory of the uncanny. Freud remarked that we have 'surmounted' certain convictions in order to be sensitive to the feeling of the uncanny (Sigmund Freud, 'The Uncanny' [SE XVII], pp. 247ff). In the fairytale world, on the contrary, where the existence of ghosts, fairies, and so on, is assumed, there is nothing uncanny. This means that, according to Freud, only those who do not believe in ghosts can be afraid of the uncanny. The concept of 'surmounting', by the way, corresponds perfectly with the concept that Freud introduces in 1927 as 'disavowal/denial'. On theological paradoxes, see the beautiful study, 'The God of the Transvestites', by Miran Božovič, in his *An Utterly Dark Spot: Gaze and Body in Early Modern Philosophy* (Ann Arbor: University of Michigan Press), pp. 3–14.

28   See Mannoni, *Clefs pour l'Imaginaire*, p. 20.

29   Ibid.: 'Je sais bien que ces coincidences n'ont aucun sens, mais quand même elles me font plus ou moins plaisir.'

displeasure, which can appear in disconcerting forms, such as in Freud's study of the 'Rat Man', for example. Freud's patient is to stay at a hydropathic clinic where he has previously been treated. Upon arrival, he finds out that an older man has already taken the room he wants, which would have been favourable for his amorous plans. He says, jokingly, 'I wish he may be struck dead for it!' But when the older man then actually dies, the analysand – against his better knowledge – is plagued by uncanny feelings and guilt about the omnipotence of his thoughts.[30] In this variant, the completion of the formula suggested by Mannoni must be slightly different: 'I know that these coincidences mean nothing at all, but nonetheless, they disturb me.'[31]

The strong affective impacts that are associated with *croyance* can strike in both pleasurable and unpleasurable ways. The remarkable strength of these affects forms a further characteristic attribute of this type of illusion.

MANNONI'S CRUCIAL DISTINCTION – THE TWO TYPES OF BELIEF: *CROYANCE* ('BELIEF') AND *FOI* ('FAITH')

Following Mannoni's presentation of the problem of a belief that is produced through disavowal on the basis of the term *croyance*, and his explanation of the paradoxical characteristics of this belief, he comes to an original and momentous conclusion. Mannoni distinguishes between two types of belief. He separates *croyance* from *foi*. What he identifies as *foi* seems easier to characterize – mainly because the corresponding version of religious or other conviction seems more trusted and comprehensible. *Foi* is the type of conviction that its representatives openly admit to. In the case of *foi*, there is no difficulty in finding carriers for the belief. Also, should the belief be attributed to others, it is not at all enigmatic in such cases: there are simple, easily verifiable institutional criteria for it (such as baptism certificates, membership cards, and so on).

But with the addition of the counter-term *croyance*, Mannoni describes the paradoxical, provisional form of the imagination that is

---

30   See Sigmund Freud, 'Notes upon a Case of Obsessional Neurosis' (SE X), p. 234.

31   The reason that Mannoni barely mentions this unpleasurable variant of *croyance* seems to be that he does not consider the obsessional neurotic forms of illusion. In what follows I will examine in greater detail this unpleasurable form, in which neurosis functions as an exact 'negative of perversion'.

created through disavowal. An unprofessed belief (*croyance*) is the opposite of a religious conviction, or faith (*foi*). The attitude of the respective carrier is the criterion that distinguishes the two: whereas one usually embraces a *foi* directly, with pride, generally no one wants to have anything to do with a *croyance*. The latter exists merely in a transient form that is difficult to grasp, is often ascribed to other carriers, yet nonetheless often exhibits impacts (say, in the form of inexplicable joy, excitement, or enthusiasm) among those subjects who, in disavowal, repudiate the *croyance* and are in full possession of better knowledge.

With *foi*, it seems as if the respective carriers have it as a clear and desirable picture in front of them that they are attempting to catch up with – which, when accomplished, brings feelings of triumph. A *croyance*, on the contrary, they seem to have put behind them, without possessing a clear picture of it – although it seems that sometimes it catches up with them.

THE PROBLEM OF TERMINOLOGY

A third term crops up in Mannoni's theory: 'superstition'. This term is so common in everyday language that a theory of illusion is hard-pressed to avoid it. Instead, such a theory is compelled to supply an answer to the question of what a superstition actually is. It must localize what the superstition describes in relation to the theoretical concepts *croyance* and *foi*, and declare whether it describes something else – a third thing – or is already correctly and completely encompassed by either of these two terms.

Mannoni, in any case, did not introduce any arguments for a conceptual differentiation between *croyances* and superstitions. For that reason, it seems plausible that superstitions take the same conceptual position in his theory as *croyances*: *every superstition is, in truth, a croyance.* The terms 'superstition' and *croyance* describe the same thing – but they offer two different perspectives on it. 'Superstition' describes the everyday type of perception of certain *croyances*. A 'superstition' is commonly spoken of when an illusion is manifest and it seems as though it would be possible to find its carriers. A 'superstition' is therefore an illusion that seems as though it were the *professed faith* of others. (Those people who would seem to make a 'superstition' their professed faith would, for example, be the ones whom Freud described as having 'the superstition of uneducated people'.[32]) But, as we have seen, it is in no way certain that such people always exist or, therefore that it is always possible to trace a 'superstition' as a professed faith, back to the faithful. To this extent, Mannoni modified the meaning of the term 'superstition': whereas everyday language understands it to be a peculiar view – that is, the *faith* of other people – Mannoni uses the term to describe an illusion that others *seem* to be captivated by.

The term *croyance*, on the contrary, is a generic concept in Mannoni's theory. It includes those *croyances* that are perceived as 'superstitions' as well as *others*. Everything that is not a *foi*, and is therefore not claimed by anyone, would be assigned to the realm of *croyance*. For Mannoni, *croyances* would thereby be all forms of non-faith-like illusions: on the one hand, so-called superstitions, which are manifest as illusions and usually assigned to an unidentified someone else; and, on the other hand, also those illusions in which no illusion is manifest for the actors – such as in Mannoni's example of the dead actor on the stage – which are therefore not assigned to anyone else.[33] Perceived as a *superstition*, the illusion would be manifest, but falsely understood as a faith. Perceived as a *croyance*, on the contrary, the illusion would be latent and would (outside of psychoanalytical theory) mistakenly not even be recognized as an illusion. Two typical misjudgements thus seem to be tied up with *croyances*: either they are perceived distortedly and identified as superstitions, and thereby assumed to be the faith of others, or they are not perceived at all.

By turning the everyday expressions *croyance* and 'superstition' into rigorously defined concepts, Mannoni's theory thereby changes the meaning of both. Common sense systematically fails to recognize the reality that this theory reveals, and this lack of recognition finds expression in everyday terminology: whereas common language describes superstitions as the more foolish, more disdained understandings of some people, as opposed to 'faith', Mannoni's theory understands 'superstition' (as well as belief) to denote exclusively

---

32   See Freud, 'Notes upon a Case of Obsessional Neurosis', p. 229.

33   The latent illusion in this example consists in the precautions taken to make the stage death believable for an 'unseen third person'. The illusion's subject is not the death of the character, but instead the existence of someone who 'really' believes in this death.

those illusions that no one claims – in contrast to 'faith', which always finds people who declare that they truly believe in and stand by the belief in question.

THE PROBLEM OF PLURALS: THE STRUCTURAL AND HISTORICAL DISTINCTION BETWEEN BELIEF AND FAITH

Along with this initial terminological question – which, as a factual problem, can be traced back to the common failure to recognize Mannoni's discovered reality – there is yet another problem. It has to do with the plural forms. In French, as well as in English (in contrast, for example, to German), there is a plural form for *croyance*; and it appears as such in the first sentence of Mannoni's text. *Foi*, on the contrary, seems – at least linguistically – to possess only a singular form. This poses the question of whether we have caught sight of an accidental characteristic of the French language or a thesis proposed by Mannoni that is linked to this characteristic. In other words: Is it characteristic, for the differentiation that Mannoni has decided upon, that that which he describes as *croyances* exist in the plural, whereas those things called *foi* can, according to their nature, only exist in the singular?

Mannoni's selected example seems to hint in this direction. According to Mannoni, the Bible states that the Jews had superstitious *beliefs* in the existence of many gods ('les Juifs croyaient en l'existence de tous les dieux'), but their *faith* was in only one single one ('Mais ils ne gardaient leur foi qu'à un seul.'[34]). That would suggest a far-reaching conjecture – namely, that polytheism corresponds with an attitude of superstitious beliefs, but monotheism, on the contrary, with an attitude of faith. The two types of belief, superstition and faith, would accordingly correspond with different forms of religion, and could (perhaps with the exception of transitional periods, such as the example that Mannoni introduces of the biblical Jews) also be assigned historically to the epochs and regions of polytheism and monotheism. The differentiation between the two types of belief would thus itself be an historical one: polytheists would be superstitious, while monotheists would be faithful believers.

Yet we must still ask whether this is necessarily so – that is, whether the history of religion confirms this conceptual differentiation in all

---

34 Mannoni, *Clefs pour l'Imaginaire*, p. 14.

cases, or if there might not be at least one example in which people have *superstitious beliefs* in one God, or *faithful belief* in many gods. What must also be explained is the type of belief that exists in those religions in which gods play no role.[35]

BELIEF WITHOUT FAITH, BUT NO FAITH WITHOUT BELIEF

Whereas Mannoni's text initially seems to categorize beliefs together with polytheistic religions and faith with monotheistic religions, Mannoni himself subsequently offers another way of assigning the types of belief that he has discerned. According to Mannoni, the only reason that *foi*, faith, is understood as though it had to do with the *existence* of God is a distortion owing to Greek ontology.[36] The issue of existence, however, is a subject of *croyance*, of belief: the biblical Jews believed – in the form of superstitious beliefs – in the existence of many gods.

But what constitutes the defining trait of *foi*, faith, is *unconditional commitment*. The biblical Jews devote this to only one God. Thus, the two types of belief – superstitious belief and faith – are answers to two different questions, which can exist side by side in one and the same religion. A historical division of religious epochs into those of beliefs and those of faith is therefore not possible. The difference would be structural and not historical. It would have to do with the differences between the various levels of existence of a single religion, not the difference between various religions.

An important and farsighted comment made by Mannoni with reference to religious faith strengthens this interpretation. At the beginning of his differentiation between belief and faith, Mannoni emphasizes that it is necessary to maintain a distance between the problems of faith and those of belief, as they are of different natures – although, in practice, every faith is mixed with belief: 'Problems connected with religious faith have to be put aside at the outset; they are of a different nature, even if it is a fact that faith is always mingled

---

35   Émile Durkheim can be credited with making clear that gods are not an essential, necessary characteristic of religions. See Émile Durkheim, *The Elementary Forms of Religious Life*, trans. Karen E. Fields (New York: Simon & Schuster, 1995), pp. 27–32.

36   See Mannoni, *Clefs pour l'Imaginaire*, p. 14.

with belief."[37] There is, therefore, no faith without belief. It is apparently the prerequisite for a faith's formation. Whenever there is faith, there is also a belief. Perhaps we can illustrate this thesis through the following observation: those elements appearing in all religions that can be described as 'behaviouristic', although usually painstakingly followed, are regularly explained by their practitioners as being something that is certainly a part of the religion, but nonetheless not the real heart of the matter. These dismissed elements (that is to say: the majority or even all of a religion's rituals, as well as all of its myths) would accordingly make up the required share of *croyance*; and, conversely, that which this dismissive gesture aims to make more precise would be the share of *foi*.

These conditions do not seem to apply in the opposite direction. It seems entirely plausible, as Mannoni determined, for belief to appear alone, without faith: the biblical Jews, for example, believed superstitiously in Baal without professing their faith in him.[38] Although belief is a necessary condition for the emergence of faith, it is obviously not a sufficient one. Apparently, not every belief leads to faith. We must therefore investigate the additional conditions that are necessary for a belief to turn into a faith.

Nonetheless, two structural models of religion have been described that seem to enable a classification of historical epochs. There is one type (1) in which belief exists alone, and another type (2) in which belief and faith exist side by side. Historical religious epochs could be described and differentiated from one another in this way. There would be, accordingly, epochs in which religion consists of belief alone, and epochs in which it consists of faith mixed with belief. With his concept of belief as well as the differentiation between belief and faith, Mannoni made clear that faith is, by far, not the only form in which a 'belief in' – that is, a conviction – exists, that it is even a relatively rare form of conviction. Also, it is not characteristic for all cultures, and even where it does exist it relies on the accompaniment of belief.

---

37   Mannoni, *Clefs pour l'Imaginaire*, p. 13
38   'The subject to hand is belief: the belief that, for example, allowed the Jews to believe in the existence of Baal, although they had no faith in him.' (Mannoni 2003, p. 73).

IMAGINING AND ACTING

Since Mannoni relates *croyance* to the issue of the existence of gods and *foi* to the issue of (unconditional) commitment, it seems at first as though a difference has been identified between imagining and acting, between theoretical and practical religions. Mannoni's examples, however, already point in another direction. *Croyance*, too, leads to actions – in the case of the mask cult, which Mannoni discusses at the beginning ('autrefois on croyait aux masques'), for example, it leads all the way to colourful theatrical performances. The difference cannot simply rest on the distinction between mere idea and substantive action. Instead, we have to look for it in the various types of commitment.

In addition, as we have seen, Mannoni also problematized the category of imagining. Belief (*croyance*) is a belief in something that is assigned to the other. When *croyance* refers to God's existence, then it can only be referring to *the other's belief in* this existence. Also *foi*, for its part, would not be possible without the idea of the existence of that God to whom one devotes unconditional commitment. This imagining of existence, however, in contrast to the previous sense, would be *one's own belief in* this existence.

This more precise explanation, easily detectable based on the text, shows that Mannoni's first determination of the conceptual pair *croyance/foi* with the help of the distinction 'belief in the existence [of God or gods]'/'unconditional commitment', is only an initial, provisional determination. Mannoni himself replaces, or sharpens, this first determination in the further course of the text by means of another far-reaching psychoanalytic definition. Mannoni says that *foi* leads to a commitment by installing a law. The commitment contingent on *foi* is, accordingly, a commitment in the sense of a law, an action conforming with one's duty. Necessary for this is not only a law (underwritten by society), but also a psychological agency (on the part of the individual) that controls behaviour's dutifulness. In the terminology of Freud's second topical model (*topography*), this agency is the superego. Mannoni thereby detects that the emergence of a *foi* recalls the process of instituting a superego (*surmoi*).[39]

---

39   See Mannoni, *Clefs pour l'Imaginaire*, p. 17. Mannoni speaks about a memory (*rappel*), in that the emergence of *foi* in the scene he describes is due to a youth's

Religious faith (*foi*) thus generates a sense of duty as well as a corresponding commitment, and is topically bound to the agency of the superego. On the other hand, in Mannoni's account, behaviour with regard to belief (*croyance*) remains oddly indefinite. If belief lacks all the qualities of faith, which qualities does it then have? If believers do not act out of a sense of duty, why do they act? What is the opposite of a sense of duty? Should we say (following Kant's terminology) that non-professing believers act out of inclination (*Neigung*)? And if not to the superego, to what agency would the belief be bound? To the ego? Or to the id?

THE CONCEPTUAL PAIR 'BELIEF'/'FAITH' AND LACAN'S TOPOGRAPHY

These questions seem at least partly answerable, in that Mannoni focuses his differentiation between the two types of belief (*croyance* and *foi*) on a Freudian, and also Lacanian, topography. Mannoni assigns *croyance* and *foi* to the categories that Lacan distinguishes of 'imaginary' and 'symbolic'. Belief, *croyance*, is situated at the level of the imaginary, and faith, *foi*, at the level of the symbolic.[40] Mannoni seems to rely mainly on the fact that Lacan defines the 'symbolic' (among other things) as a law, as an obligation[41] – which, in turn, seems to refer to the dimension of (dutiful) commitment.

Yet, in making this categorization, Mannoni appears mystified by the originality of his own discovery. The specific thing that he discovers about the 'imaginary' – i.e. 'superstition' – is that it is a *disavowed imaginary*. It comprises illusions, but only those that are the 'illusions of the other'. They are 'attitudes in accordance with wishes' that anyone can adopt: ideas of wishes that some indefinite other could believe in. According to Lacan, such 'illusions of the other' are missing the one

---

initiation. The founding of the super-ego, on the contrary, must occur much earlier, based on psychoanalytic theory, at the end of the Oedipal phase.

40   Ibid.: '. . . le moment où la *croyance*, abandonnant sa forme *imaginaire*, se *symbolise* assez pour ouvrir sur la *foi*, c'est-à-dire sur un engagement' (p. 17, my emphases); compare ibid., p. 33.

41   See, for example, Lacan's differentiation between adult, binding speech and childish, non-binding speech, in Jacques Lacan, *The Seminar of Jacques Lacan: Freud's Papers on Technique*, vol. I, ed. Jacques-Alain Miller, trans. John Forrester (Cambridge: CUP, 1988 [1953–54]), p. 229.

element that is characteristic of the imaginary: the reference to an 'ideal ego'.[42] The ideal ego is that picture to which the subjects attempt to correspond, which allows them, in brief moments of such (imagined) correspondence, the narcissistic triumph of being their own ideal. The 'illusions of others' have no such image. They are not composed in such a way that subjects consider being adherents to such illusions as part of their ideal image. On the contrary, these illusions contain an image that subjects in fact try to escape from. They take great pains to make clear that they are not the ones who correspond with what they feel is a disdainful image of a person who believes in the illusion. As Mannoni notes at one point, they even find frightening the thought that the belief might possibly fall back onto them.[43]

Unlike belief, however, faith necessarily contains an ideal ego. The subjects take on a faith because they are pleased to be in the position of those who belong to that faith. The faith affords them the narcissistic satisfaction of self-respect: to be in accordance with the declared faith, or at least to think that they are in accordance, signifies a narcissistic triumph.[44]

It is therefore not possible to maintain Mannoni's order of the pair belief/faith with the pair imaginary/symbolic. Not belief, but rather faith, reveals the traits of the Lacanian imaginary. Consequently, the reverse of Mannoni's arrangement is what seems most likely: accordingly, *faith belongs to the imaginary and belief to the symbolic*. Two aspects of Lacan's theory seem to speak for this reverse order: on the one hand, his theory of the imaginary *moi* as one of the agencies of misrecognition; and on the other hand, a factor related to the meaning of Lacan's concept of the symbolic – namely, establishing it as an order of the illusions of the other.

---

42   On this concept, see Sigmund Freud 'On Narcissism: An Introduction' (SE XIV), p. 94.

43   See Mannoni, *Clefs pour l'Imaginaire*: '. . . si sa croyance à la magie retombe pour ainsi dire sur lui-même, il est saisi d'angoisse . . .' (p. 30).

44   This is also the basis for the statements made in a negative form, of the type 'I fear that I am not a true Christian', which Kierkegaard considered to be the only reliable signs of true Christianity. For a discussion of this reliability, see Slavoj Žižek, *Tarrying with the Negative: Kant, Hegel and the Critique of Ideology* (Durham, NC: Duke University Press, 1993), pp. 9ff; Robert Pfaller, 'Negation and its Reliabilities: An Empty Subject for Ideology?' in Slavoj Žižek, ed., *Cogito and the Unconscious* (Durham: Duke University Press, 1998).

Agencies of Misjudgement: Moi and Foi

The arrangement of faith together with the imaginary and belief with the symbolic coincides initially with Lacan's determination of the two subjects: *je* and *moi*. Faith contains a narcissistic ideal image, as does the imaginary *moi*; belief, on the contrary, proves to be a reality that is difficult to grasp, usually covered over by faith – just like the symbolic *je*, which is difficult to grasp and is usually covered over by the image of *moi*.[45] Faith (*foi*) thus corresponds with the imaginary (and the arrangement of *moi*), and belief (*croyance*) with the symbolic (and the arrangement of *je*).

This is relevant mainly because Mannoni's theory of belief is likewise a theory explaining how difficult it is to discover a belief in action. This difficulty was already present in the terminological problems related to common sense in everyday language. Furthermore, it became evident in the paradoxical formulation: 'I know quite well . . . but still . . .': contrary to the common assumption, belief is apparently not hindered by knowledge. And in the end, Mannoni sketches out a theory relating the forms in which belief/conviction can be found – a topography of social illusion – whereby belief can either exist on its own or be covered over by a faith, whose prerequisite it constitutes. Whereas in the former situation its nature seems evident, in the latter situation, its being covered over by a faith makes it difficult to recognize both the existence and the nature of the belief. Something in the nature of faith must make it inauspicious to recognize the belief – and especially faith's dependence on belief. For this reason, 'civilized' people, as members of a faith-culture, are incapable of recognizing the magic they perform.

In a similar way, Lacan defined *moi* as an instance of misrecognition within the topography of the individual.[46] Based on the new, reversed arrangement, Lacan's theory of *moi* as an instance of personal misrecognition can thus be mobilized to analyze the misrecognitions proper to social illusion starting from *foi*.

---

45   See Lacan, 'Mirror Stage', p. 76.

46   Ibid.: '. . . the limits of a self-sufficiency of consciousness which . . . ties the illusion of autonomy in which it puts its faith to the ego's constitutive misrecognitions' (p. 80).

The Symbolic as an Order of the Illusions of Others

The second reason that speaks for our reversal of the arrangement of Mannoni's categories with regard to those of Lacan can be found in a certain aspect of meaning occasionally exhibited by Lacan's concept of the symbolic. Lacan's 'symbolic' is a diverse concept. It makes an appearance not only in the defining of laws (especially the incest prohibition), but also in the sense of declaring an *order of fictions* that are always 'the others' fictions'. Slavoj Žižek frequently highlights this aspect of Lacan's concept of the 'symbolic' (as well as the synonymous Lacanian term of the 'big Other'), which is congruent with Mannoni's concept of beliefs. For example, Žižek has explained that the political value of the Clinton–Lewinsky affair was not in revealing to voters that the president had a less than respectable private life. According to Žižek, voters never had the illusion that he did. Instead, the 'exposure campaign' was about revealing these facts to an authority other than the voters – namely, the 'big Other'. There, the president had a reputation that could be tarnished: even if everyone knew (or suspected) that the president had extramarital affairs, there was an agency from whom this knowledge was kept a secret. The president's agency, as far as the real citizens go, relies on his impeccable appearance in the eyes of this virtual 'big Other'. The president's agency was, to this extent, symbolic: it rested on an 'illusion of the other', a fiction – namely, the fiction that there is someone from whom the embarrassing knowledge must be concealed. The president's symbolic agency was not destroyed when voters knew, but when the secret could no longer be kept from the 'big Other'. (And the attempt at destruction was aimed not only at President Clinton's symbolic agency, but also at the symbolic nature of agency in society in general. It was an attempt to make symbolic agency, per se, impossible, and to replace it with real agency.)[47] Later I will attempt to show that establishing Lacan's concept of 'symbolic' as an order of fictions has entirely different consequences from those of equating the symbolic with a prohibiting law and the psychological agency of the superego. A complete organizational

---

47   See Slavoj Žižek, 'Ein Plädoyer für die ehrliche Lüge. Bill Clintons Affäre und das Freudsche Gespenst des Urvaters', *Die Zeit*, 8 October 1998. In the same sense, Žižek identified use of the Tibetan prayer wheel and canned laughter as practices 'through the medium of the other' – i.e. as symbolic practices (as an order of the illusions of others). Žižek, *Sublime Object of Ideology*, p. 35.

model for social illusion ensues from the way the symbolic works as an order of fictions (including a law characteristic for this order – the law of appearances), which opposes the model that it is formed from the law of the superego.

Rather than fitting smoothly into Lacan's topography, Mannoni's theory seems to add greater precision to Lacan's theory. Defining Lacan's concept of the symbolic as an order of illusions of the other means freeing this symbolic from all of the overtones of prohibition and superego (which Lacan was not always able to achieve in an unambiguous way; the entire tradition of critique founded by Deleuze and Guattari is based on this). The symbolic law would then be exclusively the law of the pleasure principle.[48] The entire realm of the superego's imperative as well as the sense of duty, however, would oppose this symbolic law, and would be classified as belonging to the imaginary. This corresponds with Louis Althusser's theory of the imaginary subject formation (subjectivization).[49]

Specifying the relationship between the imaginary and the symbolic in this way would also subsequently affect the understanding of the psychological observing agencies discerned by psychoanalysis. It would enable a clear differentiation of these agencies, as well as their assignment to the areas: symbolic and imaginary. An omniscient observing agency, such as the Freudian 'super-ego'[50] (for example, in the topical model from 1914: the 'ego ideal'[51]) – which also knows the secret wishes, thoughts and intentions of the subject and punishes the individual with guilt not only for their deeds, but also for their wishes and intentions – would be assigned to the imaginary.

Lacan's 'big Other', on the contrary, would not be this kind of omniscient agency – contrary to the tenor of the predominant interpretations. The 'big Other' would, instead, be an entirely naive observer who is completely oblivious to the subject's secret wishes, thoughts and intentions; one who judges exclusively on appearances (the perceivable, set signs – for example, of a president's respectability). Precisely here, in this function of naive observer and judge, the 'big Other' equates with the symbolic order.

---

48 For more, see Evans, *Introductory Dictionary*, p. 99.
49 For more, see Althusser, 'Ideology and Ideological State Apparatuses'.
50 See Freud, 'The Ego and the Id' (SE XIX), p. 28.
51 See Freud, 'On Narcissism', p. 94.

In his analyses of those illusions that are always illusions of the other, Mannoni has thereby discovered an observing agency that is characteristic of an entire type of social institution. Later in this chapter, I will examine in greater detail this type of institution, and the peculiarity of the observing agency on which it rests (see section 9, p. 231ff).

INITIAL CONSEQUENCES OF MANNONI'S CONCEPT OF BELIEF FOR CULTURAL SCIENCES

Mannoni's identification of superstition as an illusion for others contradicts a series of common assumptions. It seems appropriate at this point to summarize the theoretical gains that we are already able to draw from Mannoni's hitherto presented theses, and to show which traditional understandings they oppose.

The Issue of the Form of Social Illusions

Convictions, illusions and ideologies are traditionally understood as part of the faith paradigm, which is regarded as universal. No other type is entertained than one associated with a professed carrier. All convictions, illusions and ideologies have (at least) one *subject*. The only possible question would thus be which convictions exist in a given society, which means: the *content* of given conviction.

Mannoni, on the contrary, shows that there are convictions, illusions and ideologies that exist without subjects, as illusions of the other. Here we are dealing with a type of conviction that has no carrier – or at least not one who professes the conviction. This opens up a new question – namely, that of the *form* in which a conviction exists within a given society. Mannoni's discovery makes it necessary to create classifications that reveal not only *what convictions* can be found in a given society, but also *the form in which* these convictions are present. Two different societies can have the same conviction, but in a different form. That which might be a *foi* for one can present itself as a *croyance* for another. For example, according to Engels' bon mot, the belief in Greek gods had the status of a *foi* for nineteenth-century scholars, but, for the ancient Greeks, most likely merely that of a *croyance*.

The Transformed Concept of the Believer:
Believers Believe in Nothing At All

Mannoni's discovery that conviction can exist in various forms also changes the traditional picture that cultural theories have produced and assumed to be obvious of the carriers of belief. Not least because of the contempt in the concept of superstition against its carriers, some cultural sciences tended to strike this term from their vocabulary.[52] Since Mannoni supplies this term with a totally transformed meaning, he not only frees it from all contempt directed against the carriers, but also makes it possible to derive from it an entirely new, emphatic concept of the believers in superstition.

According to Mannoni, belief consists of delegated illusions: they are illusions of the other. It is therefore not what is believed, but rather, in what form it is believed, that decides whether it can be classified as belonging to the category 'superstition'. For example, the uneducated believers in superstition whom Freud speaks about are therefore not at all superstitious according to Mannoni's new definition, since they 'feel themselves at one with their belief'.[53] Their convictions – whether illusions or not – are their own, and not those of the other. They are forms of faith, and not beliefs or superstitions. On the contrary, in Mannoni's strict, theoretical sense, believers in superstition never feel at one with their belief. They are therefore exactly the opposite of that which linguistic usage considers them to be: they are people who do not believe – or, in any case, not in that which forms the content of their superstition. The believers do not imagine any such thing; they operate exclusively with illusions of others. Their belief is a purely *foreign belief*: a belief that is comparable with an export good – never for one's own use, but instead always produced for the other.[54]

---

52   This problem will be discussed in greater detail in Chapter 6, section 2, on p. 139ff.

53   See Freud, 'Notes upon a Case of Obsessional Neurosis', p. 229.

54   This can be explained based on Walter Benjamin's differentiation between 'cult value' and 'exhibition value'. The illusion of the other is assigned cult value – one's own illusion, on the other hand, exhibition value. This explains the seclusion of artworks in cultures that are based on the principle of superstition: 'Today the cult value would seem to demand that the work of art remain hidden. Certain statues of gods are accessible only to the priest in the cellar; certain Madonnas remain covered nearly all year round; certain sculptures on medieval cathedrals are invisible to the spectator on ground level.' Walter Benjamin, 'The Work of Art in the Age of Mechanical

Critique of the Perspective-Based Illusion

With this characterization of superstition, and also examples from theatre and the mask cult, Mannoni formulates two interconnected theses: *That which is considered to be the conviction (faith) of the so-called 'savages' is in truth their superstition*; and: *The 'civilized' also have superstition.*

Both theses are far from obvious. And even where they are understood, they will long be accompanied by an opposing expectation. The illusion of the other seldom appears as what it is – a mere export good. Instead, a double misjudgement usually takes place, a 'perspectival illusion' conditioned by one's own standpoint: one's own superstition is overlooked, but foreign superstition is understood as faith.

The Perspectival Illusion's Intercultural Variant: The Myth of a Magical World View – Mannoni and Wittgenstein

This problem that Mannoni has clarified is of extreme significance for the cultural sciences. For example, it is at the root of Ludwig Wittgenstein's critique of James George Frazer's view of magic.

Frazer attempted to grant the 'savage's' magic a certain rationality, in that he viewed it as a technology based on false, quasi-natural-scientific theoretical premises. Thanks to these albeit errant theoretical elements, according to Frazer, magic is closer to science than religion. In contrast to religion, magic assumes that the same causes will always evoke the same effects:[55] '. . . as a system of natural law, that is, as a statement of the rules which determine the sequence of events throughout the world, it may be called Theoretical Magic.'[56] To be sure, the theory developed from magic is merely implicit: its status is that of a silent conviction.[57] As conviction, however, it is false. The

---

Reproduction' (Scottsdale: Prism Key Press, 2010), p. 21. In superstition, the artworks are only shown to others, which is why cult value dominates. In faith, one must see them personally, just as one must believe personally – which is why exhibition value dominates.

55   See Frazer, *Golden Bough*, Chapter 4.

56   Ibid., Chapter 3, Section 1.

57   Frazer writes: 'In short, to him magic is always an art, never a science; the very idea of science is lacking in his undeveloped mind. It is for the philosophic student

'savages', accordingly, have false convictions or faiths, which include corresponding techniques – of which nothing is false other than their 'theory'. The practices of 'practical magic' would thus be 'applications' of the fundamental convictions that they are based on. Practising magic would thereby be no more irrational than, for example, building a bridge that then collapses because the calculations on which it is based are wrong. The error is in the theory, not in its technical application. The practice of magic is therefore an 'abortive art', because it is based on 'false science'.[58] The 'civilized', on the contrary, have true convictions due to their knowledge of natural science, and to what are now correct, no-longer-magical techniques (to the extent that these techniques are no longer applications of false, magical convictions, but instead of true, scientific ones).

Wittgenstein contradicts Frazer on all points. First, he contests Frazer's thesis that the 'savage's' idea of magic exists in the form of a conviction. The 'savages' do not believe in their idea of magic in the same way that one believes in natural science's knowledge. They do not think that the contents of 'theoretical magic' are true, and they also do not draw any self-esteem from the possession of these supposed truths (in contrast to members of scientific cultures). For that reason, they do not consider their magic as a technique – and rightly so. They instead differentiate it from technical practices, which they also have available. Wittgenstein shows this by examining several cases in which both a magical and a technical practice, which seem to serve the same purpose, exist side by side: '[T]oward morning, when the sun is about to rise, rites of daybreak are celebrated by the people, but not during the night, when they simply burn lamps.'[59]

Were Frazer correct in his explanation of magic, then every time someone needed light they would have to celebrate the ritual of daybreak, and the actors would be unaware of the technology of using

---

to trace the train of thought which underlies the magician's practice; to draw out the few simple threads of which the tangled skein is composed; to disengage the abstract principles from their concrete applications; in short, to discern the spurious science behind the bastard art' (ibid.). Theory is faced with precisely the same problem faced by the everyday magic of civilized people – for example, as observed in the practices of interpassivity. Moreover, civilized magicians, as a rule, do not develop an idea of 'spurious science' that is at the base of their 'bastard art'. Instead, they operate with an illusion that has no image.

58   Ibid.
59   Wittgenstein, 'Remarks on Frazer's *Golden Bough*', p. 137

lamps. Yet, according to Frazer, as soon as this technology is discovered, the rites cease to exist – they disappear like an outdated technology in the face of a newer one, just as the post coach made way for the van, or the typewriter for the personal computer.

The fact that these practices, magical and technical, are present side by side, shows that the actors know how to distinguish between them and furnish each with a different status, which they are able to determine precisely, based on each particular occasion: 'The same savage, who stabs the picture of his enemy apparently in order to kill him, really builds his hut out of wood and carves his arrows skillfully and not in effigy.'[60] Wittgenstein hereby showed that Frazer's original assumption was untenable: the magical practices of the 'savages' do not rest on false conviction; they most certainly have access to the corresponding better knowledge.

But Wittgenstein goes on to demonstrate that Frazer is also wrong in his view of the 'civilized'. It is not at all true that 'civilized' people have no magical practices. Wittgenstein remarks: 'When a man laughs too much in our company (or at least in mine), I half involuntarily compress my lips, as if I believed I could thereby keep his closed.'[61] And one could continue: 'but nonetheless, I would fiercely contradict any ethnologist who says that I have such a belief'. There is an illusion in the situation, but that does not necessarily mean it is the illusion of the actors themselves – their own conviction. Nonetheless, at issue is an example of a magical practice: it is treated as though the presentation of one's own silent lips would have an influence on what is represented (the other's lips).[62]

Wittgenstein's critique of Frazer can thereby be summarized as: the 'savages' are not convinced of magical views, nor are 'civilized' people any freer of them than 'savages'. Or, in Mannoni's terms: the supposed faith of the 'savage' is only belief, and precisely the same

---

60   Ibid., p. 125

61   Ibid., p. 141

62   For more, compare Wittgenstein's other examples from the 'civilized' world: 'When I am furious about something, I sometimes beat the ground or a tree with my walking stick. But I certainly do not believe that the ground is to blame or that my beating helped anything' (ibid., p. 137); 'Burning in effigy. Kissing the picture of one's beloved. That is *obviously not* based on the belief that it will have some specific effect on the object which the picture represents' (p. 123). In the words of Frazer, these civilized practices were also a 'bastard art', behind which a 'spurious science' was hiding (Frazer, *Golden Bough*, Chapter 3, Section 1).

form of belief exists among the 'civilized'. With this critique, Wittgenstein clarifies the difference between the 'language game' of magic and other practices – for example, technical ones – that Frazer overlooked. But Wittgenstein also shows here that *there is a form of illusion that is not that of conviction*. Ritualistic acts and also 'mythical' remarks[63] (among both 'savage' and 'civilized' people) reveal the effectiveness of an illusion that is revoked by 'better knowledge', and that actors do not claim as faith. In his critique of Frazer, Wittgenstein also simultaneously delivers a case study on the power of 'perspectival illusion' with regard to belief. Frazer overlooked his own beliefs in an exemplary way, and misunderstood those of others as their convictions.

The Historical Variant of Perspectival Illusion: The Myth of the 'Enlightenment Process' – 'Mythologists' and 'Ritualists'

The perspectival illusion, to which some ethnologists, including Frazer, have fallen victim, leads not only to intercultural misunderstandings, but also to an incorrect historical awareness, to an erroneous historical picture. The forms of belief are thought to be *early forms of faith*; the fact that they also exist in the present as beliefs is overlooked. This leads to the erroneous view that the history of convictions brought an 'enlightenment process'[64] along with it: earlier, people believed *more*, whereas today, they believe *less*.

Mannoni's theory of belief and faith, however, allows the reverse assumption to appear plausible: faiths are 'later' products.[65] They

---

63   On the 'mythical' variant, see Wittgenstein, 'Remarks on Frazer's *Golden Bough*': 'If I, a person who does not believe that there are human-superhuman beings somewhere which one can call gods – if I say: "I fear the wrath of the gods", that shows that I can mean something by this, or can give expression to a feeling which is not necessarily connected with that belief' (p. 131). See also p. 129: 'Rather, the characteristic feature of ritualistic action is not at all a view, an opinion, whether true or false, although an opinion – a belief – can itself be ritualistic or part of a rite.'

64   See Mannoni, *Clefs pour l'Imaginaire*: '. . . une sorte de progrès de lumières' (p. 9).

65   The fact that, under certain conditions, illusions, which are initially without owners, will one day actually be adopted by specific carriers must be understood as a late historical result. Contrary to the expectations suggested by the concept of 'enlightenment', there is a process of *increasing appropriation* of illusions. See Mario Erdheim, *Die gesellschaftliche Produktion von Unbewußtheit*, 3rd edn (Frankfurt: Suhrkamp, 1990): 'In any case, among the Selk'nam, all initiated men knew that there were no spirits, however, later, when the system of control became more extensive, the men, or the majority of them, also had to believe.' (p. 228, my translation).

emerge on the basis of superstitions, which necessarily continue to exist as such. But it is conceivable that there were previous periods in which illusions existed exclusively in the form of belief, without being covered over by faith. 'Earlier', not only did people not believe in the masks, but they also did not possess any other belief (in the sense of a faith). 'Today', on the contrary, the apparent disbelief in masks seems to have been bought at the price of being subjected to another faith – and beyond that, having to subject other cultures to a belief in the masks as their faith. Dogmatic, aggressive faith cultures (as well as cultures of concealed beliefs – see Mardi Gras festivals, Santa Claus, and so on) thereby replaced non-dogmatic, less aggressive cultures of solitary and open superstition.

Mannoni thus renders an unusual idea of history conceivable. Accordingly, the members of so-called 'primitive' cultures (but also of some so-called 'high cultures', such as that of ancient Greece) would be satisfied to function as *objects* of illusions: the actors in the superstition make themselves marionettes in a play, as it were, that they offer to a – usually undetermined – other. On the other hand, the actors do not seem eager to become subjects of their superstition and take on its content as their faith. Instead, it seems that they devote considerable effort to keeping the illusion at a distance, to avoid becoming its subjects.

Émile Durkheim offers some support for Mannoni's theory on this point. According to Durkheim, the fundamental characteristic of all religions can be found by drawing a border between the sacred and the profane.[66] But how does this happen if, in some cultures, these operations of demarcating borders mainly serve the purpose of keeping the sacred at arm's length from people? Durkheim remarks that the sacred – entirely contrary to its supposedly fragile nature, rendering it in need of protection[67] – tends to spread, in a threatening way: 'And in fact, paradoxically, the sacred world is prone by its very nature to infiltrate that same profane world it otherwise excludes. Even as it repels it, it tends to flow into it as soon as it comes near.'[68] Durkheim concludes from this: 'This is why they must be kept apart from one another and a kind of gulf must be maintained between them.'[69]

---

66 See Durkheim, *Elementary Forms*, p. 36.
67 Ibid., p 38
68 Ibid., p. 237.
69 Ibid.

Religious practices serve, as Durkheim explains, to set limits to the spread of the sacred world, to build up buffer zones against it. Is this not what constitutes the fundamental 'interpassivity' of certain religious practices? Do the Tibetans not achieve an off-putting resistance to their religion with their prayer wheels, just as consumers of canned laughter resist television entertainment in Žižek's example?[70] Does their religiosity not consist of a similar mischievous pleasure in having slipped past religion? Is that not also the clear purpose of the prayer flags driven by the wind? And can we not find traces of this resistant behaviour even in religions in which faith already dominates over superstition? Do the burning candles in a sacred Christian site not replace a pious person who has long since gone home?

Is this not the basis for the outbreak of animosity towards rituals, myths and images that springs up in the history of several religions?[71] Did these religions not use such 'reform phases' in reaction against the suspicion that their own practices might present a resistance movement against the sacred?[72] Are these reform phases not clear

---

70   As Günter Thomas has quite correctly remarked with regard to the 'liturgy' of television, 'The permanent contemporary liturgy is like much of ritual-religious communication: a given that in its occurrence and course is removed from its own disposal; something that neither has to be shaped nor can be destroyed . . . Since this situation of not being at its own disposal can also be experienced as a relief, it is necessary to place a clear question-mark on the hope of a broad acceptance and use of interactive forms of television. Interactive television assumes that there was a need to create, which in the current organization of television would necessarily lead recipients into a position of refusal.' Günter Thomas, *Medien – Ritual – Religion. Zur religiösen Funktion des Fernsehens* (Frankfurt: Suhrkamp, 1996), pp. 472–3.

71   For more, see the precise remarks in Caroline Humphrey and James Laidlaw, *The Archetypal Actions of Ritual: A Theory of Ritual Illustrated by the Jain Rite of Worship* (Oxford: Clarendon Press, 1994): 'What happens in religious traditions when the nature of ritual is questioned, but the practice of performing rituals is not itself abandoned? Much anthropological analysis simply equates religion and ritual, or regards them as forming some kind of indissoluble whole, yet in many cases a religious attitude, a searching for spiritual perfection perhaps, can turn upon its own vehicle, ritual, to regard it with distrust, depreciation, or even fear . . . We think that these reactions to ritual tell us about more than just particular religious ideologies, for there is a sense in which, when different religious traditions act in this way, they are reacting to a common phenomenon. Such reactions therefore reveal the essential features of ritual action' (p. 1). Here I might simply add that a religion's own rituals are not its only objects of mistrust – its own myths can be, too.

72   For more, see the analysis by Miran Božovič of David Hume's anti-ritual theism: '[T]he Humean philosophical theist is someone who believes in God, someone who knows that God exists – yet for that very reason he acts as if God did

signs of a transition from a model of religion that was intent on resisting sacredness to another model that attempts to appropriate it – a transition from a model of belief to one of faith?

Considerations of this kind emanating from Mannoni's theory shed a new light on a crucial discussion within ethnology – the debate between 'mythologists' and 'ritualists' at the end of the nineteenth century. Ethnologists, such as Frazer and Edward Burnett Tylor, assumed that every ritual act is a sacrificial act and therefore requires a myth: there must first be ideas, such as those of a 'holy being', in order to begin with the attempt to please this being with gifts and reverent behaviour.[73]

Orientalists and theologists such as Julius Wellhausen and William Robertson Smith countered this double thesis about the precedence of myths over rituals and the sacrificial character of rituals, formulating the thesis that ritual meals were not sacrifices, but instead 'communions', and also that they were not 'vertical' activities addressed to a higher power, but rather 'horizontal', community-building social activities. This new interpretation makes plausible a different relationship between rituals and myths; it abolished the 'vertical' interpretation of meat preparation as an activity addressed to a higher power, as well as the thesis of the precedence of myth over ritual. Instead, it stated that ritual acts may have existed for a long time without creating a system of myths. If such a system did happen to come together, then it might often have been only much later than the rituals[74] – and possibly also as a strongly distorted rendering of what the rituals were about.[75]

This controversy attains a new, intensified meaning in the context of Mannoni's contemplations: Is the real issue not that of the debate about the succession of 'rituals' and 'myths' whether the 'savages' believed in anything at all? Is the striking part of the theses by

---

not exist, for any worship that is more than mere indifferent, disinterested cognition offends him and incurs his disfavor, wrath, contempt, et cetera' (Božovič, *An Utterly Dark Spot*, pp. 3–14).

73   See Edward Burnett Tylor, *Primitive Culture* (Gloucester: Peter Smith, 1970), p. 376; compare Frazer, *Golden Bough*, Chapter 4.

74   See Smith, William Robertson, *Religion of the Semites*, (New Brunswick, NJ: Transaction Publ., [1894] 2002), p. 16. Compare Kippenberg, Hans G., *Die Entdeckung der Religionsgeschichte: Religionswissenschaft und Moderne* (Munich: Beck, 1997).

75   See Smith, *Religion of the Semites*, p. 13. Compare Freud, 'Obsessive Actions', pp. 122–3.

Wellhausen, Robertson Smith, and others, not the ill-concealed claim that 'savages' were atheists? But Mannoni's concept of belief allows this question to part company with the opposition 'ritual/myth'. Both parties in the dispute concerning the religiosity of 'savages' seem to have unquestionably assumed that 'myth' always exists in the form of faith, and that those who follow myths subsequently become believers. The theses from 'mythologists' and 'ritualists' can therefore be framed as reciprocal formulas: 'first believing, then acting'/'first acting, then believing'. Yet, for both parties, ritual seemed to have a discordant, insufficiently religious nature. Myth, on the other hand, was not exposed to this suspicion with the same radicality.[76]

But Mannoni's concept of belief would enable just that: just as ritual allows actors to distance themselves from the apparent content of belief, so also can myth. It, too, can take the form of an illusion of the other.[77] One sign that actors are distancing themselves from their myths in this way is the well-known preambles and introductions that begin: 'There once was . . .', 'As they say. . . .'[78] Also with the help of

---

76   See, for example, Durkheim, *Elementary Forms*: 'All myths, even those we find most unreasonable, have been objects of faith' (p. 80). In a note, Durkheim then makes an interesting differentiation between myths and 'fables', which 'were not believed, or at least, were not believed to the same degree and in the same manner and for that reason were not religious' (ibid., note 36). But here we could ask, with Mannoni, whether there were not also types of religiosity that were exclusively of a 'fabulous' nature. Durkheim's seemingly questionable answer is his identification of 'relationship to cult' as the decisive characteristic of myth (ibid.): are fables not just as capable of promoting cults? The 'Perchtenlaufen', for example, still practised in some regions in Austria, have all of the characteristics of a cult. Nonetheless, according to Durkheim's terminology, they are based not on a myth, but a fable.

77   William Robertson Smith comes ever closer to such a 'superstitious' concept when he writes: 'But, strictly speaking, this mythology was no essential part of ancient religion, for it had no sacred sanction and no binding force on the worshippers . . . Belief in a certain series of myths was neither obligatory as a part of true religion, nor was it supposed that, by believing, a man acquired religious merit and conciliated the favour of the gods.' William Robertson Smith, *Lectures on the Religion of the Semites* (London: Adam & Charles Black, 1894), p. 17. The criterion of 'commitment' corresponds with Mannoni's concept of 'engagement' (*Clefs pour l'Imaginaire*, p. 17), and refers to the form of faith that Smith here denies. Nonetheless, this argument merely serves the author in situating the 'commitment' in ritual rather than myth. But I would like also to remove the 'duty' from ritual, and instead see its 'binding power' as a *compulsion*, which is characteristic of the illusions without owners, and which can be observed still in many daily rituals (see, in this book, Chapter 4, sections 5, p. 111ff, and section 6, p. 112ff).

78   See Veyne, *Did the Greeks Believe in Their Myths?*, p. 23. The opposite of such

myth, a culture's members can distance themselves from the cultural content of belief; there is also an interpassivity of myth. Along these lines, Veyne remarks: 'The essence of a myth is not that everyone knows it, but that it is supposed to be known and is worthy of being known by all. Furthermore, it was not generally known.'[79] Veyne also quite correctly notes the same interpassivity as a characteristic of theoretical ideologies when he states: '[L]et us say the ideologue calls Heaven itself to witness (since bourgeois publicists did not imagine that the proletariat would read their octavos).'[80] For that reason, it is not only rituals that are exposed to reform phases in the history of religions. There were also reform phases directed against myths.[81]

Conversely, however, rituals are not, per se, bastions of belief. Quite obviously, there are rituals that are expressions of faith. Just as there are people who use canned laughter on television to stimulate their own laughter, rather than repressing their own merriment through it, there are also practitioners who use their religious exercises to assure themselves of their faith rather than to keep the sacred at a distance. The opposing pair 'rituals/myths' was, to this extent, only a provisional formulation of that which ritualists and mythologists actually fought over. Their concept of ritual represented Mannoni's concept of belief, that of myth represented Mannoni's concept of faith. But this arrangement is incorrect. Although the interpassive, belief dimension of rituals might catch someone's eye more quickly than that of myths, it is necessary to emphasize its possibility in both areas. Disavowal can exist as ritual or as myth. An illusion suspended by knowing better does not necessarily have to be found at the level of action; it can also be located at the level of narration.

In relation to illusions found in 'civilized' actions, Žižek showed with extreme lucidity, on the basis of commodity fetishism, the extent

---

formulations is the vernacular expression 'I tell you . . .' Almost like an oath, it is an expression of faith.

79   Ibid., p. 45.

80   Paul Veyne, 'Ideology According to Marx and According to Nietzsche', trans. Jeanne Ferguson, in *Diogenes* 25 (1977), p. 91.

81   See Veyne, *Did the Greeks Believe in Their Myths?*, p. 41 on the ancient Greek religion: 'the most pious minds would have been the first to remove from the so-called heroic epoch the childish interventions, miracles, and battles of the gods that Homer presents in the Iliad.'

to which people who most certainly have better knowledge can still be caught up in illusions without ever having thought of the content of these illusions. As he explains, the bourgeois individual is, in theory,

> definitely not a speculative Hegelian . . . He is, on the contrary, a good Anglo-Saxon nominalist . . . The problem is that in his practice, in his real activity, he acts as if the particular things (the commodities) were just so many embodiments of universal Value . . . [T]he illusion is not on the side of knowledge, it is already on the side of reality itself, of what the people are doing.[82]

The opposite of an illusion that is situated in action, however, is not merely misconception located in theory. The 'mythological' pendant to Žižek's identified 'ritualistic' illusion is, instead, the illusion *that remains situated in the narrative despite better knowledge*. An example of this would be a myth explored by Veyne – that of the Ethiopian Dorzé about the 'Christian' leopards. In the myth, the Dorzé speak of the predator's observance of the commandment to fast, yet at the level of action they behave in accordance with their knowledge, and protect their herds.[83]

The actual stakes of the debate over whether 'savages' were atheists, which is argued based on an opposition between 'ritual' and 'myth', can be more precisely reformulated using Mannoni's terms: Were the 'savages' professed believers, or were they superstitious? Did they actually believe, or not? Were they endeavouring to be the subjects of their illusions, or were they satisfied with remaining their objects? Did their illusions contain a self-image, an ideal ego from which they attempted to gain self-esteem, or were they simply illusions of the other from which they were pleased to distance themselves?

Through the critique of the 'perspectival illusion' with regard to history, Mannoni's theory makes it plausible that the history of illusions is in no way subject to a continuing 'enlightening, dismantling process'. Instead, it leads us to ask if perhaps exactly the opposite might be the case: Might it be possible that societies organized their illusions according to the belief mode for a long time before they began to build up faith? Is it conceivable that 'illusions for others' long

---

82   Žižek, *Sublime Object of Ideology*, p. 32.
83   See Veyne, *Did the Greeks Believe in Their Myths?*, p. xi.

fulfilled the ideological function of social illusion, promoting cohesion, and that the model of faith, which we find to be so familiar and capable of generalization, presents a relatively late and special product?[84] Might it be possible that, for a long time, people truly believed quite little, and did so more only later? Is it conceivable that only certain societies completed a late transition from a system of pure foreign belief to a system of foreign belief covered over with one's own belief?

An indication of this sort of assumption can be found in the controversy between Norbert Elias and Hans Peter Duerr over the 'myth of the civilizing process'. Whereas Elias attempted to describe the history of Western European societies as a history of the progressive taming of drives,[85] Duerr was able to make a plausible case, mainly with numerous examples of excessive violence among so-called 'civilized' cultures, that the talk of a 'civilizing process' is a myth.[86] In quantitative terms, far from lessening, violence shows more of a tendency to intensify; and in terms of violent content, it seems to preserve a certain iconographic cultural continuity, for example, in (as Duerr names it) 'the fucking of enemies and rivals'.[87] Duerr thus correctly charged that Elias had done no more with his theory of 'civilizing process' than give a theoretical formulation to a deceptive self-image of so-called 'civilized' cultures – breaching a

---

84   Michel de Certeau approaches this theory when he writes: 'belief becomes an utterance (an affirmation) when it ceases to mesh with some contractual practice . . . This sundering has given rise to . . . representations known as "beliefs" precisely because we do not believe them any longer.' Michel de Certeau, 'What We Do When We Believe', in Marshall Blonsky, ed., *On Signs: A Semiotics Reader* (Oxford: Blackwell, 1985), p. 196. 'Belief' in Certeau's sense is mere belief; the later 'affirmations', on the contrary, are faith. Nonetheless, Certeau errs when he grants the status of superstition exclusively to what he conceives as rituals (which are, in addition, conceived as sacrificial practices). The myths that he subtly analyzes under the formulation 'Other people believe in it' (ibid., p. 202) are a 'contractual practice', too. Precisely because both have the status of mere belief, and are thereby based on the principle of distance to their carriers, Certeau's declared separation between 'superstitions' and the 'mental landscapes' surrounding them has always existed, and is not a phenomenon of more complex societies. The so-called 'survivals' have always already been 'survivals' (compare ibid., p. 197).

85   See Norbert Elias, *The Civilizing Process: Sociogenetic and Psychogenetic Investigations* (Oxford: Blackwell, 2000).

86   See Duerr, Hans Peter, Obszönität und Gewalt, *Der Mythos vom Zivilisationsprozess* (Frankfurt/Main: Suhrkamp, 1995).

87   Ibid., pp. 242ff.

fundamental materialist rule, and judging the being of these cultures according to their self-consciousness.[88]

It is therefore necessary, as Duerr demonstrated, to recognize the idea of a progressive 'taming' of people throughout history as an illusion. At the same time, we must honour *the appearance of this illusion* as a cultural fact, and explain how we arrived at it. What reality is revealed by its materialization, when, already at the level of content, it appears to dispense with all reality? Where does the idea of 'civilizing' come from? When the counter-evidence is so astonishingly obvious, how do certain cultures arrive at the idea that a 'civilizing process' underlies them, thanks to which they have arrived at a greater control of their drives than others?

It seems possible to offer an answer to these questions based on Mannoni. The fact that certain cultures consider themselves to be 'civilized' points to the fact that here we are dealing with cultures of faith. These are cultures that do not produce their illusions merely for foreign use, but instead draw self-esteem from them. This self-esteem is expressed in the 'consciousness' of 'being civilized', and in the contemptuous treatment of other cultures. In what follows, I will also attempt to show the way in which the emergence of faith is tied to the origin of an ascetic ideal. Rather than the reality of controlling drives, it is a reality of the desire to do so that characterizes 'civilized' faith societies.

In this regard, it also seems interesting to apply Mannoni's conceptual pair 'belief/faith' to the issue of racism. At first glance, it might seem plausible to identify racism as a form of belief. Preambles such as, 'I am certainly not a racist', which are unavoidably followed by a 'but still . . .' cannot be ignored. They seem to correspond exactly with Mannoni's formulation 'Je sais bien . . . mais quand même. . . .'[89] Nonetheless, it appears rash to characterize racism as exclusively a belief formation. In racist actions there is apparently a noticeable constant: Is

---

88 See Althusser, Louis, *Écrits sur la psychanalyse: Freud et Lacan* (Paris: Stock/IMEC, 1993), p. 234.

89 Žižek was the first to point out this disavowing, belief dimension of racism. See Slavoj Žižek, *For They Know Not What They Do: Enjoyment as a Political Factor* (London/New York: Verso, 1991), pp. 51–2. This is one of the reasons that racism cannot be overcome through explanation: all explanatory information meets an already-existing 'I know, but . . .' For more, see David Signer, *Fernsteuerung. Kulturrassismus und unbewußte Abhängigkeiten* (Vienna: Passagen, 1997), pp. 135ff.

there not always a strange 'consensus' that racism cannot rest on mutu-
ality? Is it not remarkable that when two different groups meet (even if
they mutually abhor each other), it is immediately obvious to all parties
involved which group it is that can be racist with regard to the other?
On what criteria, then, do protagonists, as well as victims, 'realize' who
alone can take on the role of protagonist? Apparently it is not a question of power alone: the powerful are not always poised against the
powerless, nor is the majority always poised against the minority.
Racists can most certainly find themselves in the weaker position; they
conceal their racism, and only allow it to appear at those moments
when they feel themselves to be the stronger. Could this strange criterion in which victim and protagonist uphold the 'justification' for
racism again be found, perhaps, in the perception of 'being civilized'?
Are those cultures and groups who are racist against others not those
whose illusions are largely organized according to the model of faith?
Is a racist position dependent on the existence of a faith culture?

Without being able to discuss these issues here, we must simply
note that Mannoni's theory of covering over earlier forms of belief
with faith makes it possible to view in a new light several, exclusively
'later' cultural forms. For example, we can view the deceptive perception of being civilized, or even the practice of racism, in a new way,
and offer an explanation.

The Perspective-Based Illusion Theory

Based on the historical hypothesis founded on Mannoni's theory,
according to which the initially universal belief-form of organization
of social illusions was later covered over by the faith-form in some
societies, it is also possible to formulate a theory for how the 'perspectival illusion' came about. The question is raised of whether all cultures
are subject to this illusion to the same degree. In other words: Are all
cultures equally incapable of grasping the other's belief *as belief* (and
not as faith)? And are they all equally blind to their own belief? Faith
cultures are possibly affected by this misjudgement to a much greater
degree (as is shown by the fact that 'civilized' people do not recognize
that they perform magic, whereas 'savages' recognize that they do').
Misjudgement would therefore be an effect caused by the predominance of faith. It is possible that faith finds it that much more necessary
than belief to be deceptive about the existence of belief.

The reason for that might be found in the fact that the faith-form, as Mannoni detected,[90] can never exist without forms of belief. Even if faith covers over previous belief, or partially destroys it (in 'reform phases' directed against rituals and myths), this covering, control and destruction can nonetheless never be complete without simultaneous self-destruction. For that reason, even those religions starkly opposed to rituals cannot exist without them, and even those strongly opposed to myths cannot survive without any myths at all.

But there seems to be an element in the nature of faith that makes it necessary to be deceptive about a faith's actual reliance on belief. Not only the historical genesis of faith from belief, but also – and more importantly – its structural, dependent coexistence with belief, must be an embarrassing situation that faith tries to conceal. Accordingly, faith seems to have to produce a necessarily false image of belief in order to maintain its own false but flattering self-image. This necessity might therefore rest on the fact that faith, as Mannoni shows, fulfils a function that is alien to belief – that of providing its carrier with self-esteem. Belief, however, also contains an element of ludicrousness, which faith must suppress if it is to fulfil this self-esteem function.[91] The imaginary function of faith, aimed at developing and supporting an ideal self-image, an ideal ego (*moi*), would therefore be the reason for the misjudgement coming from it – for the perspectival illusion.

If this construction, developed from Mannoni's considerations, proves somewhat sustainable, then it might be used to explain how certain barriers to knowledge have been raised in philosophy and the cultural sciences. For example, why was Blaise Pascal capable of determining, in the mid seventeenth century, that the ritual practices of Christianity possess the power of producing true Christian belief, while the same thought from Immanuel Kant, at the end of the eighteenth century, seems unthinkable?[92] Why is it so difficult to grasp in

---

90   See Mannoni, *Clefs pour l'Imaginaire*, p. 13.

91   Pascal, for example, refers to this ludicrous moment of superstition when he suggests that his imaginary conversation partner follow the rituals: 'Cela . . . vous abêtira' ('This will . . . dull you'). Blaise Pascal, *Pensées*, ed. Jacques Chevalier (Paris: Livre de Poche, 1965), pp. 227–8 (§ 451). See also Chapter 8, section 4, pp. 222ff.

92   See Robert Pfaller, 'Das Undenkbare, die Höflichkeit und das Glück', in Brigitte Felderer and Thomas Macho, eds, *Höflichkeit. Aktualität und Genese von Umgangsformen* (Munich: W. Fink Verlag, 2002).

the twentieth century that 'playing' at a reality has effects on this reality? Why are areas in which such knowledge is applied and used (for example, Feldenkrais methods, Alexander technique, psychodrama, autosuggestion, and so on), often half-esoteric nowadays, developed by lonely 'gurus' – remaining practices carried out in sect-like formations, often without corresponding theory? Why is it nearly impossible to recognize the actual success of such practices and develop an explanation for them, without having the attempt at such an explanation immediately run the risk of being considered a departure from any respectable, scientifically acceptable cultural standard?

An answer to these questions that have been gathered with the help of Octave Mannoni's theory seems possible when the *affective or libido-economic conditions of belief – the pleasure in the suspended illusion* – are examined and explained. The issue of such conditions seems most clearly formulated in Johan Huizinga's theory of play. Huizinga's theory grasps play, on the one hand – echoing Mannoni[93] – as a practice of dealing with suspended illusions. On the other hand, however, with its concept of play's 'sacred seriousness', it considers play in terms of the extent of its libidinal affect, and thereby facilitates an explanation of the specific pleasure found in the illusion of the other.

---

93 See Mannoni, *Clefs pour l'Imaginaire*, p. 162.

CHAPTER THREE

Play: Johan Huizinga – The Suspended Illusion and Sacred Seriousness

Johan Huizinga published his studies of play in 1938, in the book *Homo Ludens: A Study of the Play Element in Culture*.[1] These studies seem to add key information to Mannoni's theory of illusions suspended by knowing better. Huizinga's work is particularly valuable for explaining affective aspects of such suspended illusions – i.e. pleasure.

Huizinga's play theory can be summarized in two theses that reveal its audacity and also the difficulties it encounters: (1) the thesis of play's 'sacred seriousness' as the origin of culture, and (2) the thesis of play's tendency to recede from the culture that it has created. It seems that, with these assertions, Huizinga's theory of play runs up against an epistemological obstacle. For this reason, these two decisive pillars of his theory appear isolated, and their function perplexing. Huizinga also fails to answer the questions raised by his two main theses. This is probably why he complained of the incomplete character of his work despite the enormous wealth of empirical material and accomplished presentation in *Homo Ludens*.[2]

Subsequent theories, as far as we can see, try to reduce the isolating, enigmatic aspects of these foundational elements by limiting their line of questioning to more trusted areas of play theory that are less of a challenge to common ways of thinking. Yet it is precisely these two 'isolated' assertions in Huizinga's theory that appear to be its most valuable achievement – the needles, as it were, by which the theory pierced the 'fabric of misconceptions' in which multifarious views of play remained entangled, replacing traditional, misleading questions with new, egregious ones.

The enigmatic, inexplicable, seemingly indigestible facet of these two theses rests on the fact that they break from common assumptions

---

1   See Johan Huizinga, *Homo Ludens: A Study of the Play Element in Culture* (Boston: Beacon Press, 1950).

2   Ibid., p. 8

– not only those found in the theory of play, but also in numerous theories of illusion and the pleasure derived from illusions. Yet, since not only misconceptions but also truths form a 'fabric', it seems worthwhile to embark on an attempt to point out the ties that bind these two 'indigestible' theses in Huizinga's theory. Through the connection of these two theses, it might be possible to solve the riddle that they present, to elucidate their theoretical value, and to protect them more effectively from the temptations of reductionism in the future.

THE INDIGESTIBLE: ON *HOMO LUDENS*'S TWO CENTRAL THESES

First Thesis: Play's 'Sacred Seriousness' as the Origin of Culture

The first of the two ponderous theses that Huizinga presents in *Homo Ludens* is: *the psychic intensity produced during play – among both players and spectators – is greater than the extent of affect that appears otherwise in life.* We can readily observe that play can lead to very intense emotions. This is true of all types of play: at the opera and in the theatre people throw bouquets of flowers; at concerts they trample seats and their shouts drown out the music; in the cinema they shed silent tears.[3] Yet often the audience's intense involvement in play is explained by the fact that play is similar to life: we cry at a scene in a movie because it seems so much like the death of a loved one; football and chess players tear their hair out because, for a short moment, they mistake their game for the seriousness of life.

Huizinga protests decisively against these kinds of common-sense explanations that attempt to relegate all forms of play to a mere shadow of everyday, earnest life, and establish everyday life as the only life capable of provoking real and dedicated sympathy and

---

3 Huizinga draws from this the following conclusion: 'Play is a thing by itself. The play-concept as such is of a higher order than is seriousness. For seriousness seeks to exclude play, whereas play can very well include seriousness' (ibid., p. 45). Similarly, Freud argues: 'The opposite of play is not what is serious but what is real. In spite of all emotion with which he cathects his world of play, the child distinguishes it quite well from reality; and he likes to link his imagined objects and situations to the tangible and visible things of the real world' (Freud, 'Creative Writers and Day-Dreaming' [SE IX], p. 144).

worthy of further contemplation. At the beginning of *Homo Ludens*, under the title 'The Insufficiency of Prior Definitions', he collects a proper 'shop of horrors' – a panorama showing those inadequate, primarily placatory answers that various theories have offered in response to the question: Why does play generate such intense involvement? Huizinga lists the following answers: 'discharge of superabundant vital energy', 'imitative instinct', 'training for serious work', 'self-control', 'innate urge to exercise a certain faculty', 'desire to dominate or control', 'outlet for harmful impulses', and 'a fiction designed to keep up the feeling of personal value'.[4] Countering such attempts at explanation – or, rather, reduction – Huizinga insists on three simple but precise questions: 'So far, so good, but what actually is the *fun* of playing? Why does the baby crow with pleasure? Why does the gambler lose himself in his passion? Why is a huge crowd roused to frenzy by a football match?'[5] Play is apparently the preferred, perhaps even the only, situation in which people are capable of such extreme feelings (and their expression).

The *excessive amusement* ('crowing with pleasure') emanating from play as well as the – obviously equally possible – *excessive, more or less pleasurable seriousness* ('frenzy') therefore refer to characteristic dimensions of play that cannot be derived from the proposed definitions mentioned above.

Play can cause the participants (and even those participating merely as spectators) to be 'enchanted',[6] to be 'captivated'.[7] And this intensity that regularly occurs in play is in no way the result of a misunderstanding. We do not take the game seriously merely because we forgot for a moment that, in reality, it is not serious (as is everyday life). For if play were simply to borrow its entire strength from life, its ability to excite could be no greater than life's ability to excite. We would then be only as moderately absorbed by play as we are by life outside of play.

As experience shows, however, we take play much more seriously than we do life. At a game of cards, the best of friends can have an irreconcilable argument, while they would probably have remained

---

4   Huizinga, *Homo Ludens*, p. 2.
5   Ibid.
6   Ibid., p. 8.
7   Ibid., p. 10.

friends through conflictual situations in other parts of life. The reason they argue in the game is not because they have confused the game with life. In life they would not have fought at all. Similarly, when watching the sad scenes of bad movies we burst into tears; in real life, and in even sadder situations, we would probably stay in control – and with a better film we would not even cry. As Huizinga particularly emphasizes that side of play that tends to extreme affects, he recognizes play as a distinct theoretical entity. His theory thus has the anomaly of excluding almost all other theories of play. These theories have largely circumvented the problem of affect caused by play and treated it as the affect problem of life (or have handed it over for others to deal with). They do not regard play as an independent theoretical object in light of the affect resulting from it.

Huizinga describes the increased intensity of affect that play generates as 'sacred seriousness'.[8] This sacred seriousness – the fascination, the extreme involvement and celebratory affect that is initiated by play – is at work in all forms of culture, including religion, art and sport. Huizinga thus concludes *that play presents the origin of all culture*.[9] Huizinga even sees religious cults as especially a consequence of the 'sacred seriousness' yielded from play. 'Sacred seriousness' communicates one of play's fundamental operations in establishing spatial and temporal borders – between the playing field and its environment, between the length of the game and the time beyond it.[10] This demarcation establishes the decidedly celebratory atmosphere, and the greater involvement of participants as well as spectators – which also applies among religious cults. The particular affective conditions of religions are also the result of such spatial and temporal demarcations. Huizinga therefore concludes: 'The hallowed spot [is essentially] a playground'.[11]

Émile Durkheim had already come to this conclusion in his attempts to identify a universal characteristic of religions. He concluded that, contrary to expectations, there is no evidence that all religions are characterized by having an idea of the supernatural, a mystery, one or more gods, and so on. The first positive trait of all

---

8   Ibid., p. 18.

9   Ibid., pp. 20ff.

10   See ibid., p. 189: 'The sense of the game is already stated from the marking out of the ideal room'.

11   Ibid., p. 20.

religions, according to Durkheim, consists much more in the fact that they draw a spatial and temporal line between the sacred and the profane (secular).[12] In the same way, Huizinga remarks with reference to religion and other forms of culture: 'Formally speaking, there is no distinction whatever between marking out a space for a sacred purpose and marking it out for purposes of sheer play. The turf, the tennis court, the chess board and the pavement-hopscotch, cannot formally be distinguished from the temple or the magic circle.'[13]

According to Huizinga, all cultural genres, religions, magic, sports and children's games, as well as art,[14] are marked by a 'sacred seriousness' that operates through demarcation and rests on the principle of play. The 'sacred seriousness' of play forms the origin of culture.

Problems with the First Thesis

This conclusion, pertinent for cultural theory, renders the questions posed by Huizinga's first thesis even more explosive. These questions, which Huizinga himself leaves unanswered, are: What stirs this excessive dimension, the 'sacred seriousness' of play? How do such intense affects arise, and why is it specifically play – and nothing else – that can set them loose? Which affects (or which affective dynamics) are generated by play's spatio-temporal demarcations? What is it about play that works so strongly to the advantage of culture?

The Second Thesis: Play's Tendency to Recede from Culture

Huizinga's second thesis says that, although play forms the origin of all culture, it has the tendency to recede from the culture it has created.[15] All cultural institutions exhibit the phenomenon of a loss of play throughout their history. In all cultural fields – including religion,[16]

---

12 See Durkheim, *Elementary Forms*, p. 36.

13 Huizinga, *Homo Ludens*, p. 20. See also p. 25, where Huizinga describes the genetic relationship between these two phenomena: 'The concept of play merges quite naturally with that of holiness'; and Freud, 'Obsessive Actions', p. 122.

14 On the origin of art in play, see Huizinga, *Homo Ludens*, pp. 158ff, 173ff.

15 See ibid., p. 46: 'As a culture proceeds, either progressing or regressing, the original relationship we have postulated between play and non-play does not remain static. As a rule, the play-element gradually recedes into the background'.

16 See ibid., p. 136.

art[17] and sport,[18] but also, for example, fashion[19] – Huizinga notices the disappearance of play and the advancement of profane serious-ness and slackness. He notices this type of anti-play impulse especially in the nineteenth century: 'utilitarianism', the 'welfare ideal', the progress of science and technology, cause people 'to mould the world after the patterns of their own banality'.[20] Huizinga also detects the same tendency in earlier epochs:

> But as civilization increases in spiritual amplitude, the regions where the play-factor is weak or barely perceptible will develop at the cost of those where it has free play. Civilization as a whole becomes more serious – law and war, commerce, technics and science lose touch with play; and even ritual, once the field par excellence for its expres-sion, seems to share the process of dissociation.[21]

Huizinga's findings can be easily augmented. Is it not apparent that even the main cultural genres that Huizinga lists show a characteristic tendency towards 'disintegration'? Does that not also lead to the disappearance of the element of play? This disappearance seems to take on the form of a displacement, in which the play element constantly wanders from one cultural genre to another: in *religions* in earlier periods, such as antiquity and ancient Asian cultures, there were *arts and sports* (for example, the Olympic Games, martial arts such as karate, Zen archery, and so on), then later just *arts* (dance, music, architecture, sculpture, painting, poetry); but then, even later, the arts seemed gradually to disappear from religion. In today's Christianity or Islam, for example, sports and the arts do not even remotely approach their earlier, dominant roles.

Like religion itself, art that was originally included in religion shows a tendency towards a loss of play. This problem, which

---

17   See ibid., p. 164: '[I]t is certain that the play-quality tends to be obscured in modern forms of dancing'; p. 143: 'The epic severs its connection with play as soon as it is no longer meant to be recited on some festal occasion but only to be read. Nor is the lyric understood as a play-function once its ties with music have gone.'

18   See ibid., p. 195: '[Sport is pushed] further and further away from the play-sphere proper'.

19   See ibid., p. 192: 'From then on men's dress became increasingly colourless and formless and subject to fewer and fewer changes.'

20   Ibid., p. 191.

21   Ibid., p. 134

Huizinga noticed and documented in much detail, appears to be particularly explosive in contemporary art. Especially in recent decades, the desire for scientific validity and political involvement, a professional media presence, the awareness of the division of labour and relativity of artistic intervention, the search for new, collective authorial positions, and so on, have spawned a steady growth of incompetence in the areas of formalism, curiosity, charm and elegance, and a practical ban on almost all kinds of extravagances.[22] Rather than elevating scientific validity or boosting the political relevance of art, these reflexive tendencies in contemporary art seem to be the results of increasingly narcissistic self-deception and the (un-self-reflexive) social primacy of ascetic ideals.

One could have drawn the conclusion from religions' loss of play that not the religion itself, but instead the art that was inherent to it, was the play element. But art's tendency towards a loss of play reveals that art is also not play, per se; art cannot be seen as its genuine, inviolable site. Even art palls on occasion and loses the excessive joy, the 'sacred seriousness', the element of play.

Ultimately, the same is true for sport, as Huizinga shows. Even sport is marked by a tendency towards the loss of play; here, too, the 'sacred seriousness' of the game threatens to retreat in favour of the profane seriousness of life. One piece of evidence for Huizinga's thesis is that the rules within sport have to be constantly changed in order to keep up a certain, steady enthusiasm. ('It's not a game anymore', the spectators say, disgusted – when faced, for example, with a football match that is overly dictated by tactics.) The fact that sports are also affected by temporary losses of their play element shows that sport is also not play, per se.

Problems with the Second Thesis

Huizinga's second thesis, asserting play's tendency to recede from all forms of culture that it has created, also poses a series of questions, which he also left largely unanswered. First of all, this thesis makes it difficult to *specify what comprises play*. This is because Huizinga's observed tendency of play to recede means that play does not have its

---

22   On the problematic of the loss of play in art, see Andrea van der Straeten, ed. *Die sentimentalen Favoriten. Spiele in der Kunst* (Vienna: Triton, 2000), and Hughes, *Culture of Complaint.*

own genuine cultural form: not religion, or art, or sport. All of these practices are founded through play and its characteristic 'sacred seriousness', yet play once again retreats from all of them. Huizinga's so-called play-sphere[23] is therefore more of a psychic state than a real situation that can be described through constant characteristics: one and the same practice can be play at one moment and, at the next, no longer play. Indeed, what is play for one person may in fact be something entirely different for someone else.[24]

Huizinga's failure to provide a useful definition of play, which Roger Caillois would later point out,[25] cannot be attributed to negligence or conceptual weakness. Rather, it appears, due to these findings, to be structurally impossible to cite rules or descriptions of practices that would be sufficient to define play. If play is its own, fleeting substance, which can disappear again from all the different forms that it assumes and founds,[26] then it appears that there is no characteristic form for play. Ultimately, every attempt to cite definitions of its form is doomed to failure. The only accusation that can be made of Huizinga is that, contrary to the conclusions of his second thesis, he attempted to arrive at a general definition of play focusing on its form.[27]

Moreover, Caillois's conclusion that a uniform definition of play is impossible, and that a 'multiple' definition must therefore be

---

23   See Huizinga, *Homo Ludens*, p. 195. Compare pp. 137–8, where Huizinga speaks of the 'play spirit' and the 'play-sphere'.

24   This can also be decisive for the fascination that play holds for a person. Sexual fetishism behaves similarly. See also Freud, 'Fetishism', p. 154: 'The meaning of the fetish is not known to other people, so the fetish is not withheld from him . . . What other men have to woo and make exertions for can be had by the fetishist with no trouble at all.' Compare Jean-Bertrand Pontalis, *Objekte des Fetischismus* (Frankfurt: Suhrkamp, 1972), p. 12. Also in aesthetic practices – especially that of 'bad taste' such as 'camp', as well as in the 'aesthetics of the sublime' – this happiness plays a crucial role by virtue of the fact that it cannot be shared. See also Susan Sontag, 'The Pornographic Imagination', in her *Styles of Radical Will* (New York: Picador, 2001); Jean-François Lyotard, 'The Sublime and the Avant-Garde', in Andrew Benjamin, ed., *The Lyotard Reader* (Oxford: Blackwell, 1989); and compare Pfaller, *Interpassivität*, pp. 58–61.

25   See Roger Caillois, *Man, Play and Games*, transl. Meyer Barash (Urbana/Chicago: University of Illinois Press, 2001), p. 4.

26   See also Huizinga, *Homo Ludens*, p. 19: 'We said at the beginning that play was anterior to culture; in a certain sense it is also superior to it or at least detached from it.'

27   See ibid., p. 10.

attempted, appears utterly inadequate when confronted with Huizinga's radical second thesis. The question is not merely whether play can be defined by one criterion or whether multiple criteria are necessary, but, instead, on what terrain to search for such criteria – at the level of practices or psychic states. Anyway, Caillois is entirely aware that he has not achieved a definition of play with his 'multiple' criteria, but at most has introduced a classification of diverse types.[28] Although games can be classified according to characteristics – similar to the very useful criteria developed by Caillois of competition, simulation, chance and vertigo[29] – nothing guarantees that these classified attributes can be seen as sufficient, constitutive criteria for the presence of play. The fact that something is, for example, a competition (and not a masquerade) does not necessarily mean that it is play. The fact that there are white chess pieces (as opposed to black pieces) does not necessarily mean that everything that is white is a chess piece.

The only possible definition of play that follows from Huizinga's theory of play's tendency to retreat consists in defining it in terms of that which is lost when it retreats from cultural forms, rather than in terms of cultural forms themselves. Huizinga obviously sensed this necessity, and for this reason made a number of attempts to define play in his text.[30] Just as psychoanalytic theory reveals that repetition refers to a continued lack of something,[31] the repetition that occurs in *Homo Ludens* of the attempt to define play can be traced back to something that Huizinga himself felt to be missing.

This type of play-definition that leaves aside cultural forms does not, however, have to be exclusively negative. If it is true that play is characterized above all by the emergence of a 'play-sphere', and if this constitutes more of a psychic state than a set of applicable forms or rules, then play must be determined by this special psychic state. This state is Huizinga's so-called 'sacred seriousness'. Several further criteria introduced by Huizinga can also be seen in conjunction with a definition referring to this psychic state. The feelings of players (and observers) of being 'enchanted' or 'captivated'[32] by the game are two

28   See Caillois, *Man, Play and Games*, p. 11.
29   Ibid., p. 12.
30   See also Huizinga, *Homo Ludens*, pp. 10–11.
31   See also Freud, 'On the Universal Tendency to Debasement in the Sphere of Love' (SE XI), p. 189.
32   See Huizinga, *Homo Ludens*, pp. 10–11.

such manifestations. They are also what is lost when a cultural form loses its play element. Other criteria can also be derived from these psychologically orientated criteria – for example, 'knowing better', which will be described in more detail in the next section. These criteria are what lend the most general gestures of demarcation their play-specific meaning, and demarcate them from other – for example, geographic – gestures of demarcation.

In addition to the difficulty of giving a definition of play, Huizinga's second thesis conjures up further, more general cultural-theory problems. Huizinga, too, was unable to resolve these questions in *Homo Ludens*: What is it about play that appears to work so strongly to the advantage of culture? And what is it in culture that seems to work so strongly against play? Why does culture cause play's 'sacred seriousness', from which culture originates, to disappear? Can it be that play works against itself here? Is there a 'dialectics' of play?

THE INDIGESTIBLE: TO WHAT EXTENT DO HUIZINGA'S THEORIES TOUCH ON AN EPISTOMOLOGICAL OBSTACLE?

On the basis of Roger Caillois's critique, it is possible to make clear that Huizinga's theses – of the 'sacred seriousness' of play and the tendency of play to retreat from the culture that it has founded – present the most valuable assertions of his theory because they touch on, and perhaps even overcome, an epistemological obstacle. Caillois's critique aims accurately at exactly the most difficult and 'indigestible' assumptions that Huizinga makes. We must therefore credit him with having detected the most important and disturbing aspects of this theory – even if he does not, as a consequence, follow Huizinga's advances and develop a new view, attempting instead to find arguments to eliminate the causes of disturbance and preserve the common view.

What Ferdinand de Saussure once noticed seems to apply to Caillois's critical argument – namely, 'that it is easier to discover a truth than to assign it to its rightful place.'[33] These critical arguments thus have value as symptoms. They are in no way false; they are merely not, as Caillois believed, critical. They answer questions other

---

33 Ferdinand de Saussure, *Cours de linguistique générale* (Paris: Payot, 1987), p. 100.

than those they intend to answer. They are therefore not counter-arguments, but, rather, valuable refinements and complements to Huizinga's assertions.[34]

The Problem with the Definition of Play

One of Caillois's first specifications was mentioned in the previous section: Caillois correctly noticed that Huizinga's definition of play is problematic. Yet, rather than undertake a 'multiple' definition of play, he should have confronted the fact that Huizinga's second thesis does not allow for any such definition (and that Huizinga should be criticized – if at all – for attempting such a definition). The consequence would have been to move away from the attempt to arrive at a definition of play through the description of practices (as Huizinga's own, largely unsuccessful attempts at definition have repeatedly shown), and to develop instead a definition of play as a psychic state. Caillois's dissatisfaction with Huizinga's definition certainly marked the point at which Huizinga, without completely recognizing it, indeed achieved a new breakthrough in the theory of play.

Play and the Sacred

Caillois's second critique refers to what Huizinga formulates as the *classification of religion as play* (as 'sacred seriousness'). Whereas Huizinga described the 'sacred site' as a 'playground', and thus radically localized the origin of religious feelings in the play-sphere, Caillois sees a difference here:

> Through the sacred, the source of omnipotence, the worshipper is fulfilled. Confronted by the sacred, he is defenceless and completely at its mercy. In play, the opposite is the case. All is human, invented by man the creator. For this reason, play rests, relaxes, distracts, and causes the dangers, cares and travails of life to be forgotten. The sacred, on the contrary, is the domain of internal tension, from

---

34   This is also true for the points on which Caillois agrees with Huizinga. But even here he is mostly commenting on a problematic point in his theory – for example, when he supports Huizinga's view that the professional athlete 'is not a player in the actual sense but much more a worker' (Caillois, *Man, Play and Games*, p. 6). I will return to this in much more detail later in this chapter.

which it is precisely profane existence that relaxes, rests, and distracts. The situation is reversed.[35]

Caillois thus draws the picture of a series of declining states of human tension, from the sacred to the secular, right down to the distractions of play. This theoretical categorization into a sacred sphere that is more serious than life and a play-sphere that is less serious appears necessary in light of Caillois's original assumption – namely, *that what is most serious could not be deemed relaxing.*

But this is not the case at all. Here, Caillois overlooks a paradoxical situation. Exactly that which 'overcomes' people – the power that they feel 'at the mercy of', and so on – can, at the same time, be where they find 'relaxation' from profane life. This is what characterizes, for example, the comforting and reproductive functions of religious ideologies that seem to operate with what at first glance appear to be not very comforting ideas of almighty, punishing and angry gods. This seemingly paradoxical logic of relaxation through a fear-inspiring religion was elucidated by Slavoj Žižek in reference to Lacan,[36] in a comment on Racine's drama *Athalie.* In the play, Abner, an officer of the tyrannical queen Athalie, approaches the high priest Jehoiada, a well-known opponent of the queen, and offers to join him in a pact against her. He is full of fear due to the impending danger, yet Jehoiada answers him: 'I fear God, dear Abner, and have no other fear' (*Je crains Dieu, cher Abner, et n'ai point d'autre crainte*).[37] As Žižek subsequently shows, the priest Jehoiada is able to transform the fearful Abner into a calm and devoted disciple through this intervention. By evoking the fear of God, as if by a miracle, the whole situation is turned around, and fear is transformed into bravery.[38] Žižek elucidates the paradoxical aspect of this intervention: 'Jehoiada does not simply try to convince Abner that divine forces are, despite everything, powerful enough to gain the upper hand over earthly disarray; he appeases his fears in a quite different way: by presenting their very

35   Roger Caillois, *Man and the Sacred* (New York: Free Press of Glencoe, 1959), p. 158.

36   See Jacques Lacan, *Le séminaire III: Les psychoses* (Paris: Seuil, 1981 [1955–56]), p. 203.

37   Žižek, *For They Know Not What They Do*, p. 16.

38   Ibid., p. 17.

opposite – God – as a thing more frightening than all earthly fears.'[39] Religion is thus entirely capable of 'relaxing' people in light of the dangers of profane life. It is thus not profane life (as Caillois believes) that relaxes people from the tensions of religion, but, on the contrary, religion that provides an opportunity for relaxation from the tensions of life. Yet it achieves this by mediating to people the feelings that Caillois aptly identifies as 'defenselessness' and 'being at the mercy of'. The comfort is found in the prospect of an even greater horror.[40]

This refutes one side of Caillois's critique: religion does not differ from play because it is incapable of providing relaxation from profane life; instead, it is capable of doing so, just like play. The second side of Caillois's critique, however, must also be amended: play is in no way something that is pursued with less exertion than mundane life. The core of Huizinga's thesis of play's 'sacred seriousness' deals with exactly that. Caillois thus ignores those paradoxical elements surrounding play that Huizinga perceived, and that led him to his thesis. Caillois appears grossly to underestimate the involvement that play produces when he writes: 'In play, man is removed from reality. He seeks free activity, which does not involve him more than he has decided in advance . . . Play . . . constitutes a kind of haven in which one is master of destiny.'[41]

Accompanying the questions posed at the beginning of his treatise, Huizinga had listed a series of arguments refuting this trivializing view of the reality, seriousness and power of play.[42] One of these arguments consists of the observation that numerous games – duels, for example, but also guessing games[43] – were once played for life or death. This alone makes clear the impossibility of upholding Caillois's

---

39   Ibid.

40   Žižek draws from this a general ideological-theoretical conclusion: 'Here the common Marxist formulation of the consolation in religion as "imaginary compensation" for worldly suffering is considered from a more complex point of view . . . That is the basic operation of ideology: "reality" is not rendered bearable by offering an imaginary consolation that makes the horrors bearable – in which a "deeper meaning" annuls the experience of senselessness; rather, an uncanny, unbearable point is constructed – a traumatic "Real" that effaces the horror of reality.' Slavoj Žižek, 'Hegel mit Lacan', in *Wo es war* I (1986), pp. 59–60 (my translation). Compare Žižek, *For They Know Not What They Do*, p. 17.

41   Caillois, *Man and the Sacred*, p. 158–9.

42   See Huizinga, *Homo Ludens*, p. 2; and see above, pp. 74ff.

43   Ibid., pp. 89, 105ff.

assumption that play is characterized by less exertion or tension than profane life. Furthermore, in the ambit of mass sporting events in today's industrial and service society, the stakes are even sometimes life or death: for example, when fans of opposing football teams attack each other (such as in the 1985 massacre at Brussels's Heysel Stadium, which was broadcast for hours on live television).[44] Racing around in cars and on motorcycles, so popular among rural youth, which leads to exorbitant death rates, also belongs to this category of deadly (and apparently also unavoidable) games.

For a precise understanding of the role of play in these life-threatening and deadly activities, it must be made clear that play does not derive its "kick", its joyful, sacred seriousness from the element of mortal danger. (After all, life-threatening situations in mundane life are not made more appealing by the moment of danger.) Instead, exactly the opposite is true: even the risk of death is endured because play has tempted the actors into a sphere in which it appears to them to be the lesser evil, or in which they fulfil a role that does not allow them any other option. Just like the 'fear of God' in *Athalie*, the play-sphere seems capable of transforming normal fear into murderous or suicidal foolhardiness.

Further evidence of the power that Huizinga attributes to the 'sacred seriousness' of play can be found in the spell that the game casts over players and audience alike. Contrary to Caillois's view of the 'free activity' that involves the player only to the extent that 'he has decided in advance', and also Huizinga's own formulations about play as 'free activity' or a 'voluntary occupation',[45] it is necessary to emphasize that play has an inherent tendency to slip from the participants' power.[46] The most superficial glance at a video-game hall can confirm this: perhaps the game begins voluntarily, yet the players suddenly cannot get enough; and often they begin to

---

44   It is amazing that such relevant processes in their own cultures have not given ethnologists more to think about, when, for example, one still hears that the ritualized athletic ball games played by the Mayans were accompanied by 'human sacrifices' offered to the gods. Instead of insisting on the problematic concept of sacrifice in this context, cultural scientists would do better to investigate and to recognize the laws of such processes: where there are mass sporting events, people are killed on a regular basis.

45   See Huizinga, *Homo Ludens*, pp. 10, 28.

46   See also chapters 4 and 9, below.

play without intending to – such as when automobile drivers suddenly *cannot help* but enter into a passing duel. Regarding this, Huizinga notes: 'Play casts a spell over us; it is "enchanting", "captivating".'[47]

The effects of pathological gambling, and also of those ceremonial acts of obsessional neurotics that Freud likewise deciphered as play,[48] ultimately form further strong evidence against Caillois's assertion that play 'constitutes a kind of haven in which one is master of destiny'.

Even with regard to its second half, Caillois's attempt at resolution must be viewed as a failure. Play is in no way tackled with less seriousness or tension than profane life. Instead, it has an inherent intensity that seizes players even more strongly than everyday life, and even leads them to disregard all considerations of that life. Precisely this powerlessness and defencelessness of the players against play prove that, in this regard, play cannot be differentiated from the sacred. Just like the sacredness of religion, which, according to Caillois, renders the worshipper helpless, the 'sacred seriousness' of play renders the player helpless.

Rather than suggesting a proper differentiation, Caillois has instead contributed by concealing a fundamental commonality, and clouding Huizinga's discovery of the founding of the sacred through play. His attempt to differentiate between the sacred and play belongs more to the way that certain religions imagine themselves to be, rather than to the realm of theory.[49] In fact, following from this is another interesting question in cultural theory, which Huizinga himself has asked: Why is it that some religions (and some sciences of religion) believe that religion is something fundamentally different from play?[50] And why, contrary to this (and even contrary to the sciences)

---

47   Huizinga, *Homo Ludens*, pp. 9–10.

48   See Freud, 'Obsessive Actions', pp. 115–27.

49   This relapse of Caillois's into the religious object's perception of itself becomes especially evident when he comments: 'In play, the opposite is the case. All is human, invented by man the creator.' (Caillois, *Man and the Sacred*, p. 158.) After all, some centuries before him, enlightened religious critique had already noted that in religion, much appears 'human' and from 'human creation'.

50   See also Huizinga, *Homo Ludens*, p. 20: 'It is surprising that anthropology and comparative religion have paid so little attention to the problem of how far such sacred activities as proceed within the forms of play also proceed in the attitude and mood of play.'

are other religions thoroughly capable of comprehending themselves as play?[51] What motivates some religions and theories to present the sacred as something higher than or superior to play?

The fact that Caillois took the 'sacred seriousness' of play postulated by Huizinga as his starting point, and that all arguments employed to differentiate the sacred from play are arguments about their identity, once again shows that his critique has value as a symptom. Here it has – in the form of the 'negation',[52] so to speak – once again precisely grasped the point at which Huizinga achieves a decisive discovery and, with the means available to it – *ex negativo* – has elucidated and confirmed this discovery, even in opposition to some of Huizinga's own formulations.

Play and Secrets

A third element of Caillois's critique, which appears to be more a refinement of Huizinga's theory than a point of contention, questions the role of the secret in play. Huizinga related the group-forming function of play – an especially interesting observation from the perspective of the theory of ideology – to the situation that, in play, a unique world is created that is known to the participants, yet kept as a secret from others. The 'special world of play'[53] is generated through a secret that connects the players: 'Even in early childhood the charm of play is enhanced by making a "secret" of it. This is for *us*, not for the "others".'[54] Likewise, Huizinga attributes the occasional (and public) suspension of public order in 'student pranks', or in carnival rites, to their basis in the secret: 'The "differentness" and secrecy of play are most vividly expressed in "dressing up". Here the "extra-ordinary" nature of play reaches perfection.'[55] For this reason, Huizinga characterizes play as something that 'promotes the formation of social groupings which tend to surround themselves with secrecy and to

---

51   See also Huizinga's reference to Plato: ' "I say that a man must be serious with the serious," he says (*Laws*, vii, 803). "God alone is worthy of supreme seriousness, but man is made God's plaything and that is the best part of him." ' Huizinga, *Homo Ludens*, p. 18.

52   See Freud, 'Negation' (SE IXX).

53   See Huizinga, *Homo Ludens*, p. 12.

54   Ibid., p. 12.

55   Ibid., p. 13

stress their difference from the common world by disguise or other means.'[56]

Against Huizinga's characterization of play through the trait of the secret, which seems plausible at first, Caillois makes a likewise plausible objection:

> It is meritorious and fruitful to have grasped the affinity which exists between play and the secret or mysterious, but this relationship cannot be part of the definition of play, which is nearly always spectacular or ostentatious. Without doubt, secrecy, mystery, and even travesty can be transformed into play activity, but it must be immediately pointed out that this transformation is necessarily to the detriment of the secret and mysterious, which play exposes, publishes, and somehow *expends*. In a word, play tends to remove the very nature of the mysterious.[57]

Caillois correctly points out the public, institutional[58] character of play, which appears to rule out every kind of secret. To whom, then, should the secret still apply, when, due to its public character, all present are privy to it? Is it possible to have secrets from which no one is excluded? Can there be mysteries without people who are not in on them? Can such 'public secrets' produce and assure the cohesion of societies?

Rather than refuting Huizinga's thesis of play's characteristic of secrecy, Caillois's argument appears to make a decisive contribution to the understanding of it. Huizinga's 'secrecy' of play must be understood exactly in this way: as a secret that is often shared by all; as something hidden, which remains hidden only for fully unspecified others; as *an ignorance with no carrier*. The example of politeness as a playful, socially binding practice can clarify this: as Kant showed, politeness is a deception by which no one is deceived.[59] The fact that niceties are 'not real' is thus a secret that is shared by all participants,

---

56 Ibid., p. 13
57 Caillois, *Man, Play and Games*, p. 4.
58 Ibid., p. 4.
59 See Immanuel Kant, *Kant: Anthropology from a Pragmatic Point of View*, ed. Robert B. Louden (Cambridge: CUP, 2006 [1798]), p. 44. Compare Manfred Schneider, 'Der Betrug der guten Sitten', in Ruthard Stäblein, ed., *Höflichkeit. Tugend oder schöner Schein* (Darmstadt: Wiss. Buchges., 1993), pp. 44–65.

and one that is kept secret from others who remain fully unspecified. Societies can thereby produce their own coherencies by producing exclusions that do not relate to any real people.[60] They must protect their secrets only from virtual 'invisible third parties', and in this way can create a complicity bonding the 'initiated'. Even the idea that there could really be such others who do not know the secret can once again be seen as one of those illusions believed only by unspecified others. The real members of society do not have to believe in this illusion. It, too, can remain an illusion without an owner: the others' illusion.

If games – for example, the children's games that Huizinga mentions – really do exclude real, other people as the uninitiated, the unknowing others, then this seems to be preparation, as it were, for another, more general practice, whereby this exclusion no longer refers to real persons – similar to the way in which children first obey real authority figures, a behaviour which they later apply to virtual 'persons', psychic agencies.[61]

The open secret of play, which becomes visible through Caillois's refinements, forms the point at which Huizinga's theory demonstrates its most significant contact with Mannoni's theory of the 'ownerless' illusion. Like the theatre audience described by Mannoni that is 'in cahoots' with the actors in order to maintain an illusion for God-knows-who, play, too, in Huizinga's sense, is a practice that is based on the *illusion of others*. Play's culture-forming function seems to stem from precisely this: its ability to hold society together and its obvious trait of sparking off excessive happiness. This excessive happiness, which is the 'sacred seriousness' of play, as shall be demonstrated in the next section, is bound to the condition that the practising persons are initiates who see through the illusion of the game.

Huizinga's two main theses have therefore brought with them a series of disturbing, seemingly paradoxical questions (such as that of the shared secret with no outsiders). As we have seen, Caillois's critique serves more to hide these questions than answer them. However, the futility of this attempt to conceal the questions has its

---

60   This knowledge possibly produces a way out of what Freud described as the pessimistically diagnosed dilemma that the binds that tie together society at large could produce their unity only through animosity towards outsiders (see Sigmund Freud 'Civilization and its Discontents' [SE XXI], p. 114). Perhaps it would also be enough to render others virtual, rather than make them victims of aggression and silencing.

61   See also ibid., pp. 123ff.

value as a symptom: read against its intentions, it delivers clear information about where the problems can be found and what the decisive questions are.

An answer to the questions posed by Huizinga's 'indigestible' theses seems within reach when one attempts to connect these theses and the questions resulting from them. By explaining where 'sacred seriousness' comes from, it would be possible to cite the reasons why play tends to disappear. Analysis of the amplified psychic intensity of play provides the key to understanding the 'dialectics' of play. The first step in the analysis of this amplified psychic intensity consists in analysis of a moment that Huizinga clearly recognized as a necessary condition of the 'sacred seriousness' of play. This condition is that players (and spectators) know that a game is a game.

ENTHUSIASM AND KNOWING BETTER

The validity of Huizinga's first thesis – that play possesses an extreme power to fascinate, a power unavailable to all other practices – is bound to one condition. Huizinga maintains that *this fascination of play depends upon the knowledge that it is 'just' play.*[62] If this knowledge is lacking, no extreme affects emerge. A player who does not know that the game is play cannot be captured by 'sacred seriousness'. He or she remains trapped in profane seriousness.

This knowledge essential for play consists in 'knowing better' about an illusion. Consequently, every game must contain an illusion. Huizinga notes, as does Mannoni, that the term 'illusion', taken literally, refers to 'play' (*ludus*).[63] Along with the assumption of necessary knowledge, Huizinga also formulates the thesis that all play contains an illusion – *namely, the illusion that it is not just play*. This illusion, in its general form, describes not only 'figurative' play, in which something is presented, such as theatre or computer simulation games; it also characterizes 'non-figurative' games, such as football.

However, only as *a suspended illusion* can this illusion trigger feelings of desire: the illusion – that it is more than play – must be

---

62   See Huizinga, *Homo Ludens*, pp. 8–9.

63   Huizinga, *Homo Ludens*, p. 11: '[The spoil-sport] robs play of its *illusion* – a pregnant word which means literally "in-play" (from *inlusion, illudere* or *inludere*)'. Compare Mannoni, *Clefs pour l'Imaginaire*, p. 162, which speaks of the 'illusion ludique'.

suspended by the player, by the knowledge that it is really just play, so that the fascination of play and the heightened stakes, the 'sacred seriousness', can emerge. By assuming such a correlation between fascination and knowledge, Huizinga contradicts almost all classical theories of play. The classical theories, which all tried to trace play's fascination back to a fascination for real life, have always assumed that play is able to fascinate due to confusion – a short-term memory lapse: the fascination comes from confusing the game with life, forgetting for a moment that it is just a game.

Classical theories, too, claim that every game contains an illusion. But in this account, the players are always the ones deceived. Play produces the illusion of being life; the players fall into the illusion for a while and take the game as seriously as they do life. The game that *presents* something (life) is fascinating, and consequently delights only if *the presented object*, for its part, is fascinating and delightful. Play satisfies wishes that cannot be fulfilled through fiction, for example, to the extent that it presents these wishes as being fulfilled, and lets one forget that the presentation (and therefore also the satisfaction) is merely a fiction. According to this model, desire is not for fiction and presentation, but, rather, only for that which is invented and presented.[64] As a result, the affective and intellectual moments must be mutually exclusive: the feeling of fascination can only arise when intellect is suspended. Desire would be available only at the price of ignorance; knowing better only at the price of frustration – according to the motto 'sad, but true'.

Yet Huizinga's discovery of the 'sacred seriousness' in play fundamentally changes this picture: if play, as Huizinga has recognized, can be more fascinating than other areas of life, then it is not possible to explain this effect as a mix-up. Forgetting that it is 'just' play would cause one to be only as interested in it as one is in other areas of life. Instead, sacred seriousness can arise only if the players are *not* confused. Only by knowing that it is 'just' play is it possible to be more absorbed by it than by other areas of life. The players consequently cannot be those tricked by the game. Whatever play feigns for them,

---

64 The weakness in these kinds of theories can be seen already in their inability to explain the fascination with non-humorous fictions – for example, tragedies or horror films. See also Freud, 'Beyond the Pleasure Principle' (SE XVIII), pp. 15ff; 'Psychopathic Characters On The Stage' (SE VII), pp. 305–6.

they must avoid being taken in by it – otherwise they no longer see it as play.

If play fascinates and delights through presentation, then this fascination and delight are due not to what is presented, but to the act of presenting. There is a desire to feign things. There must be an advantage to the fact that it is only fiction. If the player is taken into the spell through a lapse of memory or a mistake, then this advantage is lost. But the desire for fiction and the knowledge that fiction is at play hence belong together. The affective and the intellectual moments do not exclude one another. On the contrary, the one requires the other: there can be no desire without knowing better, no naivety without losing the enjoyment of fiction. According to Huizinga, the excitement aroused by play can be achieved only by knowing better – by knowing that it is all 'only' play. The astonishing part of Huizinga's discovery is this dependence of the affective moment on the intellectual one: *we will be absorbed by the illusion of play only if and when we see through it.* Knowledge does not help us gain emotional distance – on the contrary: our intellectual distancing from play pushes us into the throes of the affective captivity of play. In order to break the spell of play, we must therefore try to forget that it is just play.

If, in the state of sacred seriousness, an error or confusion occurs, then it is only that someone mistakenly confuses a part of life for play – but not vice versa. If someone thinks that something is merely a game, then this supposed 'knowledge' of the play character of the situation is sufficient to cause excitement and playfulness. This 'knowledge' can be illusory; the mistaken reality will already be experienced as play through mere imagination. Incidentally, it is also clear that, for Huizinga, the player is no mere cynic or postmodern relativist who is 'above' everything, and who takes nothing seriously because there are no more 'big narratives', and instead only play, and understands every opinion as worth just as little, and culture as merely fun culture ('Spasskultur').[65] This vain postmodern self-image fails to recognize the relationship between intellect and affect in exactly the same way that traditional theories of play did. What it overlooks is that the strongest emotional ties to something can develop precisely when the matter – through real or imagined better knowledge – is declared to be 'foolish' fun or 'mere' play.

---

65   See also Huizinga, *Homo Ludens*, p. 195.

This picture also fails to recognize the relationships within the intellect itself: in order to relativize something intellectually – in order to identify it intellectually as 'mere play', for example – one must claim for oneself a *better* knowledge: this knowledge must be ranked more seriously than the play it devalues; it cannot be seen as play, or as a mere opinion among many. In order to experience something as play, a player does not necessarily have to have true knowledge, but they must have a serious claim to it – a claim that they cannot simultaneously relativize with the play. Playing is a language game that functions in exactly the same way as doubt: in order to doubt something, something else that is fixed must first be established – it acts like a door and hinge. Universal doubt, as Wittgenstein determined, does not have the slightest power to raise doubt.[66] Similarly, Huizinga established that the idea that everything – the whole world – is a game, or merely theatre, does not contribute at all to the theory of play.[67] Such an idea is, by the way, just as beloved among ascetic Christian metaphysicians as it is among their accomplices, the asocial postmodernists who purport to be hedonists. In the end, both share the inability to take pleasure in fiction – a pleasure in differentiating between play and knowledge, fiction and nonfiction.

Knowledge Chains Us to Illusion

Huizinga concludes that all play operates with illusion, and requires a moment in which this illusion is seen through. All play acts as if it were real and, in order to play, all players must know that this is not so. When players know (or at least believe) that it is notreal, but rather just play, then they succumb to sacred seriousness. Huizinga has herewith delivered a series of determinations that present his general definition of play. For Huizinga, unlike Wittgenstein,[68] all games have something in common (even that 'nonfigurative play' that at first glance does not appear to represent anything, such as throwing a ball against a house wall): an illusion (of being a real

---

66   See Ludwig Wittgenstein, *On Certainty* (Oxford: Blackwell, 1975), p. 164 (§625): 'A doubt without an end is not even a doubt.'

67   See Huizinga, *Homo Ludens*, pp. 3, 8.

68   See Ludwig Wittgenstein, *Philosophical Investigations: The German Text, with a Revised English Translation*, transl. G. E. M. Anscombe (Oxford: Blackwell, 1991), p. 52 (§§66–71).

issue); the claim to see through this illusion, and a resulting, intensified sacred seriousness.

But Huizinga's definition uses these criteria to describe a psychic state, and not a practice. The multiple practices that Wittgenstein introduces as examples are, according to Huizinga, not immune from one day no longer being play. The psychic state of the play-sphere, conversely, can also capture people in acts that are not generally considered to be play. A practice such as tennis, for example, can one day leave the ludic sphere; on the other hand, such mundane practices as shopping, driving a car, or investing in capital markets might one day, for some people, operate as ways of entering the ludic sphere.

In terms of the status of knowledge, this finding of Huizinga's appears extremely paradoxical and disturbing: knowledge does not create a distance from play; instead, in its function as knowledge, it chains us to the illusion of play. Instead of breaking the spell of play, knowledge entangles us in it. Huizinga's discovery of the enmeshing role of knowledge is the paradoxical element that is so difficult to imagine, and that other placatory theories of play attempt to escape. There is a strong tendency to imagine the relationships in the reverse – that is, if someone believes in something illusory, then we tend to think that they lack 'better knowledge'. If someone adheres to an illusion, then it is because they do not have the knowledge to escape it.

On the contrary, it seems much more difficult to come to terms with the fact that the attachment to an illusion can rest precisely on the knowledge of its illusory character. What Huizinga insists on in numerous examples is this specific form of existence of a belief that is relativized in this way. Here lies the significance of Huizinga's theory of play for all theories – of philosophy, psychoanalysis, and ideology, for example – that ask the question of how convictions arise and in what form they are perpetuated. Huizinga's theory makes plausible a new type of conviction: the type of illusion that is kept suspended by knowing better, yet thereby adhered to with even greater devotion.

The Theory of the Suspended Illusion: Huizinga and Wittgenstein

The kind of illusion that befalls those who know better is much trickier than a 'naive' illusion that arises due to a lack of knowledge and can be resolved by knowing better; it is much less noticeable, and thus more difficult to counter. Illusion that is kept suspended by knowledge is always mistaken either for knowledge or naive belief: we prematurely conclude from the fact that we are conscious of our knowledge that we are free of devotion to the illusion. However, we tend to accuse others – who appear to us to be under the spell of illusion with their games or their performance of petty rituals – of a lack of knowledge and an imprisonment in naive belief.

Huizinga described and criticized with great clarity this necessary 'perspectivist deception' regarding the relationship between one's own knowledge and the maintained illusion, as did Ludwig Wittgenstein (in the notes on Frazer's *The Golden Bough*). According to Huizinga, so-called 'primitives' from earlier cultures and children are not the true carriers of maintained illusions; they are not the correct owners of those illusions that all the others do not want. Against ethnologists like Frazer, Huizinga maintains, for example, that the 'mental attitude in which the great religious feasts of savages are celebrated and witnessed is not one of complete illusion. There is an underlying consciousness of things "not being real".'[69]

With reference to earlier cultures, Huizinga contends very decisively – in contrast to Paul Veyne, for example[70] – that they maintained their beliefs in a playful form; in other words, they knew better: '[W]e feel some doubt whether in fact the primitive Hindus and Scandinavians ever really believed with the full force of conviction in such figments as the creation of the world from human limbs. At any rate the reality of this belief cannot be proved. We may go so far as to say that it is extremely improbable.'[71]

With reference to children and their games, Huizinga also emphasizes the existing moment of knowing better – but also the tendency for children to construct (somewhat as Frazer did) a naive other:

> Every child knows perfectly well that he is 'only pretending', or that it was 'only for fun'. How deep-seated this awareness is in the child's soul is strikingly illustrated by the following story, told to me by the father of the boy in question. He found his four-year-old son sitting at the

---

69   Huizinga, *Homo Ludens*, p. 22.
70   See Veyne, *Did the Greeks Believe in Their Myths?*, p. 129. See also Introduction, above.
71   Huizinga, *Homo Ludens*, p. 137.

front of a row of chairs, playing 'trains'. As he hugged him the boy said: 'Don't kiss the engine, Daddy, or the carriages won't think it's real'.[72]

Thus, just like 'civilized' adults, small children also already have better knowledge at their disposal, which allows them to see through illusions as illusions without owners. On the other hand, like 'civilized' adults, they also fall into the perspectivist deception that there are other agents – in this case the 'train carriages' – that are considered the possible owners or carriers of the illusion, and for whom one must maintain the illusion.

Like Wittgenstein, Huizinga ultimately shows to himself and to us that, contrarily, even we adults and 'civilized people' are not free from suspended illusions – and that, for that matter, we usually do not notice.[73] Even fully mature 'civilized' persons are involved with ideas and practices that can appear to outside observers as a retreat into an infantile 'omnipotence of ideas' or primitive animism. Without necessarily being naive, we, too, practise quite common, everyday magic. Huizinga writes that

> personification is both a play-function and a supremely important habit of mind. Even in modern civilization it has not, by any means, dwindled to a mere artifice of literature, something to be put up with and sometimes resorted to. Which of us has not repeatedly caught himself addressing some lifeless object, say a recalcitrant collar-stud, in deadly earnest, attributing to it a perverse will, reproaching it and abusing it for its demoniacal obstinacy? If ever you did this you were personifying in the strict sense of the word. Yet you do not normally avow your belief in the collar-stud as an entity or idea. You were only falling involuntarily into the play-attitude.[74]

---

72   Ibid., p. 8

73   See also ibid., p. 24: 'A somewhat childish father can become visibly angry if his children discover that he has disguised himself as Santa Claus'. If the delegation of the illusion fails, aggression results – exactly as with the failed delegation of pleasure. See also Slavoj Žižek, 'The Interpassive Subject': '[W]hat sets aggressivity in motion in a subject, is when the other subject, through which the first subject believed or enjoyed, does something which disturbs the functioning of this transference' (at egs.edu). The illusion, then – as Mannoni (Clefs pour l'Imaginaire, p. 30) would have said – goes back to the recognized Santa Claus, for whom the amusing rebuff of the illusion through delegation thus becomes impossible.

74   Huizinga, Homo Ludens, p. 140.

Together with the insistence that this all occurs in light of better knowledge, which nonetheless exists, Huizinga's last remark – 'You were only falling involuntarily into the play-attitude' – contains a second paradoxical aspect: one plays not only contrary to *knowing* better, but also despite one's own *will*.[75] Since, according to Huizinga, play behaviour presents the origins of all culture, the result of certain persons' involuntary falling into the play-attitude is that, *against their will*, such people also become *creators of culture*. Involuntarily, in spite of themselves, they produce culture.

The desire for the maintained illusion – the sacred seriousness – therefore contains an element of *coercion*, as it were: one must play, one can't help it. The following chapter will deal in more detail with this moment of coercion, this entanglement in the others' illusion, following an elucidation of the affective conditions. Even coercion can be derived from knowing better, which presents the key to the entire paradox and to that affective state in play that Huizinga describes so precisely. Based on the moment of knowing better, which appears in correlation with 'sacred seriousness', it is possible to take the most important step in relating Huizinga's two main theses: by clarifying the affective conditions of sacred seriousness and coercion.

---

75 Wittgenstein also recognized the tendency of these mundane magical practices to retreat from decision: 'When a man laughs too much . . . I half-involuntarily compress my lips as if I believed I could thereby keep his closed' (Wittgenstein, 'Remarks on Frazer's *Golden Bough*', p. 141). What is suspended through better knowledge remains as a little 'half-involuntary' action. It is exactly these everyday, mundane practices of the 'civilized' being that seem to confirm what Hubert and Mauss noted about magic in general: 'Nobody can become a magician at will . . .'. Marcel Mauss, *General Theory of Magic*, trans. Robert Brain (New York: Routledge, 2001), p. 33.

CHAPTER FOUR

The Condition for Greater Fascination: Ambivalence – 'Knowledge' is Hatred

AMPLIFIED AFFECT

Huizinga's realization about play's unparalleled power of fascination extends Mannoni's findings. Huizinga's emphasis is on the aspect of the economy and dynamics of the libido, which Mannoni largely excludes. Suspended illusions are thus investigated in terms of the amplified affect associated with them. Whereas Mannoni had already pointed out the strong affective impacts, the feelings of satisfaction and triumph associated with disavowal (expressed in the statement 'But still . . .' – which can, for example, be completed as 'it is fantastic', or 'it is disturbing'), Huizinga added that these experiences of satisfaction and triumph, which can be attributed to play's suspended illusion, are extraordinarily great – greater than all other comparable pleasurable affects. According to Huizinga, it is impossible to achieve such extremely pleasurable experiences in any other way than play. In other words, only contact with suspended illusions, disavowal – that is, play – is capable of generating such excessive involvement and creating these kinds of satisfactions and triumphs.

Consequently, we must view Huizinga's subject (play) and Mannoni's theme (disavowal and belief/superstition) as identical. For all play is an activity involving belief (and vice versa[1]): it always contains a denied illusion suspended by knowing better. That applies not only to artistic and religious activities, but also sport. Granted, not all games are 'representative' in the manner of theatre or representational arts, but all games harbour a fundamental illusion – namely, the one that is suspended through the players' better knowledge. Because this knowledge includes the fact that the game is 'only a

---

1   Compare Huizinga's explanation of mask ceremonies in tribal cultures with the staging of Santa Claus in so-called civilized cultures (Huizinga, *Homo Ludens*, pp. 24–6).

game', the game must contain a counter-illusion, so to speak – namely, that of being 'more than just a game'. This emerges as an important observation for understanding other, non-representative practices, too (such as abstract, repetitive forms in art, obsessional neurotic acts, and religious rituals that have seemingly lost their meaning): *wherever sacred seriousness reigns, there must be a denied illusion that is kept suspended.* Sacred seriousness is a sign indicating the presence of an illusion of the other. It is its symptom.

AMBIVALENCE: ADDING UP OPPOSING AFFECTS

Under these premises, we can pose the question of the fascination with others' illusions as one of the *economy of the libido.* What special powers are at work here? What conditions lead to such an increase in the amount of affect? One answer to this question can be developed through recourse to Spinoza's theories on affect. At a time when philosophy still considered the theory of affects to be an indispensable element in the broader theorization of the parameters of human reason, it had access to a theory of the conditions for the emergence of exceptional increases in affective intensity. In Proposition 44 of the third part of his *Ethics*, Spinoza writes: 'Hatred which is completely vanquished by love passes into love: and love is thereupon greater than if hatred had not preceded it.'[2]

Consequently, love can be intensified by the hatred that preceded it, and vice versa. Here Spinoza outlines precisely the situation that psychoanalytic theory later identifies as *ambivalence.*[3] In doing so, he discovers 'overdetermination'[4] (*Ueberdeterminierung*) at work in intensified love (for it is not composed exclusively of love, but gives this illusion), and offers a sense of the general, everyday relevance of these connections of love and hatred that intensify love. Developing this insight, we can ask whether it might be a preceding moment of hatred that distinguishes love from friendship, and brings about its immensely greater intensity and also fragility. Do all love affairs not

---

2   Spinoza, *On the Improvement of the Understanding*, p. 159.

3   See Freud, 'Notes upon a Case of Obsessional Neurosis', p. 239, n. 1 (addition from 1923), as well as Freud, 'Totem and Taboo', pp. 29–30.

4   For more on the term 'overdetermination', see Freud 'The Interpretation of Dreams' (SE IV), pp. 202–3, 247–8, 479–80. See also Laplanche and Pontalis, *Language of Psychoanalysis*, p. 292.

begin with the lovers cherishing exactly those qualities in their partner that cause well-meaning friends simply to shake their heads?[5]
When we first fall in love, do we not look at certain traits in our lover,
such as stubbornness, flightiness, untidiness and boorishness as original and distinctive quirks that shape their personality?[6] And when
the relationship is over, are not precisely these quirks thrown accus-
ingly back at the once beloved and declared to be insurmountable
obstacles to continuing the relationship?

Freud's work 'A Special Type of Choice of Object Made by Men'
was, in this respect, more generally valid than its author cared to elucidate.[7] Such a moment of ambivalence could possibly be at work in all
occurrences of love, and not only in cases of perversion or with other
'special' types of object choices. The ambivalence involved in reinter-
preting drawbacks as special assets might give rise to the surplus that
delineates 'sensual' aspirations from 'affectionate' ones. This might also
explain Freud's remark that 'something in the nature of the sexual
instinct itself is unfavourable to the realization of complete satisfaction'.[8]

Nonetheless, Spinoza's remark on the ability of hate to increase
love (or to elevate its intensity in such a way that it first turns into
love) still demands an explanation. Why is love alone not strong
enough to result in this greater amount of intensity? What is the
essential condition that leads to this combining of powers? Freud
presents this condition in his theory of ambivalence. Ambivalence is
due to a conflict of aspirations of which one remains unconscious
(or, at least, for the most part). When one of the adversaries is
unconscious, then the conflict as a whole is an unconscious one, too.
Accordingly, only an unconscious conflict can form a base for
ambivalence. Freud subsequently wrote, for example, about the

---

5   Compare Freud, 'Notes upon a Case of Obsessional Neurosis', pp. 238–9: 'We
know that incipient love is often perceived as hatred, and that love, if it is denied
satisfaction, may easily be partly converted into hatred. . . .'

6   See also Žižek, *Tarrying with the Negative*, p. 125: 'Let us recall what is perhaps
the most sublime moment in melodramas: a plotter or well-meaning friend tries to
convince the hero to leave his sexual partner by way of enumerating the latter's weak
points; yet, unknowingly, he thereby provides reasons for continued loyalty; i.e., his
very counterarguments function as arguments ("for that very reason she needs even
more").'

7   See Freud, 'A Special Type of Choice of Object Made by Men', *SE*, 11:165–75,
pp. 167–8.

8   Freud, 'On the Universal Tendency to Debasement', pp. 188–9.

tender and likewise hostile feelings of survivors with respect to dead persons:

> There is bound to be a conflict between these two contrary feelings; and, since one of the two, the hostility, is wholly or for the greater part unconscious, the outcome of the conflict cannot be to subtract, as it were, the feeling with the lesser intensity from that with the greater and to establish the remainder in consciousness – as occurs, for instance, when one forgives a slight that one has received from someone of whom one is fond.[9]

In a conscious conflict, opposing aspirations are subtracted from one another. The love for a beloved person is slightly decreased by injury. In an unconscious conflict, on the contrary, subtraction never occurs. Instead, the powers are simply added together, regardless of their focus. (For example, minor, periodic insults form an essential element of some ambivalence-based love affairs.[10])

This difference between the conscious, subtracting conflict and the unconscious adding one shapes a fundamental thought in clinical psychoanalysis. As is generally known, clinical psychoanalysis is orientated towards introducing a conscious re-enactment of the unconscious conflict expressed in the symptom. This is meant to lower the intense, displeasurable tension caused by the unconscious conflict. Furthermore, discovering this unsigned mathematics operating in the unconscious also appears imperative for understanding the relationship between neuroses and perversion. If the amplitude of stimulation is more decisive than its direction or quality, then it is easy to explain that the neurosis forms the 'negative of perversion',[11] and that the forms of displeasure with which the one is afflicted (such as fear, disgust, guilt and pain) can be converted directly into forms of pleasure characteristic of the other (such as sexual desire, coprophilia, conscious and pleasurable disregard of moral principles, and partial-organic states of arousal).

---

9   Freud, 'Totem and Taboo', p. 62.

10   See also Freud, 'Notes upon a Case of Obsessional Neurosis', p. 239: 'The love has not succeed in extinguishing the hatred but only in driving it down into the unconscious ... In such circumstances the conscious love attains as a rule, by way of reaction, an especially high degree of intensity, so as to be strong enough for the perpetual task of keeping its opponent under repression.'

11   See Freud, 'Three Essays', p. 165.

The theory of ambivalence as the cause of a greater amplitude of intensity ultimately also leads to an explanation of that moment of *compulsion* that becomes manifest in neurotic forms (compulsive behaviour, obsessional neuroses), as well as in perverse phenomena (fixations, sexual addictions, apparent increase in the libido). If a greater intensity arises exclusively through ambivalence, then it is possible to derive the following paradoxical law of addiction and compulsion: as long as positive tendencies alone compel an action, this action remains moderately necessary, an object of free choice. An action becomes compulsive, however, the moment when negative tendencies directed towards a certain goal and positive tendencies conducive to it unite because of an unconscious conflict (as the perfect compromise to please both sides). Even the greatest passion for something does not lead to a compulsion or an addiction; only when this passion 'amalgamates' with an opposing one and, consequently, forces a substitute action (which not only satisfies the positive attitude towards the goal, but also the negative, defensive one) does it become unavoidable and irresistible for the person carrying it out.

Manifestations of (neurotic) compulsion, (perverse) fixation, addiction, and so on, can only emerge on the basis of an amplified dependency on an object or a practice generated by a preceding hatred of it. Relevant here are solely objects or behaviours that might come into consideration for a moment of hatred. No one becomes addicted to healthy country air, but there are most certainly people addicted to inhaling unhealthy fumes. No one develops an addiction to a game that presents no financial risks or the possibility of causing damage or injury in any other way. Yet even the intellectual mortification of being part of a 'foolish' game seems sufficient to allow addiction.

AMBIVALENCE AS THE BASE OF PLAY'S 'SACRED SERIOUSNESS': 'KNOWLEDGE' IS CONTEMPT

This theory of ambivalence also seems to allow us to explain the paradox of play that Huizinga emphasized with his thesis: players are entirely absorbed in the 'sacred seriousness', although at all times they know that it is 'only' a game. We can now give this matter a new formulation in terms of the economy of the libido: the game is more fascinating than even life's positive aspects because it unites both positive and negative aspirations, adding them together. Actors do not take the game seriously because they can think 'illusorily' of the pleasant side of life (and forget about the game). Instead, exactly the opposite is the case: precisely because the game is 'nonsense' in their eyes, a mere game, and because they therefore disdain and hate the game (while simultaneously loving it, whether for the suspended illusion that is presented in it or for the suspension of that illusion), they fall under its spell.

Looking at the situation from the perspective of the economy of the libido allows us to clarify the status of 'better knowledge' with regard to an illusion that is kept suspended: 'knowledge' is in no way knowledge as such; for a game to come about, the mere illusion that it is a game suffices. Instead, 'knowledge' is – as something *better* – a sign of *contempt*. It forms the affectless, intellectually cleansed track of the hatred that contributed to the addition of the affects. 'Knowledge' is hatred. The contempt for the illusion that is caused by this 'knowledge' is added to the love granted by the illusion. The contempt thereby makes the love of the illusion stronger than it was before knowledge followed by contempt came into the picture.

The gesture of *'intellectual' distancing* thus shapes the conditions for enormous *affective dependency* on the illusion that is held in suspense. The *symbol of negation*[12] contained in 'better knowledge' is the condition for the amplified affective affirmation. This explains what Huizinga detected as the 'sacred seriousness' of the game: the crowd is roused to a frenzy when a goal is scored precisely because they have not forgotten where they are, they know they are dealing with 'merely' a 'foolish' game in a football stadium.

Mannoni's formulation, 'I know perfectly well . . . but still . . .' can be understood in this context as an expression of ambivalence. The first part of the formulation, 'I know perfectly well', can be completed with 'that it is nonsense', and thereby expresses the subject's contempt for the idea or behaviour in question. The second part, 'but still', can be completed by stating 'it is fantastic' or 'I have to do it', thereby expressing not only the positive, desirable side of the matter, but also the overdetermined, compulsive consequences.

The apparent contradiction between knowledge and enthusiasm appearing in Mannoni's formulation can henceforth be recognized

12   The negation signifies, for example, 'this is not genuine', 'this is nonsense', or 'this is not real'. Mannoni uses the concept of the 'negation symbol' repeatedly with reference to the theatre (Mannoni, *Clefs pour l'Imaginaire*, pp. 166, 168, 304).

as a condition for the adding together of affects. The logical relationship formulated in the analysand's statement 'I know perfectly well . . . but still . . .' must be reformulated in accordance with the logic of the unconscious, which operates without countering any antagonistic or contradictory elements,[13] but in fact as a relationship of the sort 'because . . . that's why . . .'. The formulation advanced by Mannoni can therefore be reformulated as follows: 'I love it so much because I hate it.' (Such a formulation brings to mind principles at work in the aesthetics of the sublime and of camp.[14]) This explains why a person's better knowledge not only creates a possible opportunity, but even becomes a necessary requirement for a greater amount of passion, as is pointed out by both Mannoni and Huizinga, since without the knowledge that the matter is nonsense, there would be no contempt felt for it. In order to stir fascination, play requires the constant intellectual restriction, 'It is only a game.' This preamble must – in a way that I consider comparable with the Kantian 'I think'[15] – accompany all play in order for amplified intensity, 'sacred seriousness', to arise.

The same conditions as for play apply to the area of belief explored by Mannoni, which (as Huizinga had already demonstrated[16]) can be understood as a form of play. Consequently, the popular opposition between belief and knowledge ('We believe what we do not know') must, at least in terms of belief, be reversed to its exact opposite: better knowledge forms a necessary prerequisite of each and every belief; we believe precisely what we know better.[17] And this paradox now seems explicable: better knowledge nourishes contempt of the belief and keeps it alive – and does so apparently in spite of all better knowledge and all enlightenment. Therefore, superstitious believers must always be viewed as bearers of a 'cynical awareness' that elevates them above matters – and they must also view themselves in this way. There is an

---

13 Compare Freud, 'Interpretation of Dreams', p. 318.

14 See Immanuel Kant, *Critique of the Power of Judgment*, ed. Paul Guyer and Eric Matthews (Cambridge: CUP, 2008 [1790]), §§23ff; Susan Sontag, 'Notes on "Camp"', in her *Against Interpretation and Other Essays* (New York: Picador, 2001).

15 See Kant, *Critique of Pure Reason*, §16, pp. 152–3.

16 Huizinga, *Homo Ludens*, pp. 20, 25–6.

17 Kant's sanctimonious assertion that knowledge must be denied to make room for faith (*Critique of Pure Reason*, Preface to the 2nd edn, p. 29), also appears in another light with respect to this finding, or at least in terms of superstition: knowledge and belief are not exclusive, complementary territories.

'I know' here that must be able to accompany all illusions of this kind.[18]

This explains why the illusion without an owner always brings along sacred seriousness as its symptom: the suspended illusion contains 'knowledge'. The 'knowledge' in 'sacred seriousness' is contempt; therefore, the 'sacred seriousness' arises as a result of an ambivalence – an unconscious conflict between disdain and dependency. Huizinga's emphasis on the excessive intensity of the game prompted an analysis based on the economy of the libido, and this leads to the concept of ambivalence. With the help of ambivalence, it is possible to explain why certain people despise their own mindset and why, because of the fact that they despise this mindset, they are even more addicted to it than to any other mindset that they do not despise.[19]

TYRANNICAL GAMES: FROM 'SACRED SERIOUSNESS' TO COMPULSION

The 'sacred seriousness' of play caused by ambivalence often works as a spell that holds players captivated, making it impossible for them to leave the 'ludic sphere' for any considerable amount of time regardless of the great damage this may cause. For example, drivers in regular traffic often seem imprisoned in this kind of ludic sphere, which makes it impossible for them to allow other drivers to change lanes. Contrary to all reason, and apparently also against their will, they are compelled to stop anyone from passing, regardless of the risk:[20] they put 110 per cent effort into driving – perhaps even more so than professional racing drivers, who in such situations sometimes also cleverly 'hold back'.

As Huizinga remarked, play is '"enchanting", "captivating"'[21]; this spell emanating from the ludic sphere has the nature of a

---

18 Blaise Pascal once formulated this principle in the short assertion: 'The incredulous are the most credulous.' Pascal, *Pensées*, trans. with an Introduction by A. J. Krailsheimer (London/New York: Penguin, 1995), p. 71 (no. 224).

19 In Kant's aesthetics of the sublime, this intense devotion appears, as in Anthony A. C. Shaftesbury, under the concept of 'enthusiasm' (see Kant, *Critique of the Power of Judgment*, p. 154).

20 For more on this, see the precise comment by Signer, *Fernsteuerung*, p. 137ff.

21 Huizinga, *Homo Ludens*, p. 10.

compulsion. That is remarkable to the extent that it seems to contradict another conclusion reached by Huizinga about play. Like many other play theorists before and after him,[22] he characterizes play as something that is marked by freedom: 'First and foremost, then, all play is a voluntary activity'.[23] Huizinga even describes this as one of the 'main characteristics of play': 'it is free, is in fact freedom'.[24] That would mean that neither the game nor other people can force the player to play. No coercion emanates from play because

> for the adult and responsible human being play is a function which he could equally well leave alone. Play is superfluous. The need for it is only urgent to the extent that the enjoyment of it makes it a need. Play can be deferred or suspended at any time. It is never imposed by physical necessity or moral duty.[25]

A command given by another person would also destroy the nature of play: 'Play to order is no longer play'.[26] In contrast with this, I will attempt to show that it is a grave error to characterize play in terms of freedom: in this chapter by referring to the game's coercion, and later (in Chapter 9) to the coercion exerted by other people.

But Huizinga had another reason for defining play through the characteristic of freedom. What is crucial is not the idea that people cannot be forced to play, but instead the thesis that the game is played for its own sake. This thesis arose from Huizinga's examination of the fascination emanating from play: if we are correct in assuming that the game is able to fascinate us more intensely than daily life, then the seriousness that reigns in play cannot be borrowed from daily life. Because the game possesses its own unique power of fascination, it must correspondingly have its own reason for being carried out. Based on these same assumptions, Huizinga suspects that professionalization – in sport, for example – is decisive in play's disappearance from culture. When play becomes a serious occupation and is thereby no longer

---

22   On this, see for example Kant, *Critique of the Power of Judgement*, §29, B 116; Schiller, *On the Aesthetic Education of Man* (Oxford: OUP, 1982), p. 109 (15th letter; 'the freest most sublime state of being'); Caillois, *Man, Play and Games*, p. 9.

23   Huizinga, *Homo Ludens*, p. 7.

24   Ibid., p. 8.

25   Ibid.

26   Ibid., p. 7.

something done for its own sake, but is instead carried out as a necessity of life, then according to Huizinga it loses its ludic quality.[27] That could be countered, however, with the observation that even professional athletes, in spite of high material stakes, are occasionally utterly and completely absorbed in the ludic sphere – football players and ice hockey players become 'intoxicated by play' in the best cases, and in the worst start violently attacking their opponents; highly paid boxers bite their adversaries' ears even though this might lead to a suspension or ban from the sport, severely damaging or even ending their careers. Thus, even in professional sports, 'sacred seriousness' often appears to prevail over professional, secular seriousness.[28] Here, too, for the emergence of play, it does not seem decisive whether the matter is, in truth, play or a secular profession; instead, what is decisive is that those carrying it out treat it as play, regardless of what it might actually be. The 'knowledge' in this case even seems to be reversed idiosyncratically. Rather than representing the attitude *I know perfectly well that it is only a game, but still I attempt to make it seem as serious as possible (for the benefit of the paying audience),* these professional athletes assume exactly the opposite, paradoxical attitude: *I know that it is only my secular profession, but nonetheless I am caught in the spell of the ludic sphere and have to do something monstrous.*

The freedom that Huizinga speaks about with relation to play is therefore not the players' freedom from all compulsion, but instead play's freedom from all external reasons for playing. But this is precisely why it is possible for a game to captivate players. The freedom of play accords with the players' lack of freedom.

---

27   Ibid., p. 197.

28   We should not forget, however, that the ludic sphere of professional sports is superseded by that of another sphere – that of mass media in which *even bad news is good news*. Athletes who are out of control may do harm to their athletic agenda, but they benefit their publicity. Their excesses seem to be carried out with the same compulsion that is typical of captivation in the illusion of the other. This can also be seen in so-called 'Reality TV', such as the *Jerry Springer Show*. Although one could say that the episodes (of the sort: 'jealous wife demolishes the car of her unfaithful husband live, on camera') are simply acted out by those involved, at the same time a kind of 'sacred seriousness' often seems to overcome these actors and, like a drug, compel them to go further than they normally would. What began as a more-or-less staged private need for revenge is increasingly transformed into genuine rage. This emerges from a situation of acting within the medium of the illusion of the other, and having to use the currency valid there: the demand to offer the audience something, without fail, must be satisfied at all costs.

Furthermore, the freedom of the game even appears to cause the players' lack of freedom: because the game is played for its own sake, it demands absolute obedience from the players, almost like a brutal, monotheistic god.[29] In its autotelic ('end-in-itself') character, play is tyrannical. In its 'sacred seriousness', it is also, accordingly, much more serious than daily life, since it demands unconditional compliance – and remarkably, demands it *immediately*. We can see this in the dramatic forms of affect that an unhealthy game addiction gives rise to, as well as the bad conscience that befalls religious and secular neurotics when they fail to carry out their ceremonial play behaviour.[30]

The game's 'here and now' command is still evident, although in a milder form, when reasonable people abruptly end a gathering with the excuse that they have to go home to watch a football match (or the next episode of a series) on television. And what is important here is that they often introduce their departure with a preamble: 'Unfortunately, I have to go now to watch a football match.' Those present view the addiction to televised sporting events as unfortunate but unavoidable – a sure sign of the ambivalence generating the procedure. The players' own submission to play is evident in an expression of contempt – revealing a disdain for the game and for oneself, which contributes significantly to dependence on the game.[31]

This demand that play makes of the viewer is even more clearly evident when, for example, the Olympic Games are broadcast live on television at the most outrageous times of day. No company could ever motivate its employees to work during these hours, whereas the appearance of star athletes inspires them 'voluntarily'[32] to keep a diligent night watch over the television. For example, in spring of 1998, the Austrian public awaited with particular interest the men's downhill section of the Alpine ski competition at the

---

29   The demand for unconditional, immediate obedience reveals a structural similarity between the spell cast by the game and the significant 'fear of God', as Žižek illustrated with recourse to Lacan (see Žižek, 'Hegel mit Lacan', p. 59; and compare Žižek, *For They Know Not What They Do*, pp. 16–17).

30   See also Freud, 'Obsessive Actions', p. 119.

31   Christof Siemes offers a very good and humorous description of this in his 'Sieg ohne Tor', *Die Zeit*, 8 June 2000, p. 41.

32   This 'voluntariness' is typically expressed more accurately by phrases such as 'I have to watch it'.

Nagano Olympic Games (an Austrian skier was poised to win). The scheduled broadcast time on Austrian television was approximately 3 a.m. The event was repeatedly cancelled because of snow storms. First it was postponed for an hour at a time, then cancelled altogether and rescheduled for the next day. This went on night after night; the enthusiastic Austrian news reporter was on location, standing in the snowstorm urging the audience to hold out and stay awake for the broadcast of the race, which would, with any luck, take place later. Apparently, a significant amount of the workforce was moved by these appeals. In the following weeks, several spokespeople for industry appeared in the Austrian media to point out the downturn in production – the effects of which were great enough to have already affected the economy – caused by the week-long vigil, during which employees had showed up for work exhausted from staying up all night.

What seems particularly remarkable in this context is that even the copious spread of recording devices has not put an end to the habit. Apparently, there is something about the game that cannot be recorded and repeated later[33] – something that demands the viewers' live presence in front of the television screen. This tyrannical moment of mass media play seems conditioned by a belief, an illusion without an owner – and, for that matter, an extremely absurd illusion: it is necessary to watch the football match live because otherwise there is no chance of influencing the course of the game.[34] Of course, no one seems really to believe that their gaze at the television is capable in any way of affecting the events shown on the screen. Everyone 'knows' that such a conjecture is utter nonsense. Nonetheless, the majority of sports fans act as though there were a reason for this belief. This also explains the 'endless depths' that seem to engulf television viewers as they sit on their couches, not to be disturbed under any circumstance – reminiscent of a ritual practice. They are, after all, grasped by a sublime task; every disturbance would impede their impact on the course of the game.

---

33   Televised sport is one of the few areas in which there is no interpassive use of recording devices. This may be attributed to the fact that watching live sports programmes is already an interpassive act (as will be shown in what follows). It contains a suspended illusion delegated to someone else. The unsuitability of sporting events for recording means that there is no interpassivity of the interpassivity.

34   I am grateful to my friend Ulf Stengl in Berlin for this paradoxical insight.

This puzzling symptom of a relentless command to be present for sporting events on television can be categorized together with a number of other symptoms in which the enthusiasm for sport rears its head more readily and clearly as a form of common magic of the civilized: television viewers often call out commands such as 'Run!' or 'Shoot!' to the little figures of the athletes running across the screen. They seem incapable of refraining from these kinds of invocations when watching television, although they know very well that the pixel-based depictions cannot hear them (and, even if they were face to face with the real person, they would not shout for fear of disturbing them). In this case, the game turns out to be something that 'mature and reasonable people' are in no way able to 'just as well do without', as Huizinga believed. To make matters even worse: they cannot even leave it temporarily to then catch up later. The game's command for presence 'here' and 'now' abides no postponement. Even educated, politically active people regularly turn *first* to the sports and horoscope pages as they leaf through the daily paper, and not to those parts that report on the things that are relevant for their lives or their way of thinking.[35] Free play, an end in itself, renders its fans willing, pliable slaves at all times – to a much greater extent than the secular seriousness of life is capable of doing.

COMPULSION, ADDICTION, AND THE ILLUSION OF THE OTHER

This perspective that Huizinga opened up with the concept of the 'play sphere', as well as his remark about players being seized by the game, seems interesting in that it might also shed a new light on other obsessive phenomena that are apparently unrelated to play. As it turns out, play is not the only massive and regular phenomenon (regular, that is, not only in the pathological form of game addiction) that is bound to compulsion. Instead, based on this finding, we must pose the question the other way around: Can all phenomena of

---

35 Roger Caillois clearly noticed this moment, which contradicts his own assumption of the 'freedom' in play, based on the example of the horoscope: 'To be sure, the reaction of the majority of the public is to smile at such puerile predictions. But it still reads them. And more important, it keeps on reading them. At this point, many begin [by] reading the astrological section of their newspaper.' Caillois, *Man, Play and Games*, p. 47.

compulsion and addiction be understood based on an understanding of play?

That would mean that obsessive and addictive phenomena are caused by ambivalence – that they show the character of 'sacred seriousness' and that, like play, they contain a suspended illusion. In other words, like play, they would also always be 'representational', and would be steered by an illusion without an owner. Huizinga's concept of 'sacred seriousness' would thereby build an overall formula for those psychological states that are at work in obsessive neurosis, addiction, and perverse fixation, as well as in their normal, hardly watered-down, but socially more acceptable forms (such as the – nevertheless occasionally deadly – rioting of soccer fans at a match).

Therefore, we must be able to establish the previously stated thesis – that wherever sacred seriousness reigns, a suspended illusion is at work – for the area of compulsion in general: the suspension of an illusion creates the decisive condition for the compulsion – *everywhere compulsion reigns*, it is possible to uncover the presence of an illusion suspended by knowing better. If the compulsion is sacred seriousness, and sacred seriousness arises through the suspension of an illusion, then the suspension of the illusion – in other words, the other's illusion – is the cause of compulsion. Freud, too, established this thesis that obsessive neurotic acts, as inconspicuous and senseless as they might seem, are always of a symbolic nature.[36] Following Huizinga, it seems possible to take up the same thread at the other end – that of the suspended illusions of the game – and explain *why suspended illusions in particular lead to the spell of the play sphere*. In other words, from this angle it would be possible to explain *why symbolic acts, in particular, prove suitable for obsessive behaviour*.

CAPTURED IN THE ILLUSION OF THE OTHER:
DELEGATED ADDICTION, UNAVOIDABLE
PLAY, INVOLUNTARY POLITENESS

By showing 'that the consecrated site cannot be distinguished from the playground', Huizinga traced the sacred back to play. He thereby also related ambivalence – which had previously been recognized by numerous authors as a character trait of the sacred, and from which it

---

36   See Freud, 'Obsessive Actions', p. 120.

is possible to explain compulsions emanating from the sacred – beyond the sacred, to play.[37] According to Huizinga, play is a symbolic practice in which the players present and maintain a suspended fiction; therefore, symbolic behaviour must contain something that accommodates – or even evokes – ambivalence.

Symbolic behaviour begins as soon as special attention is given to form – for example, in obsessive neurotics' 'ceremonial actions'.[38] Since form is something that points beyond an object at hand, rendering it a sign or symbol of something else, all formalism is symbolization. Every carefully nurtured form – whether in common compulsions, design or art – contains a 'myth', in the sense intended by Roland Barthes.[39] This 'myth', this fiction, is presented in play, and is situated as an illusion of the other through the 'knowing better' that is necessary for play.

Identified by its form as a replacement and disdained by the superior knowledge as *mere substitute*, the matter becomes susceptible to ambivalence. It can thereby evoke compulsion, addiction and 'sacred seriousness'. The minimum condition necessary for an object to provoke addiction is the ability to associate it with contempt and hatred – before love for the object emerges. For this reason, the nature of a substitute – regardless of what it replaces or what is being used as a replacement – is inherently suitable for addiction. The fact of being a symbol creates the practical element for this amplification of affective value. Something can be hated because it is 'only a replacement', and thereby have amplified powers of attraction. The fascination emanates from the fact that it is a depiction and not the thing or actual content that it depicts.[40] Because play depicts something, and through

---

37   See also Freud, 'Totem and Taboo', pp. 311ff; Roger Caillois, *Man and the Sacred*, trans. Meyer Barash (New York: Free Press of Glencoe, 1960), pp. 37ff.

38   See also Freud, 'Obsessive Actions', pp. 117ff.

39   See Roland Barthes, *Mythologies* (New York: Hill & Wang, 2001).

40   A corresponding misunderstanding underlies a great number of the currently booming beauty practices, such as cosmetic surgery – as though someone will become more beautiful by virtue of a closer resemblance to their idol. The fascination, however, does not arise through similarity but through depiction. The attraction does not lie in the achieved 'natural form', but in the charming action of depiction – since, as Spinoza has pointed out, we do not love things because they are 'good' in themselves, but, on the contrary, we love them because we strive for them. Likewise, the magic of cosmetics does not involve promising that someone will look like a certain celebrity, but the promise of allowing people to participate in the 'glamorous life'. The formalism of cosmetics generates the 'myth' of a big, wide world.

'knowing better' suspends the depicted fiction (by identifying it as an illusion of the other), it is capable of stirring ambivalence, and along with that compulsion, addiction and tyranny.

Accordingly, this background is necessary for explaining the particularly paradoxical-seeming phenomenon of interpassive, 'delegated' addiction: the former alcoholic can only remain 'dry' by constantly filling his or her guests' glasses. It is an alcoholism that is lived out through other people – an interpassive alcoholism 'for others' and 'through others', a substitute alcoholism; a 'more objective' alcoholism that serves the illusion of the other, so to speak, in the same way that Žižek shows the amusement from canned laughter on television as an 'objective' amusement, carried out for the sake of the other.[41] Along the path of displacement (comprising substitute behaviour), addiction can progress from a 'subjective', self-practised alcoholism to this 'objective', interpassive variant. All toxicological explanations are useless when confronted with this phenomenon. An explanation of addiction based on its ludic character and the libidinal cause of ambivalence, however, can reveal the extent to which love and hate unite, and thereby also become irresistible in this interpassive behaviour. The symbolic, substitute activity of pouring another glass serves to ward off an impulse of hatred of drinking by offering the appearance of a continued, endearing occupation with the drug.

Phenomena of interpassive addiction thereby form a key to understanding other forms of addiction. The delegated alcoholism of the interpassive drinker allows for a better understanding of the more common alcoholism of someone who actually does their own drinking. The alcoholic's drinking, too, is caused in part by a persistent hatred of drinking (as well as of one's own person). Drinking, too, is based on a latent hatred of the drug, a desire to 'obliterate' it.[42] This dominates over manifest, positive references to stimulants. Drinking is thus already a substitute activity. As a symbolic 'protective measure' it serves – more than the enjoyment of the apparently so well-loved drug – primarily to destroy it. However, as in the practices of interpassivity, a strong devotion to the relevant matter is staged for the illusion of the other.

41   See Žižek, *Sublime Object of Ideology*, p. 35.
42   See also Heinrich, *anfangen mit freud*, p. 55.

For the same reason, interpassive practices – such as bibliomania, photocopying, collecting video recordings, and so on – must also be understood as forms of addiction that rest on the principle of play. They are all substitute activities. As symbolic, protective measures, they serve to overcome an impulse of hatred towards something that is outwardly loved but latently hated: bibliomania and photocopying serve as a defence against the rising hatred of reading; video-recording serves to ward off the persistent hatred of television. According to the well-known logic of obsessional neuroses, this kind of defence always brings the emergence of exactly that which is being warded off.[43] That is also why, in the case of interpassive substitute activity, the replacement of the delegated pleasure is preferred to what is being replaced: one's own pleasure. For that reason, with the help of their recording devices, interpassives prefer to 'stage' the activity of watching television for the illusion of the other, rather than actually carrying it out.

This moment of defence and hatred is also clearly shown in practices of a less obviously interpassive nature, such as taking pictures of tourist attractions. With the help of a camera only a few inches tall, the pyramids, a hundred meters high and dwarfing the viewer to only a miniscule detail, are then shrunk to a trifle, their fate in the hands of the viewer holding the camera. The compulsion expressed in phrases such as 'I have to take a picture of that' is based on a similar latent hatred of the object that is manifestly loved or reviled. The manifest respect for an object is expressed by professing 'esteem' with the help of the camera. The latent hatred, however, is satisfied in that the tourist attraction has now been shrunk, and only the camera has had to look at it and not the camera's owner.

In order to understand addiction and compulsion, it seems utterly necessary to highlight the decisive role of play – including the illusion of the other. Every addiction *is a form of play*. Among other things, this also helps to explain a phenomenon discovered by addiction research: the addict's inability to play.[44] Addicts cannot play because, in their addiction, they are already *living* a game. At the

---

43   See Freud, 'Notes upon a Case of Obsessional Neurosis', p. 225.

44   See Hannelore Albrecht, 'Analytisch orientierte Beratung für Patienten mit Folgeschäden eine Suchtmittelmißbrauchs in einem Allgemeinkrankenhaus', Bremen (psychology diploma thesis, 1995), p. 29.

same time, perverse people, for example, also seem incapable of fantasizing. The so-called 'average Joe' perhaps fantasizes at times by
imagining perversions. Perverse people, on the contrary, live these
perversions out – there is no room left over for fantasizing. Clarity
could also be given to common, everyday forms of addiction, such as
smoking and the difficulty in quitting, through a theoretical approach
beginning with the illusion of the other addressed by play – an approach
that is not accessible through 'substance-based' theories. Smoking is
not only (due to the release of neurotransmitters) a pleasurable inges-
tion of more or less harmful substances; at the same time it is also a
symbolic procedure. The subtlety of the materials used practically
demands a certain care in its execution – a formalism that characterizes
symbolic practices. Combustion in miniature, which also appears in
many religious practices, intensifies the ceremonial character of the act.
There is also an entire series of well-established iconographies à la
Humphrey Bogart and Lauren Bacall that are available for integrating
the consumption of tobacco products. We are dealing with an *illusion
containing an image*, not with an 'imagination without an image': the
practice of the ceremonial act assures participation in a widely known
and accepted myth – participation that is thoroughly conscious, which
is not necessarily true of all ceremonial acts.

Even more important than this iconographic aspect, however,
seems to be the fact that smoking – according to Jenny Holzer's
formulation – 'keeps something going':[45] the ceremonial act enables
a seemingly magical transformation of the situation. While
awkwardly waiting for another person or for an inattentive
bartender, for example, reaching for a cigarette can turn the situation into one of self-contented, seemingly philosophical calm.
Rather than simply sitting or standing there like someone who has
been stood up, the person has something to do. Instead of being
peered at and scrutinized for what they are doing there, they
become an agency against which the situation has to measure up,
and show its reason for being there.

The conspicuous exchangeability of forms of addiction also ultimately supports this interpretation of addiction, which rests on its
symbolic rather than chemical aspects. Hannelore Albrecht has

---

45   See Jenny Holzer, *Truisms and Essays* (New York: Barbara Gladstone Gallery,
1983), p. 3. See also Chapter 6, below.

remarked: 'An example of this might be the dependency of many recovering alcoholics on their regular Alcoholics Anonymous meetings and the ritualized self-presentation that takes place there.'[46]

In direct accordance with this remark, David Fincher's film *Fight Club* offered a humorous presentation of such a phenomenon of replacing one form of addiction or compulsion (insomnia) with another (visiting self-help groups), and led the story to its logical conclusion: a violent excess of 'sacred seriousness' in play. [47]

The ability to replace one form of addiction with another indicates that it was already a form of substitution – and hence, symbolic. Under this condition, and this condition alone, not only do other practices that are likewise substitutes seem attractive – so also does the replacement of the one by the other. The fact that the illusion of the other can become obsessive for precisely those who seem above it by virtue of 'knowing better' is also shown in the example of the peculiar compulsion emanating from symbolic social forms of behaviour: politeness, too, can be an addiction-like, obsessive behaviour. Polite people become or remain polite, unwittingly. Henri Bergson considered this sort of 'automatism', illustrated clearly in the example of unwitting politeness, to be a main source of comedy.[48] Walter Benjamin, one of the few theorists of politeness, pointed out the ambivalence that is integral to the polite form, and that is the cause of the compulsion it evokes.[49] Žižek considered the fact that, despite knowing better, we treat unintelligent or incompetent superiors with respect – and apparently are unable to do anything but treat them that way – as evidence that we often do not (consciously) know how things appear to us:[50] by showing respect for someone who is a renowned idiot, we are prisoners of an illusion of the other (an imagination which, for us, remains without an image). This illusion becomes compulsive for our behaviour – opposing all of the freedom that our knowledge seems to

---

46   Albrecht, 'Analytisch orientierte Beratung', p. 25.

47   *Fight Club* (dir. David Fincher, USA, 1999).

48   See Henri Bergson, *Laughter: An Essay on the Meaning of the Comic* (Whitefish, MT: Kessinger, 2004), p. 33.

49   See Walter Benjamin, 'Höflichkeit', in his *Gesammelte Schriften* (Frankfurt: Suhrkamp, 1980), vol. IV.1 (wa 10), pp. 402–3; see also Huizinga's remarks about 'exchanging civilities with the enemy' (Huizinga, *Homo Ludens*, p. 98).

50   See Slavoj Žižek, 'The Interpassive Subject', .egs.edu/faculty/slavoj-zizek/articles/the-interpassive-subject/; cf. Introduction to this volume.

grant us. It is precisely this knowledge that renders the illusion suspended by it a compulsion. For this reason, polite people (for whom the fictive essence of politeness based on social convention is evident) find it much more difficult to set aside their politeness than, for example, good-natured people their good nature (which they regard as their true character). The compulsion of the outer forms (which are subject to the illusion of the other) is stronger than the obligation evoked through internalized principles (corresponding with one's own illusion).[51]

With the help of the psychoanalytical concept of ambivalence, the secret of 'sacred seriousness' has seemingly been decoded. The concept of ambivalence also furnished an explanation of the tyrannical tendencies of play that Huizinga detected – despite his own intentions. Both, ambivalence and compulsion could then be traced back to play's symbolic nature – i.e. its reference to the illusion of the other.

In this way, it is possible to shed light on those aspects of addiction phenomena that stem from the illusion of the other, and thereby highlight the significance of the illusion of the other, as opposed to addiction's commonly emphasized, substance-related, toxicological aspects.

Above all, the concept of ambivalence offers an explanation of the paradoxical 'logic' of suspended illusions detected by Mannoni and Huizinga – that is, the circumstance that an illusion that has been seen through is more compulsive for those who have seen through it

---

51   Thomas notices this difference between the *obligation* based on internalized, subjectifying ideologies and the *compulsion* of external, non-subjectifying ideological forms (see Thomas, *Medien – Ritual – Religion*, p. 474). With regard to the 'liturgies' of television he remarks: 'Due to the perpetuity of the liturgical order, the structuring of time emanates from the individual rituals that constitute it, which, however – and here lies an important difference to the rituals studied by Rappaport from earlier societies – do not necessarily disrupt everyday life since they do not demand compulsive participation.' Television can be described as the progression of individual rituals, '[r]hythms, cycles, and repetitions, although their observation and the participation in them is not made socially mandatory' (ibid.). Yet, contrary to what Thomas states, the 'liturgical' order of television is based on the principle of compulsion rather than a casual commitment. In this particular respect, television culture is comparable with the tribal cultures of earlier societies. As Marshall McLuhan established in his pioneering work (*Understanding Media*, pp. 29ff), both cultures are shaped by the predominance of 'cold' media. Sports fans must watch television live, just as the members of tribal cultures have to carry out certain rituals immediately, and polite people have a compulsion towards immediate politeness.

than for all others. Since the 'better knowledge' suspending these illusions is – in emotional terms – contempt, it intensifies the emotional ties to the illusion. Owing to this contempt, an intensified overall affect arises through a moment of hatred. And it is more difficult to escape from this ambivalent affect, composed of hatred and love, than from any non-ambivalent affect, no matter how strong. Since it carries within it a moment of contempt, the illusion of the other is more compelling than any illusion of one's own.

CHAPTER FIVE

Dialectics: Sigmund Freud – Ambivalence and the Loss of Play in Culture

FROM 'SACRED SERIOUSNESS' TO THE DISAPPEARANCE OF PLAY: IS THERE A 'DIALECTIC' OF BELIEF?

By tracing Huizinga's concept of 'sacred seriousness' back to the psychoanalytical concept of ambivalence, it seems that we are on track to finding out why, as Huizinga discovered, play tends to disappear from the culture founded upon it. In what follows, I will attempt to show that, by means of this ambivalence, it is possible to explain the tendencies to miniaturization and invisibility. This will substantiate the connection between the two main problems in Huizinga's theory – the problem of 'sacred seriousness' and that of play's tendency to disappear. And this connection of the problems simultaneously forms their solution: 'sacred seriousness' would accordingly contain that specific moment that pushes for play's retreat from culture. The ambivalent 'sacred seriousness' of play exerts a tyrannical force on players, subjecting play to a dynamic that is comparable with that of obsessional neurosis. In accordance with this dynamic, the practitioners, throughout the course of cultural history, gradually 'play' themselves free from the constraints of play. But what I aim to show is the price they pay for this.

A theory of the disappearance of play as a result of ambivalence would also present an explanation for a problem emerging from my investigation of Mannoni's theory, in which I reconstructed belief as an independent form of ideology. An illusion of others kept at a distance through better knowledge, belief, like play, proved to be compulsory for its actors – more so than faith is for the faithful. Belief – a compulsion that the believers themselves hold in contempt – appeared as a universal early form of ideology; the respected conviction, or faith, on the contrary, appeared as a later form typical only of certain cultures. Whereas belief can stand alone, faith always presupposes belief – as both a background context and a base that remains standing, though it is now subjected to a necessary misconception.[1] In addition, ritual practices, images and myths were all founded on belief, and thus are gestures of distancing. They thereby seem to have served as defences against the formation of faith.

These conclusions raised the question of what causes the transition from belief to faith-like forms of ideology, and whether it might be conceivable that belief (the illusion of others) would tend in any way to switch over to faith – that is, to one's own belief, despite defensive motions? If it is true that belief, like play, is caused by ambivalence, and if ambivalence is capable of generating changes, then it is possible to infer that belief itself is inherently inclined to being overlaid by faith. Rather than external causes alien to this form of ideology, it would thus be partly a tension inherent to the form of belief itself that leads this form to transform into one of faith. We can thus speak of the 'dialectic of belief' (in a sense analogous to that of Adorno and Horkheimer's 'dialectic of enlightenment'[2]). Corresponding with this dialectic, the contempt inherent to belief would gradually evolve into the self-esteem typical of faith. Precisely those rituals and mythical practices that we have interpreted as defence mechanisms against the emergence of faith due to their 'interpassive' character will, as a consequence, always cumulatively bring about that which they are acting as a defence against. The measures taken so that the illusion of others continues to retain its status as the others' illusion will ultimately lead to the formation of illusions that are one's own. In the same way, perhaps, that repeatedly playing a favourite CD not only allows one to love it, but also finally to grow weary of it, the persistent defence against subjectivization also helps create ideological subjectivity.

Freud's study 'Obsessive Actions and Religious Practices' offers an exemplary depiction of this sort of process caused by

---

1   See the examples from Durkheim, *Elementary Forms*, p. 34, which also draws the conclusion, for deistic religions, that there are 'rites that are entirely independent of any idea of gods or spiritual beings'.

2   Theodor W. Adorno and Max Horkheimer, *Dialectic of Enlightenment: Philosophical Fragments*, trans. Edmund Jephcott, ed. Gunzelin Schmid Noerr (Palo Alto, CA: Stanford University Press, 2002). The 'dialectic of belief' is, however, not a complete one. Faith builds up over belief, but belief is never entirely abolished within it. There is no faith that does not have superstitious elements of belief. However, every faith must increasingly conceal the persistence of belief. An *imaginary* abolition of belief takes place.

ambivalence, and explains the tendency to 'switch' into the opposite. Freud's text first gives an account of the typical development of an obsessional neurosis, from the repeated obsessive actions to their ultimate disappearance. In this text, Freud also develops the beginnings of a theory of the history of religion based on the individual dynamics of obsessional neuroses. These beginnings seem capable of confirming and clarifying the relationship between belief and faith that we have been able to work out from Mannoni's theory. First, however, some precision should be added to a few of Freud's explicit statements by using his own suggestions, and also by applying Mannoni's observations.

In drawing parallels between neuroses and major areas of social production, Freud conceived of religion as the 'normal model' ('Normalvorbild') for obsessional neurosis.[3] For the time being, however, I need to emphasize those elements in Freud's depictions that identify *magic* rather than *religion* as the counterpart of obsessional neurosis. This is necessary for interpreting the parallels between developments in obsessional neurotic history and cultural history described in 'Obsessive Actions and Religious Practices' as the explanation of a 'dialectic' that leads to magic and belief suddenly being overlaid by religious faith. After all, there are numerous indicators for justifying such a classification of obsessional neurosis together with magic and belief.[4] First of all, as Freud remarked, there is the 'private nature' of obsessive actions 'as opposed to the public and communal character of religious observances'. The obsessional neuroses are preferably practised 'hidden from view like Mélusine', and therefore deliver 'a travesty, half comic and half tragic, of a private religion.'[5] Yet such privacy is characteristic of magic, not religion.[6]

Moreover, Freud's comparison of obsessional neuroses with a system of taboos points more to belief and magic than to religion. Taboos are not religious, but rather magical: they are not commandments from a God, and they provide their own sanctions. Neither are they moral prohibitions: they have no arrangement in any

---

3   See Freud, 'Totem and Taboo', pp. 73–4.

4   Thus, Freud remarked that the 'primary obsessive acts of these neurotics always have a magical character' ('Totem and Taboo', p. 87).

5   Freud, 'Obsessive Actions', p. 119.

6   See also Durkheim, *Elementary Forms*, pp. 43, 223.

substantiating system.[7] An especially remarkable fact about taboos is the mechanism whereby they apply regardless of whether someone has guilty intentions or not. For example, those who have eaten from the plate of the chief will be punished, regardless of whether they knew it was the chief's plate, and regardless of whether they intended to insult the chief. And often the punishment is not an act, but instead a state: the poor person who was hungry does not have to go to prison, but instead becomes sick and dies, as though having consumed poison.[8] The taboo's mode of action thus seems closer to that of medicine than to that of religion or jurisprudence. This would correspond with what some authors notice as magic's character as a 'quasi-natural science'.[9]

In 'Totem and Taboo', too, Freud confirms the classification of obsessional neurosis together with belief and magic. Evidence is provided by his obsessional neurotic patient, the 'Rat Man': 'All obsessional neurotics are superstitious in this way, usually against their better judgement.'[10] Once again, through this turn 'against their better judgment', we meet the characteristic of 'better knowledge', which we have learned to interpret as an expression of contempt and as a component of ambivalence. In accordance with this contempt, the obsessional neurotic practices, just like the magical, are carried out not only without reference to any type of god, but also without reference to an ideal of a believer. Not only are magic and obsessional neurosis 'religions' without a god – they also do not even have a self-image that their adherents can refer to, and proudly live up to when they have satisfied all of its demands. With the help of Mannoni, we discerned this lack of an 'ideal ego' as a typical characteristic of belief, and as the criterion differentiating it from a religious faith. Based on the absence of such an ideal, the corresponding concept of 'guilt' associated with it also presents a problem in connection with the taboo-arrangements – it makes just as little sense in this context as it does in a medical one: when someone eats the wrong thing, they die.

---

7   See Freud, 'Totem and Taboo', p.18.

8   Ibid., pp 42–3

9   See Frazer, *Golden Bough*, Chapter 3, Section 1. Durkheim notes, in *Elementary Forms*, pp. 222–3: 'By contrast, a magical prohibition is sanctioned only by material consequences . . . disobedience incurs risk, like those run by a patient who does not follow his doctor's advice.'

10   Freud, 'Totem and Taboo', p. 86.

This simple rule again points out that, in the area of belief, the practitioners remain *objects* of an illusion. They do not attain a subject state that is regulated by reference to an ideal, which would imply concepts such as responsibility, intention, guilt, self-esteem, and the like.[11]

The fantasy of 'omnipotence of thoughts' that appears in obsessional neurosis likewise refers much more clearly to a parallel between obsessional neuroses and magic than to one between obsessional neuroses and religion – also according to Freud's own version. This is so strong that, for Freud, the real social 'normal model' for the obsessional neuroses was, in the end, not religion (with its spiritualizing tendencies), but instead art (which produces material).[12]

If this parallel announced in Freud's title between obsessional actions and religious practices actually exists, then it is not something that is present from the outset. In the beginning, obsessional actions are magical. It is only later, after a very definite switch, that something emerges in obsessional neuroses to make them comparable with religious faith. The interesting thing in Freud's text is the theory of this switch.

WITHIN COMPULSIVE DYNAMICS, RITUALS BECOME FOOLISH

The object of Freud's study are those small gestures that shape the clinical picture of the obsessional neuroses and, as he established, share structural features with performances 'by means of which believers give expression to their piety'.[13] As Freud discovered, others before him – possibly even several of his analysands – had identified obsessional actions with the term 'ceremonial', and thereby first established an analogy between neurosis and religious (or magical) rituals. Freud took up this analogy and examined it for possible justification beyond the level of formal comparison – with regard to an identity of the respective motives, i.e. the drive or defence dynamic.

As a result, Freud hit upon an initial obstacle in his comparison: the neurotic ceremonial actions defy their actors' comprehension – in seeming opposition to the practices of religion, they appear 'foolish

---

11   See Durkheim, *Elementary Forms*, p. 223: 'There is no sin in magic.'
12   See Freud, 'Totem and Taboo', p. 90; see also Chapter 9, below.
13   Freud, 'Obsessive Actions', p. 117.

and senseless'.[14] Freud not only countered this impression of foolishness and senselessness with the fact that, in the majority of religious communities, ignorance of the meaning of one's own rituals is characteristic (and perhaps is simply concealed better through the collectivity).[15] Even more decisively, according to Freud, this impression is a complete deception: like the impression of senselessness in a dream, it is itself a result of the censorship, and thereby a part of the object to be interpreted. It conceals the fact that the obsessional actions, as Freud noted, 'are perfectly significant in every detail, that they serve important interests of the personality and that they give expression to experiences that are still operative and to thoughts that are cathected with affect'.[16]

Relying on several examples, Freud shows, with a precise, virtually art-historical formalism, the finely detailed legibility of obsessional actions. In many cases these actions deal with a literal figurativity controlled through wording (for example, the idiom 'bed and board' is translated into action[17]). Yet obsessional actions and religious practices are alike in more ways than one. They share not only 'meaning', but also 'motives'.[18] They coincide not only in their thoroughly meaningful, symbolic character, but also in terms of their motivation by drive-dynamics. As Freud shows, neurotic as well as religious acts are to be understood as 'an *action for defence* or *insurance*, a *protective measure*'.[19]

Although, until this point in Freud's study, religious practices served as a model for understanding neurotic obsessional actions in terms of the *meaning* of the ceremonial, at this point the explicative relationship reverses: neurotic obsessional actions now serve as an explanatory model for religious practices with regard to *motives*.[20] These, too, Freud concludes, are to be understood as substitute-actions, with all of the consequences intrinsic to this term: religious rituals, too, are compulsive, evoked by an 'unconscious sense of guilt';

---

14   Ibid., p. 119–20.
15   Ibid., p. 122–3.
16   Ibid., p. 120
17   Ibid., p. 121.
18   Ibid., p. 122.
19   Ibid., p. 123 (emphasis in original).
20   Ibid., p. 123: 'Analysis of obsessive actions has already given us some sort of an insight into their causes and into the chain of motives which bring them into effect.'

they serve as defence – although as compromise formations, which always also grant access to what is to be defended against; and the mechanism of their genesis is that of psychic displacement.[21]

Starting with this point, Freud explores several extremely interesting perspectives from religious studies. Since religious practices are compromise formations, just like obsessional actions, and are caused by an 'unending conflict',[22] it is possible to understand their tendency towards miniaturization – which is also, in the histories of many religions, a process of increasing 'displacement from the actual, important thing on to a small one which takes its place'.[23] The little gestures of religion continue to shrink because the conflicts on which they are based first realize already miniature-like symbolic solutions through displacement – yet, after a certain time, these solutions must be further miniaturized through renewed displacement. In this way, displacement is at the beginning of symbol-formation, and goes on to form the mechanism through which continually smaller symbols are generated.

This tendency towards greater reduction, however, is accompanied by a tendency for that which is fended off to become increasingly assertive – and in some cases even acts as the driving force behind the miniaturization process. The defensive conflict must be constantly resumed – not only because new temptations surface[24] and these new occasions cause a sharpening of the prohibition,[25] but also because the achieved solutions increasingly prove to be unfit forms of defence: 'They . . . always reproduce something of the pleasure which they are designed to prevent; they serve the repressed instinct no less than the agencies which are repressing it. As the illness progresses, indeed, actions which were originally mostly concerned with maintaining the defence come to approximate more and more to the proscribed actions. . . .'[26]

Miniaturization seems necessary as soon as the old solution, with its compromise character, is too easily identifiable as a return of that

---

21   Ibid., pp. 125–6.
22   Ibid., p. 124
23   Ibid., p. 126.
24   Ibid., p. 123.
25   See Freud, 'Totem and Taboo', p. 30: 'Any fresh advance made by the repressed libido is answered by a fresh sharpening of the prohibition.'
26   Freud, 'Obsessive Actions', p. 125 (compare 'Totem and Taboo', p. 30).

which is to be fended off. The defence then takes refuge in an even smaller, temporarily less transparent solution, which nonetheless exhibits the same inappropriateness as the former. Its manifest defensive character also increasingly moves behind its latent, drive-serving aspect, and the defence must consequently search for greater credibility in a new, even more extremely miniaturized compromise formation, in which the intrusion of what is to be fended off is even less visible.

As time goes by and displacement increases, the symbols thus generated become increasingly less legible. The development of religion tends, therefore, towards a decrease in legibility – that is, comprehensibility – while the scale of its actions increases. If there was perhaps once a clearly legible scale of 1:10, then that is followed by a less legible 1:100, and then a completely foolish-seeming 1:1000, as Freud establishes, 'so that the petty ceremonials of religious practice gradually become the essential thing and push aside the underlying thoughts'.[27] Not only do obsessional actions tend to become increasingly 'foolish' and 'senseless' in appearance – so do religious practices.

For Freud, these tendencies towards miniaturization make it possible to understand the reforms in religious history: 'That is why religions are subject to reforms which . . . aim at a re-establishment of the original balance of values.'[28] Such reforms can be perceived as procedures of increasing internalization: rituals are replaced by an ethos (conviction), which prohibits the rituals. Reforms turn against form: formal elements disappear in favour of content. Such 'antiritualistic' reforms that aim at the repeal of 'foolish'- and 'senseless'-seeming formal procedures and customs, such as Protestantism's reformation of the defining formalities of Catholicism, begin at a point of advanced miniaturization.

Surprising theories, with relevant consequences for both the theories of belief and interpassivity, arise from Freud's thoughts on this matter. The picture that Freud drew of the anti-ritual reforms implies, first of all, that emphasis on 'sense' over 'form' represents a later result. The idea, for example, that believers should themselves carry out the act of prayer, or even think and believe the content of certain beliefs, appears as something secondary or supplementary to

27   Freud, 'Obsessive Actions', p. 126.
28   Ibid.

the possibility of personal delegation (for example, to a priest) or mechanical delegation (to a prayer wheel). Moreover, myths are thus something secondary in relation to practices; they are to be understood as belated 'rationalizations' of prior practices, whose sense they are capable of reproducing in a distorted form, at best: 'In all believers, however, the motives which impel them to religious practices are unknown to them or are represented in consciousness by others which are advanced in their place.'[29]

As a consequence, we can rule out an understanding of the custom, so important for the theory of interpassivity, of using representative mechanical devices in various religions – such as prayer wheels, prayer flags, rosaries, burning candles, and so on – as a partial result of 'industrialization', a further development or progression as opposed to an earlier stage of 'manual' religious production. For example, Villiers de l'Isle-Adam interpreted the use of ritual devices in this sense as a phenomenon related to industry's cheapening of religious values, as cultural decay, and as the loss of a former authenticity. Because of their use of prayer wheels, the 'Chinese' appeared to him as 'our precursors in all issues having to do with progress'.[30]

By contrast, Freud's theory draws the opposite picture: in religion, the introduction of machines comes earlier than the idea of an individualized 'manual' religious practice. The dominance of 'form' precedes the emphasis on 'meaning'.[31] In Christianity, for example, the idea that one needed a personal conviction in religious ideas appears to have emerged relatively late, with Protestantism. The production of ideology thereby had a dynamic opposed to economic production. Whereas economic history is characterized by a progressive division of labour, delegation, and the increasing introduction of

---

29   Ibid., pp. 122–3.

30   Auguste Villiers de l'Ilse-Adam, 'La machine à gloire', *Contes cruels*, 6th ed. (Paris: Calman Lévy, 1893), p. 79; cf.

31   Through this theory, Freud accounts for that paradigm change that had taken place just a few years before in anthropology. Scholars, such as E. B. Tylor had interpreted rituals as 'survivals' of prior systems of ideas, and assumed a primacy of rituals over myths. See E. B. Tylor, *Primitive Culture: Researches into the Development of Mythology, Philosophy, Religion, Art, and Custom*, 2 vols (London: John Murray, 1871), vol. I, pp. 63ff. A new generation, however, led by Julius Wellhausen and William Robertson Smith, began to invert this perspective, viewing the rituals as a starting point and even to conceive of religions that rested solely on rituals and did not have any evidence of myths.

machines, the history of ideology seems to be determined by a retreat in all of these things. At first, religion was left to the priests and the mechanical rituals; it was only later that people became involved as the holders of beliefs. First of all was replacement, then that was followed by something that considered itself to be the original thing.

Like Wittgenstein,[32] Freud also maintained that, with regard to rituals, there is no 'progress'. On the contrary, however, there are reforms – but they are backward-looking. They aim at the dissolution of the collective and its internal hierarchies, and the abolition of its instruments and formalism. As Freud writes, they 'aim at a re-establishment of the original balance of values'.[33]

RELIGIOUS HISTORY AND ITS MINIATURES: IS THERE A LIFE-SIZE ORIGINAL?

At first glance, however, this concept of an 'original balance of values' seems to relativize the astuteness of Freud's theory. Was there really a first stage of full, transparent sense, which only later, through continuous displacements, degenerated ritualistically into increasingly less sensible forms? Did the goal of the late reforms have an original model in the beginning of history? Was the myth really there at the beginning? Would myth represent the original dimensions miniaturized in subsequent rituals?

This same text of Freud's delivers an implicitly negative answer to these questions, and further evidence to support this argumentation is available in Freud's other texts. The key to answering the questions posed can be found in the following consideration: Could there ever have been a religion at a scale of 1:1, under the premise of the Freudian assumption? Could a genuine state have existed prior to all displacement? Let us recapitulate the Freudian assumption: if religious practices, like obsessive actions, are compromise formations, and thus originate in a defensive conflict, then ambivalence is at the beginning of religious activity and obsessional neurosis. This corresponds with the elevated 'sacred seriousness' of the former and the compulsive character of the latter. Without ambivalence, there would be no sacred seriousness and no religion.

---

32   See Wittgenstein, 'Remarks on Frazer's *Golden Bough*', p. 141.
33   Freud, 'Obsessive Actions', p. 126.

Moreover, ambivalence and its corresponding conflict of defence carried out through displacement form the 'motor' of the history of religions. Without it, the process of continual displacement would never have begun. From these two arguments, it is possible to derive the following. First, without ambivalence there would be no first link in the miniaturizing series. The first link must already be formed through ambivalence (and consequently through displacement, as something miniaturized), or none at all would form. And second, with an initial link on a scale of 1:1, no movement would ever take place. A non-ambivalent, non-miniaturized first link would not only be the beginning, but also simultaneously the end of the history (of religions) – it would not press for any further displacement. An 'original balance of values', first of all, would not have been a religion, and second, could not have been original, because nothing else would follow from such an origin.

The idea of such an 'original balance of values' must therefore be viewed as a product of 'retroactivity' – as an idea that first becomes possible at a later point in development, transposed to prehistory, which is now depicted, for the imagination of this later point in time, as its real preliminary stage. This idea describes an imagined first link that could never actually have existed. Nonetheless, this imaginary original formation has a decisive function in the case of religious reform: it conceals the fact that the reform itself is also a product of the history of subsequent substitution – that the transition from foolish rituals to proud ethos is also a result of displacement. As much as an ethos may want to exclude itself from what came before, it nonetheless still forms a miniaturization of the last little ceremonial action. It is nothing more than a more compact, even more miniature than the ceremonial action.

Displacement thus leads through increasingly smaller rituals and through prohibitions towards an ethos. Displacement shapes the process of all 'dialectics' in the history of religions, which first precipitate rituals and then behave in a hostile way with regard to those rituals. This faith, which considers itself to correspond with an 'original balance of values', and sees the rituals merely as disfiguring miniatures, thereby misconceives its own character as a miniature and its own nature as one more step in deforming the sense of the rituals.

In this way the moment of misconception, as well as the fantasy of greatness associated with it, is newly added to the process. Whereas all previous miniatures were simply miniatures, now a miniature has emerged that regards all other small forms as miniatures, but itself as their life-size model. In the process of continued displacement, a qualitatively new element has entered in the form of faith. The apparent senselessness of the obsessional performances seems to have abruptly given way to sense. The contempt inherent in the rituals, which were becoming increasingly foolish, has now suddenly switched to respect (for the meaning). The discontent with rituals – which had hitherto seemed just as senseless as the rituals themselves, and was compulsively enacted as the search for new forms of defence not yet corrupted by that which was to be fended off – seems to be replaced by something that radiates self-sufficiency. The previous replacement of rituals is now no longer carried out 'blindly', but instead in the name of a binding sense.

The hostility towards rituals that characterizes the entire course of religious history until now, enters a new stage with the appearance of such a 'push for reform' to re-establish an 'original dimension'. In terms of its gestures, at least, it must no longer push for miniaturization, but instead for the complete removal of rituals. To the extent that rituals appear senseless – that is, as an object of an illusion of others – they must be purged. All that is allowed to stay are those ritual behaviours that appear as a perfect expression of assumed sense or meaning – or, as we would say, as one's own, sincerely believed illusion. Yet, since every formalism produces an excess (a surplus) of content, since the form of an action is always something that stands for something else, and since this symbolic element tends to free itself of all predetermined sense, this strict imposition of meaning upon the forms often signifies their total abolition.

The idea of exclusive, religious self-conviction experienced its most radical implementation in the eighteenth century – for example, in the philosophical theism of David Hume. The 'invisible religion' that Hume's theism depicted would be the most extreme point in a reform aimed against religious performances. It would represent faith's complete absorption of pious exercises – the perfect dissolution of belief in faith. The conception of such an educational, rational religion aimed to achieve the complete disappearance of all of the religious realm's visible ritual manifestations. The principle of this theism thus allowed Miran Božovič to characterize a Humean philosophical theist as someone who 'knows that God exists – yet for that very reason . . . acts *as if God did not exist*'.[34]

Damned to invisibility, this purely internal form of religiosity seemed fundamentally less viable than its 'barbaric', heathen ritual forms. It even seems possible to ask whether, through its attempt at total 'reappropriation' – that is, the complete retraction of ritual alienation and delegation – it lacked the essence of religion entirely. Even the most radical religious strivings, pushing for an extreme internalization, could only have been preserved historically to the extent that they were aware, in practice, of the necessity of developing what is called a pragmatic attitude towards their ritual parts.

With his theory of 'reforms' in the history of religions, Freud showed how magic practices transform at a certain moment into religions, and how these religions, from this point on, behave in a permanently hostile manner towards those magical practices that they nonetheless never completely abandon. He made it conceivable that the obsessional actions caused by ambivalence push for their own partial abolition. If Freud's analysis is correct, then that would mean, for Huizinga's theory of play, that the 'sacred seriousness' of games is what causes the dynamic by virtue of which play tends to retreat from culture. In Freud's cultural theory-based thesis, we found evidence for Mannoni's theory that belief (the illusion of others), contains within it moments through which it tends to become faith (one's own illusion). The dynamics of obsessional neuroses thus make the 'dialectics' of belief and play comprehensible.

---

34   See Miran Božovič, *An Utterly Dark Spot: Gaze and Body in Early Modern Philosophy* (Ann Arbor: University of Michigan Press, 2000), p. 14.

CHAPTER SIX

The Pleasure Principle:
All Cultural Enjoyment is 'Fetishistic' –
The Other's Illusion:
Civilization and Its Contentments

Up to this point I have attempted to uncover the structure of the illusion of the other, to distinguish it, and to disclose its affective conditions. Yet I have only briefly touched upon the central function of the illusion of the other within culture. Mannoni and Huizinga are in complete agreement with regard to this function as embodied in *croyance* and 'sacred seriousness', through which it shapes culture's decisive pleasure principle.[1] It causes the 'baby to coo with pleasure', and a 'mass of thousands [to be driven] to a furore' at a sporting event. We can thank it for the delight we glean from reading our horoscope and the pleasure that a magic trick brings, as well as the enjoyment we get from theatre's 'comic illusion'. We can even thank it for the resounding laughter that erupts from an audience when there is a mishap on stage – for example, when an actor depicting a dead person suddenly has to sneeze.[2] Contemporary literary theory offers confirmation of Huizinga's and Mannoni's theories of the pleasure-bringing power intrinsic to the illusion without an owner. Jonathan Culler established that it is impossible to read literature without a certain split occurring within the reader. Culler writes, '[T]o read and interpret literary works is precisely to imagine what "a reader" would feel and understand ... To read is to operate with the hypothesis of a reader'.[3] 'Fetishism', as a practice of disavowal, splitting of the ego, and operating with the illusion of the other, is in no way limited to manifestly

---

    1   When we employ the term 'pleasure principle' differently than in the Freudian usage, it is to identify a technique for gaining pleasure (and not, like Freud, the orientation of the psychic apparatus towards gaining pleasure).

    2   See Mannoni, *Clefs pour l'Imaginaire*, p. 163.

    3   Jonathan Culler, *On Deconstruction: Theory and Criticism after Structuralism* (London: Routledge, 1983), p. 67.

'perverse' sexual practices; as Mannoni has already made clear, it is instead at the base of even the most 'sublime' and respectable pastimes – for example, that of reading belletrists.[4]

In addition, the illusion of the other also structures the more sinister pleasures of superstition and perversion. And even a practice that has a slightly better reputation, such as politeness – a widespread technique for creating happiness that is seldom investigated for its incredible effectiveness – rests on the principle of an illusion that is understood by all of those present. The effects of politeness, too, are thereby due to an illusion of the other.[5] Lying behind many aesthetic products is a long cultural history of lies told with the wink of an eye, illusions and charming deceptions that have always been transparent. This tradition has perhaps found its most characteristic forms in *trompe-l'œil* painting[6] and bizarre exhibits in 'chambers of wonders'.[7] Even science and philosophy seem to have followed this artistic principle during certain epochs. Did the clever Greeks ever seriously doubt that a tortoise was capable of passing the speedy Achilles? And their stories about art and artists – tales of amazing deceptions, such as birds pecking at painted grapes – are they not also artful deceptions told without any intention of their really being believed?

Lies and illusions enjoyed great popularity in former times, and apparently formed a means of well-cultivated sociability among people who knew perfectly well what was and was not true. It seems that, with a wink of the eye, those 'in the know' presented to each other paradoxes, logical misconclusions, polite sayings, and artfully prepared objects and instruments of illusion. They were capable of enjoying these types of things and sophisticated enough not to infer

----

4   Sigmund Freud included only the neuroses (hysteria, obsession, paranoia) as corresponding with the major social products (art, religion, philosophy). See Freud, 'Totem and Taboo', pp. 73–4. I also want to grant the perversions this relationship to one of society's 'normal models'.

5   See also Chapter 9, below.

6   See also Miriam Milman, *The Illusions of Reality: Trompe-l'oeil painting.* (Geneva: Skira, 1982), and Patrick Mauriès, *Le trompe l'oeil. De l'antiquité au XXe siècle* (Paris: Gallimard, 1996).

7   On the intentional misnomer of a narwhal tusk as a 'unicorn horn' in a chamber of wonders, see Joachim Menzhausen, *Dresdener Kunstkammer und Grünes Gewölbe* (Vienna: Tusch, 1977), p. 13. See also the interpretation of Casanova's chamber of wonders episode in Mannoni, *Clefs pour l'Imaginaire*, p. 25; and Straeten, *Haus der Kälte.*

naivety in others who likewise found pleasure in them. This epoch apparently viewed culture as an exercise in the skill of observing illusions, seeing through them, and – despite knowing of their presence – accepting them benevolently, not aggressively.[8]

In sharp contrast to this epoch, not only is our contemporary, increasingly lacklustre popular culture busy abolishing courtesy, but the sciences, philosophy, and even art, are also involved in an effort to destroy illusion once and for all (to the extent that it still exists). It is as though the present had been afflicted with a lack of irony – as though we suddenly had to prove to someone that the magician's tricks do not really fool us. Yet, in the loss of pleasure, charm and glamour that results from this, we can also recognize that suspended illusions form a culture's pleasure principle.

Conversely, in collusion with the majority of the ancient philosophies of happiness, it is possible to say that the greatest unhappiness is regularly caused by one's own illusion.[9] In ancient philosophies, techniques for happiness were developed to counter this type of unhappiness caused by one's own illusion. These techniques rested on the principle of the illusion without an owner. Even religious theorists, such as Blaise Pascal, did not shy away from recommending operating with the illusion of the other as the path to happiness. And since, as I will show, apparently simple, non-representative practices in which 'something is [simply] kept going' relate to an illusion, then the illusion of the other is at work as a pleasure principle where water drips continually into a bucket in the yard; where we can watch the bees buzzing in and out; where people race aimlessly through the countryside in their cars, sit mesmerized by sporting events on the radio or television, or let the CD play on and on without paying the slightest attention to it. Even the seemingly most primitive and senseless pleasures owe their allure to a suspended illusion. As Anatole France remarked, 'You can't be sensual unless you are a bit of a fetishist.'[10]

---

8   Only a few ascetic spoilsports such as the philosopher Plato contradicted this. Plato carries his argument against art right to the heart of the matter, arguing that 'children' and 'simple persons' may be deceived by a painting (Plato, *The Republic*, 598c). We would rather expect that not even children or simple people could think such a thing. By showing us that he thinks such a thing and that there is someone 'harmed' by the illusion of art, Plato 'proves' the harmfulness of art.

9   On this, see also below, Chapter 8, Section 2, p. 213.

10   A. France, quoted in Apter and Pietz, *Fetishism as Cultural Discourse*, p. 6. In

In the following section I will return to the examples mentioned here that have not yet been discussed. First, I will take a closer look at the exact conditions under which the 'thievish pleasure' in the illusion without an owner emerges, and under what conditions it threatens to disappear. In Huizinga's 'sacred seriousness', as well as in Mannoni's formulation of deception ('I know perfectly well, but still'), I identified a moment of contempt. In its complete version, the formulation would read: 'I know perfectly well that it is nonsense, but still it is fantastic.' This contempt contributes to an ambivalence that allows us to explain the excess of affect.

The contempt that actors or players feel towards their 'foolish' games or 'nonsensical' ceremonies is, simultaneously, self-contempt. Those who enthusiastically participate in a foolish game are, in the end, no wiser for it. The illusion of the other draws part of its motivational power from the participants' humorous self-contempt. Accordingly, that particular ideological form based on the illusion of the other – belief – always works without reference to an ideal ego. Instead, participants 'live down' to an image of themselves that is less than ideal. By contrast, the other ideological form – faith – does require such an ideal: a role-model is always present, and the actors attempt to live up to its image. Whereas belief generates (object-libidinal) pleasure from the self-contempt of its actors, faith gives (ego-libidinal) rewards in the form of self-esteem. If a 'dialectics of belief (superstition)' exists, then it is based precisely on the fact that self-contempt and contempt of belief (superstition) can transform itself into a power of self-respect and respect for one's faith. The next section will deal with the transformation that occurs in the way that pleasure is experienced. First, I will highlight two steps that identify contempt's pleasurable mode of operation, and also the first variations in the ability to experience this pleasure. At the same time, it should be evident that these steps represent different ways of organizing contempt; and, according to the hypothesis of the dialectic of belief, they can perhaps be viewed as steps in the transition to self-esteem.

---

particular, the games of animals that Huizinga quite rightly emphasizes (*Homo Ludens*, p. 1) reveal this intellectual dimension based on the principle of the suspended illusion of all of the seemingly sensual pleasures.

SCIENCE AND SWEARING: SUPERSTITION AND PERVERSION – THE PHENOMENA OF SELF-CONTEMPT

In theology, the term 'belief' in the sense of superstition is just as controversial and in danger of abolition as the term 'perversion' is in sexology. In both cases, these fields appear to shy away from using a term that expresses a moment of contempt. Burkhard Gladigow, for example, remarks in his article 'Aberglaube' ('belief'/'superstition') in the *Handbuch religionswissenschaftlicher Grundbegriffe* ('Handbook of Theological Terms'):

> Belief/superstition, the word and the concept, belong in a field of expressions for interreligious polemics. Their use implies specific religious values ... Superstition is a concept from European religious history, which reaps its concrete, primarily polemical meaning from various religious reference systems. It is a term of object language and thereby itself an *object* of theological analysis – rendering it useless as a basic descriptive or analytical concept.[11]

In the case of perversion, it is not difficult to uncover similar terminological scruples among sexologists. Preben Hertoft, for example, states: 'The term perversion is unsuitable for everyday use because of its negative connotations, and should be replaced by the term sexual deviation, so that perversion is reserved for use in the psychodynamic context as a term for intrapsychological symptom formation.'[12] Bornemann argues along the same lines when he writes that the term perversion is

> the most controversial of all terms in sexology, for it has proved impossible to define medically ... One thing is clear: 'perverse' cannot be defined as something that a person does as an individual. 'Perverse' is only that which deviates from what the society considers to be correct. 'Perversion' is thereby, in the real sense, not a clinical, but rather a social phenomenon.[13]

---

11   Burkhard Gladigow, 'Aberglaube', in *Handbuch religionswissenschaftlicher Grundbegriffe*, vol. 1 (Stuttgart: Kohlhammer 1988), pp. 387–8.

12   Preben Hertoft, *Sexologisches Wörterbuch* (Cologne: Ärzte-Verl 1993), pp. 147–8.

13   Ernest Bornemann, *Ullstein-Enzyklopaedie der Sexualitaet* (Berlin/Vienna:

The arguments from theology and sexology are analogous: these are derisive terms with which one religion or form of sexuality attempts to defame another. They are terms that can therefore be allotted to the side of the respective *object* – inner-religious or inner-sexual polemics – but not its *theory*. Theory is meant to refrain from such value judgments. (It remains open whether the terms suggested as alternatives, such as 'sexual deviation', are really suitable choices with fewer negative connotations.)

The pedagogic dimension of such demands is evident, and should not be contested. It is utterly necessary that every science worthy of its name carry out an 'epistemological break'[14] with regard to supposed common sense, and not succumb to delivering seemingly scientific rationalizations for a particular society's reigning prejudices.

Nonetheless, it seems that something decisive is missing from those liberal approaches in theology and sexology. Even if entire societies were at some point to regard religious and sexual practices in a way that was similarly enlightened and non-judgmental, as the sciences demand of themselves, the question remains whether there would remain a striking difference with respect to the *attitude* with which religious and sexual actors pursue their own passions. For superstition and perversion are condemned not only by others (in fact, this does not even have to be the case), but also primarily – and necessarily – by their bearers. This self-contempt on the part of the actors is what differentiates superstition and perversion from faith-based or ego-syntonic forms of religion and sexuality.

The secretiveness and hint of deviance are thus not conditions that repressive societies have imposed on the practices from outside, but are instead these practices' intrinsic sources of pleasure. Superstition and perversion draw their special attraction for practitioners from the feeling of contempt, and of being contemptuous in the eyes of others. Therefore, we must resolutely contradict the myth of the heroic pervert, which occasionally also surfaces in psychoanalytical literature, as a person who pursues his passion doggedly, even obstinately, despite social prohibitions, remaining true to it as though it

Ullstein, 1990), p. 607.

14   On this term, see Althusser, 'Ideology and Ideological State Apparatuses', p. 45; and Étienne Balibar, *Écrits pour Althusser* (Paris: Éditions la Decouverte, 1991).

were practically an ideal.[15] The pervert pleases himself or herself through self-contempt – that is itself the perversion. As I will show in greater detail below, not corresponding with any ideal is a decisive condition for superstitious as well as perverse triumph.

The affective condition of these passions, which also leads to religious compulsion and sexual fixation, is ambivalence. It is therefore just as impossible for liberal theologians or sexologists to disagree with superstitious and perverse people who express self-contempt as it would be for a psychoanalyst to disagree with a paranoiac who is convinced of their being followed. It would be just as out of place to claim in the one case that the matter is 'objectively' not at all contemptuous as it would be in the other to mention that there is actually no stalker. The respective statements cannot be examined with regard to their truth value; instead, they must be honoured as authentic, albeit symptomatic, forms of expression of psychic realities.[16] Paranoiacs truly perceive aggression, even if it is their own; perverts truly sense contempt, even if it is chiefly their own contempt that they feel for their own position.

Those who contest the contemptuousness of superstitious people and perverts are therefore greater enemies to them than those who affirmatively express contempt. People who spurn the superstitious and perverse simply declare their dissent, leaving the universe of superstition and perversion intact, albeit banning it from the public realm. The well-intentioned liberal adversary, on the contrary, threatens to rob superstitious people and perverts of their most important source of pleasure, self-contempt, and thereby destroy their very universe.

This does not mean, however, that social contempt is a necessary or helpful linchpin for superstition and perversion. Contrary to their own assessment, superstition and perversion are even entirely capable of offering up a dominant, public model for entire societies. Their contemptuousness rests on an illusion without an owner, and not on the contempt of real members of society. Even if there came a day

---

15   See also, for example, Freud ' "Civilized" Sexual Morality and Modern Nervous Illness' (SE IX), p. 192; and Lacan's theory of the dutiful ethics of sadist libertines in Jacques Lacan, 'Kant with Sade', transl. James B. Swenson Jr., *October* 51 (Winter 1989).

16   Compare Freud, 'Formulations on the Two Principles of Mental Functioning' (SE XII), pp. 225–6.

when no one refrained from such practices, all practitioners could nonetheless still find them contemptuous. Like mass sporting events, collective magic rituals in tribal cultures – perhaps even in the case of the antique world of the gods – these models are capable of encompassing entire populations without ever having to stop creating a contemptuous pleasure premium for their practitioners through the awareness of their being part of a 'foolish game'.

Theory must account for the contempt that the practitioners have for their own position, which is a decisive indicator for its mode of existence. If this characteristic is not taken into consideration, then it is not possible to recognize the *difference with regard to the economy of the libido* between ambivalent and non-ambivalent attitudes, or the *topical difference (i. e. the difference in the involvement of the psychic instances identified by Freud[17])* between the positions of *croyance* and *foi*. The specific property of superstition and perversion that procures pleasure by undermining all ego ideals thereby remains unrecognizable.

What is therefore decisive in the use of the terms 'superstition' and 'perversion' is not whether what is believed or practised seems ridiculous or contemptuous, but simply whether the actors accompany their rites, practices and myths with contempt. We must therefore safeguard the terms 'belief/superstition', 'perversion' (and similar pejorative expressions, such as 'fetishism'[18]) from expulsion from the corresponding sciences. The science that does not want to approach its subject with contempt out of a sense of 'correctness' must account for the self-contempt of its subject.

MOVING FROM A MATERIAL TO A FORMAL DEFINITION OF THE TERMS 'SUPERSTITION' AND 'PERVERSION'

In defining superstition and perversion through the characteristic of the actors' self-contempt, the possibility of a *material* definition is brushed aside for the benefit of a *formal* definition. It is not certain rituals, concepts of belief, fantasies or sexual practices that seem

---

17   Cf. Freud, ‚The Ego and the Id' (SE XIX), pp. 3–66.

18   See also, for example, Adler, 'Der Ethnologe und die Fetische, in Pontalis', *Objekte des Fetischismus*, p. 217: 'Fetishism has lost all civil rights in today's anthropological theory' (my translation).

superstitious or perverse to us, but instead the actors' contempt for them. As in Huizinga's definition of play, we find the criteria for a definition of superstition and perversion in the practitioners' psychic states rather than in their practices. This leads to an important consequence: *one and the same practice can be proudly practised in one case and the subject of pleasurable self-contempt in another.*[19] This position is what determines whether the respective practice is perverse, superstitious, or neither of the two.

In contradiction with classical psychoanalytical theory, perversion can no longer be diagnosed based on 'deviations' with regard to the sexual object or goal. Rather than attempting such a material determination, I have carried out a formal, topical determination in accordance with Mannoni's definition of *croyance*. If actors have contempt for their practices, and thereby for themselves, this means that their gain in pleasure is organized around avoiding a reference to an ideal ego. The 'topicality' of their pleasure gain is different than for those practices that allow their practitioners to triumph by corresponding to an ideal. At the same time, there is also a difference at the level of the economy of the libido and the dynamic level: when the gain in pleasure is achieved by means of self-contempt, then ambivalence exists. The joyful overload of affect is due to an unconscious conflict of opposing forces.

However, at this point we run into a problem: in conjunction with Freud's theory of compulsive behaviour, I have assumed that ambivalence leads to displacement. And displacement means substitution. It leads to ambivalently connoted, symbolic substitute acts. Therefore, substitution does seem to bring about *material* deviations, which would characterize perverse or superstitious (magical) practices. Because the formal definition of superstition and perversion leads to the concept of ambivalence, and because ambivalence causes

---

19   This means that there are no genuinely superstitious or perverse practices. Just as Huizinga pointed out for cultural practices, superstition and perversion, too, can be afflicted by the phenomenon of the loss of play, through which they forfeit their moment of self-contempt. This seems to be the case, for example, with several of the S/M practices propagated since the 1980s in so-called lifestyle magazines. Rather than being the off-colour, secretive practices of deviant accomplices, such practices thereby increasingly become a cultural element that gives people the feeling of being part of a chic elite. A relationship to an ideal ego thus arises: being versed in 'perverse' practices becomes part of a general education, somewhat like the dexterity of eating with chopsticks.

displacement, the formal transformation also always seems to be a material one. So that there can be contempt, the objects have to be substitute objects, and they have to be small and ludicrous.

All the same, along this route I have been able to identify reference points for why certain contents appear only in the form of beliefs and others only in the form of faith. Nonetheless, my thesis that one and the same practice can be an element of superstition or perversion, but also of conviction or normal sexuality, seems to have become untenable – unless, that is, I can show that the psychoanalytical concept of displacement needs greater precision, that it requires a correction similar to the one carried out on the material conditions of superstitions and perversions. What I would have to show would be that displacement can enact replacement without causing a material change. The substitute act attained through displacement would have to resemble closely the substituted act; it would not have to contain the obsessional neurotic miniaturizations or perverse deviations noted in the previous examples. The displacement must replace without distorting. In what follows, I will attempt just such a correction of the concept of displacement. The starting point for these considerations comes from the fortuitous discovery of a metaphor without which they could hardly have occurred.

THE 'INHIBITION THRESHOLD' AND THE 'FACILITATION THRESHOLD': ON THE OPERATION OF DISPLACEMENT IN OBSESSIONAL NEUROSIS AND PERVERSION

The threshold serves as a frequent metaphor in both literature and philosophy. However, it is a certain understanding of the threshold that prevails here – namely, that of a caesura in space and time. In this sense, one could, as in German, speak of the 'magic of the threshold' (*Schwellenzauber*) and 'threshold experiences' (*Schwellenerfahrungen*).[20] Certain situations can be read or experienced as 'passages', as 'transitions' from one state to another.[21]

---

20   *Translator's note*: The German language is replete with threshold metaphors which unfortunately cannot always be adequately rendered in English. A case in point is *Bahnschwelle* (literally: train threshold, which in English is railway sleeper).

21   See Arnold VanGennep, *The Rites of Passage* (London: Routledge, 2004); Winfried Menninghaus, *Schwellenkunde. Walter Benjamins Passage des Mythos* (Frankfurt: Suhrkamp, 1986).

The use of this metaphor can often transcend the figurative – when, for instance, in the context of art and culture, reference is made to a café that has been built right next to a museum so as to 'lower the threshold' to the entire institution. Yet here the threshold (German: *Schwelle*) actually swells, becoming something that it is not – that is to say, something whose height inhibits the person trying to cross it. It thus becomes a barrier, even a hurdle. Be that as it may, this swelling of the threshold to a barrier that not only generates *symbolic anxiety of the threshold* but also demands *physical* effort and sprightliness also has its limits. A threshold is never a barricade in this sense; thus it would appear ridiculous to speak of 'freedom on the threshold', as one might speak of 'freedom on the barricades' – for example, with reference to Eugène Delacroix's 1830 painting *La Liberté guidant le peuple*.

However, this idea of threshold as barrier seems applicable only to the threshold of a door and similar types of spatial border. It seems less apt with reference to another genre of threshold, which is no less important. The *Bahnschwelle*, or railway sleeper, does not seem to represent an obstacle, but rather acts to support and facilitate.[22] At first glance, it thus seems to lend itself less to metaphorical usage than the so-often poetically deployed door threshold. Or are there conceivable cases beyond the railway sector where impassable terrain can only be travelled if thresholds have been erected, where constructing a barrier can enable one to cross it? Does it make any sense to use the threshold as a conceptual model framing it as facilitating (*Ermöglichungsschwelle*) rather than inhibiting (*Hemmschwelle*)?

One should not simply pass by a potential metaphor – especially when it seems at first glance to be without a referent. Precisely those metaphors without a specific referent – 'pure signifiers' in the terms of Roland Barthes[23] – can serve to make imaginable something that has not yet been thought. They are not simply formed according to already-known images in order to describe them at the next opportunity in a slightly contrived and distorted way in the service of greater festiveness. Instead, pure metaphors most of all generate conceivableness, for they indicate a place where a future thought can be pinpointed.

---

22   See Johannes Weidinger, 'Schwellen', in *Stahlbetonschwellenwerk Linz: Wege in die Zukunft* (Linz: SSL, 1997), p. 2.

23   See Roland Barthes, *Empire of Signs*, trans. Richard Howard (New York: Hill & Wang, 1982), p. 89.

The idea of 'facilitating thresholds', which at first seems futile, identifies this kind of place. The metaphor adds something to the theory into which it can be incorporated. It introduces conceivableness at a point at which there was previously none – or very little. The theory into which the metaphor of 'facilitating thresholds' can be incorporated is the psychoanalytic theory of compulsive acts. Small, strange, seemingly senseless acts, which nonetheless certain analysands have to carry out at all costs, struck Freud as quite meaningful, perfect representations (of desired or experienced events). The apparent contradiction between their urgency and their seeming senselessness could be resolved thanks to the fact that these small acts had the full psychological value of the other acts that they represented in miniaturized form.

This miniaturization came about, as Freud wrote, by means of *Verschiebung* ('displacement'), which is a concept that recalls the world of trains and switching tracks. The compulsive act resolves a defensive conflict by replacing one act that should not take place (since it corresponds to a suppressed wish that is to be fended off) with another, usually small act, which can be understood as the displacement of the former. The displacement often replaces something big with something small, the whole with a part (for example, the beloved with a lock of their hair), or a person with an object they have touched (for example, a spouse with a chair on which they sat), or an object with a neighbouring one with which it often appears together in a *façon de parler* (for example, a bed with a table.) The concept of displacement thus designates a certain method of representation by means of signs. It is a semiotic concept. As I will show in what follows, this semiotic concept of displacement used by Freud can be elaborated with the metaphor of the threshold. The displacements take place by way of thresholds, and whatever they perform is facilitated by thresholds.

At first glance, the axis along which the displacement runs is striking. It is, as we have seen, an axis of contact, of contiguity.[24] The relation between an object and its substitute, an act and its substitute act, is established on the basis of a frequent or even singular past contact. On the other hand – and this factor often fades into the

---

24   See Roman Jakobson and Morris Halle, *The Fundamentals of Language* (The Hague: Mouton de Gruyter, 2002 [1956]), pp. 83–4.

background in relation to the former, just as railway sleepers disappear from view for the train passenger as the neighbouring tracks speed by – displacement is also always an operation of substitution,[25] and thus a symbolic operation. The one object now occupies the place of another, absent one, with which it was once linked through contact. This is how it symbolizes the substituted object. A person kisses their absent beloved's lock of hair. Precisely where there was once a whole there is now a part that fills its place (on the lover's lips). The lock of hair now absorbs all of the attention and affection once directed to the beloved. The two elements must be separated to complete the substitution. The contact that had once been should no longer exist. While one can also kiss the detached lock of hair before the very eyes of the beloved, if the lock of hair were still on the beloved's head, it would no longer be possible to perform a substitute act upon it. The part would not represent the whole; instead, all affection would be directed at the whole.

For the lock of hair to be a symbol *of the beloved*, there must have once been contact between them. But for it to function *as a symbol*, a substitution must have taken place. While it may be important for the *creation* of this symbol that the objects once touched each other, it is decisive for the *functioning* of the symbol that they are now completely separated by a boundary. This boundary, running like the line of a numerical fraction between the designated and the designator, can and must in many cases be marked and represented by a threshold. Making this boundary recognizable, or representing it by means of a threshold, is what makes a number of strange things and processes possible.

If displacement produces a substitution, thereby adhering to the condition that the substituting element was once linked to what is being substituted, it seems to follow automatically that displacement always amounts to a miniaturization. One could assume that displacement will always replace the whole with a part, and not the other way around. The technical and economic advantage herein can be observed in more cases than just that of the love of model trains: a hobby in which it is cheaper to collect the models rather than their full-sized

---

25   The fact that he overlooked the substituting nature of displacement as well as metonymy was a grave, far-reaching mistake made by Jakobson who, as is known, saw the metonymic relation as a syntactical relation between two equally present elements (see ibid.).

counterparts. Miniaturization results in an additional advantage for obsessional neurosis: that of being unclear and inconspicuous. Especially when what is symbolized is something prohibited – such as a forbidden sexual act, for example – the corresponding substitute act can hardly be realized in a larger act – say in the form of a mass orgy. The articulation of an incomprehensible prayer or a delay in rising from a chair can, by contrast, possibly express the matter, so that a semblance of decency remains.[26]

Freud's remarks also seem to point in this direction: displacement produces miniaturization.[27] The discovery of this miniaturizing dynamic of obsessional neurosis also provided Freud with a referent for understanding a regularity in the history of religion: its tendency 'to make the most innocuous thing the most important and most pressing matter' – the increasing miniaturization of rituals, which is linked with a strange revaluation of these rituals, and has the effect 'of gradually making the simple ceremony of religious practice essential'. As a result, 'anti-ritualist' reform movements seem necessary, such as the Protestant reform movement against Catholicism, to re-establish a presumed 'original balance of values'.[28]

In order to clarify whether displacement always results in miniaturization, it seems necessary to consider the functions of both aspects of displacement – substitution and contact – from a different perspective: that of the economy (and dynamics) of the libido. Substitution corresponds to an act of defence, a process of repression. What is being substituted is the satisfaction of a desire that is not permissible. By means of unconscious defence, it is made to reside on the other side of the boundary. Thus, the boundary marks not only a 'not' (in the sense of 'here, on this side, x cannot be, for it is there, on the other side'), but also an 'against' ('here comes everything which is directed against x, there comes x').

---

26   See Freud, 'Notes upon a Case of Obsessional Neurosis', p. 225, and 'Obsessive Actions', p. 121.

27   See Freud 'Obsessive Actions', pp. 125–6: 'We have noted as a curious and derogatory characteristic of obsessional neurosis that its ceremonials are concerned with the small actions of daily life and are expressed in foolish regulations and restrictions in connection with them. We cannot understand this remarkable feature of the clinical picture until we have realized that the mechanism of psychical *displacement* . . . dominates the mental processes of obsessional neurosis.'

28   See ibid., p.126.

Since such an act of defence by means of repression is not possible without the concurrent return of the repressed, something new must appear on this side of the boundary. On the one hand, this new thing must now appear in the 'counter' position, and act as a defence against that which has been substituted. On the other hand, this something new (the substitute act) must now be connected with what was substituted (the original act). For the substitute act can only fulfil its function if it is able to return some of the pleasure that was connected with the original act.[29] This becomes possible through contact. The contact in a sense opens up the channel through which the pleasure that was connected to the repressed object can be passed on to its substitute.

The desire that is fended off and the corresponding act are so powerful that they cannot be completely dissolved, only redirected. This force merges with the force of defence, with which it collided, and together they insist on a solution that is acceptable for both, a compromise. Since forces that are involved in an unconscious conflict (even if directed against each other) are added together and not subtracted, as in a conscious conflict, the resultant force is extremely strong – that is, as strong as both forces joined together.[30] The force of defence and the force of what is to be fended off merge in the urge for a substitute act. The substitute act is now, since there are two added forces aspiring to it at once, even more urgent than the act itself, which it is replacing. It becomes pressing, even *compulsive*.

The distortion created by the displacement (the dissimilarity of the substitute with the original) has the advantage, as has been noted, of concealing the return of the pleasure that appears to have been fended off. In this sense, the compulsive acts tend both to allow an increased return of pleasure[31] and to intensify the concealment of its attainment. The more pleasure from the process to be fended off that these substitute acts allow to return, the less the substitute acts resemble the original process.

---

29   See ibid., pp. 125, 127, 'Totem and Taboo', p. 30.

30   Ibid., pp. 62ff.

31   See Freud 'Obsessive Actions', p. 125, and compare 'Totem and Taboo', p. 88: 'It is possible . . . to describe the course of development of obsessive acts: we can show how they begin by being as remote as possible from anything sexual – magical defenses against evil wishes – and how they end by being substitutes for the forbidden sexual act and the closest possible imitations of it.'

The dual condition that displacement must meet thus consists in establishing the greatest libidinal equivalence with the least possible suspicion of identity. Yet it is capable of doing this without miniaturization. While this identity can be rendered unrecognizable by continuing miniaturization, as Freud observed of the history of religious rituals, there is also another possibility. What is substituted can also appear itself, in full scale, in the role of the substitute – there need only be some feature ensuring that it is not taken to be itself. This feature is the threshold that separates the substitute from what is being substituted – or symbolizes their separation. Everything that appears in front of the threshold is assumed to be the substitute; everything that lies behind it is taken to be what is being substituted.

There are scores of examples of such concealments that are obtained not by miniaturization, but simply by means of clever localization. As Freud observed, the very acts that are forbidden by religion are practised in the name of religion.[32] In such cases – for instance, murder in the name of religion – religion gets by without any miniaturization at all. Those adamantly militant advocates of human life, for example, who oppose abortion, press on over the murdered bodies of workers from the clinic. Radical right-wing opponents of male homosexuality act in a similar way. They organize gay bashings in the course of which they beat up and sometimes rape gays. The ultimate homicidal or homosexual gratification of drives can therefore also be attained, so long as it fulfils the condition of evoking the semblance of a counter-measure. What seems to be 'opposition', then, has the effect that the x to be fended off can appear as itself and be taken for a non-x.

The same structure of making something unrecognizable by mere assignment of positions can also be found in other, less tragic contexts. Let us assume that Elvis Presley were still alive today, as some of his fans claim, he would have numerous ways of living an anonymous life. He could change his appearance and lifestyle. He could, however, also retain all of this and appear in Elvis look-alike competitions. The framework of the Elvis lookalike would then provide him with the threshold – the symbol of negation – by means of which even Elvis himself could appear as a non-Elvis (a look-alike), and be accepted as such.

---

32   See Freud 'Obsessive Actions', p. 127.

Thus, the non-identity between the substitute and what is substituted does not really have to exist – it only has to be symbolized. The symbol of non-identity is the threshold, whose presence is enough for even something identical to pass as non-identical. As a symbol – and not as real separation – the threshold evokes the idea of negation, which must accompany every x so that it can appear where no x is permitted. This idea of negation can assume various forms. It can take the form of 'this is not the truth' – a form that, in turn, has the subcategory of the form 'this is a mistake',[33] 'this is a lie',[34] 'this is only a dream',[35] 'this is only a joke',[36] 'this is nonsense'[37] – or even, as could be seen in the Elvis example, 'this is only a representation and not what is represented'.

On the other hand, the idea of negation – as the examples of the pro-lifers and the homophobes show – can also assume the form of 'this is not a measure but a counter-measure'. In this form, the idea of negation has the function of changing the way the acting subjects relate to their own actions by letting them succumb to an illusion regarding the motives of those actions. It lets them experience as their *duty* something that responds to their *inclination*. This has the advantage that they are now able to carry out the forbidden act, but at the cost of deriving not pleasure but at best self-respect. People fulfilling their duty experience what they are doing not as something they *want* to do but as something they *must* do. And after committing this act they are not happy, but at best proud of themselves. They pursue their happiness with clenched teeth, as it were. They derive pleasure in a neurotic way – that is, they enjoy without noticing it. Self-proclaimed anti-pornography activists, for instance, derive the pleasure of a protracted preoccupation with pornography by combating pornography. However, they hide this pleasure from

---

33   See Freud, 'Negation', pp. 233–9.

34   See Freud, 'Jokes and their Relation to the Unconscious' (SE VIII), p. 115. The most lucid example for the technique of such 'lying with the truth' is the 'sceptical' joke studied by Freud: 'Two Jews met in a railway carriage at a station in Galicia. "Where are you going?" asked one. "To Krakow" was the answer. "What a liar you are!" the other exclaimed. "If you say you're going to Krakow, you want me to believe you're going to Lemberg. But I know that in fact you're going to Krakow. So why are you lying to me?"'.

35   See Freud, 'Interpretation of Dreams', p. 88.

36   See Freud, 'Jokes', p. 82.

37   Ibid., p. 215

themselves with the both deceptive and sad idea of having fulfilled nothing but their duty.

The symbol of negation thus enables neurotics to transform forbidden object–libido into ego-libido – or, to put it in Kantian terms, to transform the feeling of inferior (or morally irrelevant) 'happiness' into that of moral 'perfection.'[38] Inherent in the idea of duty is thus the idea of negation. That this does not represent a final truth, but rather a quite infamous deception of self and others, hardly needs to be further elaborated in view of the cited examples. This deception became possible as a result of the fact that the threshold is not a real barrier but a symbolic one, and that, given this symbolic function, it can simulate (symbolize) non-identities where in reality there are identities.

Unlike for Kant – whose idea of duty struck him as morally irreproachable and theoretically irreducible, just as the taboo seems to the so-called savage – from a psychoanalytical perspective equipped with the metaphor of the threshold, duty represents something that is both morally and theoretically questionable. In moral terms, what Kant regarded as moral acts prove instead to be instances of immoral satisfaction of drives – which, moreover, seek in an immoral way to misrepresent their real nature. In theoretical terms, what struck Kant as an unerring sign of truth and as grounds for the non-deducibility of the idea of duty – namely, the unconditional, binding character of duty – now appears as simply deceptive and easy to deduce. The strength of duty, by virtue of which (as Kant claims) it could overcome any inclination, is indebted to the summation of the two forces resulting from the unconscious conflict. Since the obligation satisfies at the same time both the defence and that which is to be fended off, it is stronger than any possible thing to be fended off alone.[39]

Yet, from the perspective of psychoanalytic theory, this strength is not evidence of authenticity and non-deducibility, but instead a sign of the fact that two opposing forces are involved. That these merge in the final result and can appear as something singular is indebted to the deceptive 'magic of the threshold'. Thanks to this, even an act of

---

38   See Immanuel Kant, *Critique of Practical Reason*, trans. Thomas Kingsmill Abbott (Mineola, NY: Courier Dover Publications, 2004 [1788]), p. 139; A 233ff.

39   This explains the possibility emphasized by Lacan that the idea of duty can also – as Sade showed – accompany malevolent action. See Jacques Lacan, 'Kant with Sade', trans. James B. Swenson, Jr., *October* 51 (Winter 1989), pp. 55–75.

deriving pleasure in a direct sense can appear as its complete opposite. The threshold metaphor thus allows us to understand this trick, this logic of deception, and thereby contributes to overcoming the self-imposed theoretical taboos inherent to idealistic philosophy.

Outside the realm of obsessional neurosis, such facilitating acts based on symbolic thresholds play a decisive role in a different field that is also relevant to psychoanalysis – namely, the realm of perversion. As we know, Freud referred to neurosis as the 'negative of perversion',[40] and thus formulated the idea of a structural depiction of the one onto the other. Like obsessional neurosis, perversion also reveals a specific distortion mechanism. Since Freud viewed it from the perspective of the development of drives and not, as in the case of obsessional neurosis, from a semiotic perspective, he referred to the mechanism generating perversions as 'regression'.[41]

We know that Freud reconstructed the emergence of non-perverse adult sexuality as a complex, vulnerable process of concentrating and hierarchizing individual partial drives (all the way to a sexuality serving procreation under the primacy of the genital partial drive).[42] Accordingly, Freud interpreted perversions as regressions from the acquired genital sexuality to early stages of an organization of drives that is not channelled and hierarchized to the same extent. Regression thus consists (with regard to the sexual goal or sexual object) in a deviation from an already achieved genital heterosexuality and a return to an earlier stage of sexual development. Sexual narcissism, for instance, would be a perversion (deviation with regard to the object) that had its normal, primary counterpart at an earlier, childhood stage. The same would hold for various anal, oral or sadistic manifestations (as deviations in terms of the sexual goal).

Apart from the rather substantial difficulty of finding a counterpart for each perversion in a child's sexual development, the notion of regression raises another, more fundamental problem. As for the compulsive acts described above, the question that arises in connection with perverse acts is whether these, too, might appear on a 1:1 scale. In other words, is it certain that perversions always represent only a sort of miniaturized, childish, regressive form of a larger, adult,

40   See Freud, 'Three Essays', p.165, and '"Civilized" Sexual Morality', p. 191.
41   Freud, 'Three Essays', p. 240 (added in, in 1915).
42   Freud, 'Three Essays', p. 162.

genital sexuality in conformity with procreation? Or might there not also be unquestionably genital heterosexual acts that could still be described as perverse?

A passage from Marquis de Sade's *120 Days of Sodom* will serve as illustration here. In the 'stipulations' that the libertine heroes of the novel impose on themselves, one reads:

> All present shall be naked: storytellers, wives, little girls, little boys, elders, fuckers, friends, everything shall be pell-mell, everyone shall be sprawled on the floor and, after the example of animals, shall change, shall commingle, entwine, couple incestuously, sodomistically, deflowerings being at all times banned, the company shall give itself over to every excess and to every debauch which may best warm the mind. When 'tis the time for these deflowerings, it shall be at this moment . . .[43]

Even if diverse forms of sexuality may appear in this variegated confusion, genital heterosexuality (for example, in the cited acts of adultery) is by no means excluded. And from the perspective of drive theory, one can hardly harbour any objections to these heterosexual acts, at least not in the sense of judging them to be cases of regression. For nothing about these procreation-conforming examples of genital sexuality reveals a shortcoming or a regressive deviation with respect to the other, socially more accepted heterosexual acts – monogamous marital ones, for example.

Only the sacrilegious intention that the libertines pursue with a sense of duty (the obedience to self-imposed stipulations) could be noted as a difference from the consummation of a marriage. However, in drive theory this intention does not make a difference; it is only a symbolic distinction. The libertine derives pleasure from performing a completely normal heterosexual act – provided that this can be understood as directed against the social norm (which, for instance, bans incest or adultery). Like the obsessional neurotic, the libertine commits in full the act which he forbids himself from doing. He does so in full scale, provided he has only one threshold symbolically depicting the act as a counter-act.

43 D. A. F. de Sade, *120 Days of Sodom* (New York: Grove Press, 1966), pp. 246–7.

Unlike obsessional neurotics, perverts do not hide their pleasure from themselves. For only neurosis, as the 'negative of perversion', distorts the subject's experience of pleasure so that it no longer appears as pleasure. Perverts, in contrast, experience their counter-acts as highly pleasurable. The fact that they can only attain pleasure if they see it as likewise fulfilling their self-imposed sacrilegious duty – that pro is only possible in the form of con – has, in this case, the effect that they experience their pro (together with the con) as an emphatic pro, and pleasure (including its defence) as a quantitatively greater pleasure.

Like neurosis, perversion also produces a greater amount of energy emanating from an unconscious conflict.[44] That which is compulsion in neurosis is thus fixation in perversion. Fixation does not consist merely in the exclusive and detailed specification of certain sexual objects or goals, but also in a greater amount of energy (that is unknown to normal sexuality) by means of which such objects are sought and goals are pursued. In this case, too, the surplus energy is the product of an addition resulting from an unconscious conflict between two forces. Like obsessional neurosis, perversion also prohibits certain acts, fabricating instead compulsively detailed substitute acts that have to be performed at all costs. Perversion gladly contributes through substitution to the success of both sides: the defence and that which must be fended off.

Like obsessional neurosis, perversion works through the process of displacement. It builds a symbolic threshold and thus enables what is on the other side of the threshold to also appear on this side – by giving it the facilitating signs of 'non' and 'contra' thanks to the threshold.

If one questions the plausibility of Sade's libertines as an illustration, since it is taken from the realm of fiction, then it is also possible to add examples taken from the realm of life – or to be more precise,

---

44 This accounts for Lacan's lucid Kant critique: since not just the Kantian duty, which is entirely devoid of pleasure, but also the Sadean perversion, replete with pleasure, has a heightened power emerging from summation, the latter can also prevail against any threat of the death penalty. Thus even perversion is not a simple, weak 'inclination'. Thus it can stand the threat of the gallows, as in the Kantian thought experiment. See Lacan, 'Kant with Sade', in *Écrits: The first complete edition in English*, trans. Bruce Fink (London: Norton 2007), pp. 659–60; Kant, *Critique of Practical Reason*, p. 30.

from the realm of lived fiction. Is there not always a recurring element of play and fiction in erotic acts that have little or no social recognition, such as prostitution or pornography? Is this realm not characterized most of all by a *mise-en-scène* that serves as a constant long before 'regressive' deviations appear with regard to the sexual objects or goals? Has it not brought forth veritable genres (such as 'nurse and patient', 'secretary and boss', 'chambermaid and gentleman', and so on)? In his study of the cultural history of play, Johan Huizinga pointed out that this playful dimension is a special achievement of those practices 'that fall out of the framework of the social norm',[45] while they seem to be completely missing in the realm of respectable sexuality.

The threshold metaphor once again enables us to explain this peculiarity. Play is a method for creating a threshold. The game constructs a symbol of negation that signals: 'Now it is not real.' Perversion needs this symbol. Thus, not only are all playful forms of eroticism perverse, but the reverse is also true: all perverse forms of sexuality have a playful character.[46] We must read Lacan's argument in this sense: disavowal is not just the general principle of fetishism but of all perversions. Disavowal is a decisive criterion of perversion – for it *structures sexuality as a game*. As a playful sexuality, based on disavowal, perversion belongs to the order of belief in Mannoni's sense. It is a superstitious sexuality, which means it has the structure of 'I know perfectly well, but still'.[47] It avoids all reference to an ideal ego, as is characteristic of faith sexuality. And it forms illusions of others in order to achieve increased pleasure in ambivalence through better knowledge.[48]

---

45   Huizinga, *Homo Ludens*, p. 43.

46   Joyce McDougall, *Theater of the Mind: Illusion and Truth on the Psychoanalytic Stage* (London: Psychology Press), rightly emphasizes (p. 41) this aspect that is often overlooked by psychoanalytic theories – in particular of masochism.

47   Evidence of this characterization of perversion as superstitious sexuality in Mannoni's sense includes, for example, the widespread tradition of bartenders or strippers wearing Santa Claus costumes.

48   The fact that perversion always moves at a level of the illusion of the other shows how much differentiation is required in Lacan's term 'big Other'. That symbolic agency or agency that we have identified, with Žižek, as the agency over the illusion without an owner is always present in perversion. (See Slavoj Žižek, 'Ein Plädoyer für die ehrliche Lüge', and see Chapter 2, section 7, pp. 51ff, above; and compare Žižek, *For They Know Not What They Do*, p. 249.) Therefore, it must be a completely different

Once again, it is not important that this 'knowledge', this negation created by the game ('now it is not real') corresponds to a truth. What is decisive, however, is that the players see it as doing so. This explains the fact Huizinga underlines – namely, that no player, no matter how committed, no so-called 'primitive' in ritual practice, not even a child at play, ever forgets the difference between game and reality.[49] They always have this threshold in mind and derive pleasure from the delineation.[50] Whenever they are deceived, it is not because they take the game to be reality – the substitute for what is being replaced – but, rather, the other way around. Their only possible deception lies in the fact that they see reality as being a game. In this way, Yves Montand gains Marilyn Monroe's love in the film *Let's Make Love*. In reality, he is the well-known millionaire. She, however, believes that he is only a poor, bad actor amateurishly playing the role of millionaire.[51]

By analogy, perversion can also assume the form of 'normal' heterosexuality – provided that it can convince itself by means of a negation symbol that it is only playing. The decisive feature of perversion thus appears to be merely the presence of a negation symbol, rather than a 'regressive' change in sexual organization (with regard to its objects or goals). Using the negation symbol, the perverse turn their sexuality into fiction, into a representation of sexuality.[52] They achieve this by means of a subtle costume or a theatrical staging – which, incidentally, does not necessarily have to have anything fetishistic or bondage-like about it. The people involved might simply

---

agency that the pervert attempts to bring into existence, according to Lacan (compare Fink, *Clinical Introduction to Lacanian Psychoanalysis*, p. 165).

49   See Huizinga, *Homo Ludens*, p. 8

50   This could also be the reason why it is precisely eighteenth-century literature (for example, the novels of Sterne and Diderot) that constantly reflects on its form, and plays with this reflection on form, and lends itself better to dealing with libertine and perverse contents than the realist literature of the nineteenth century.

51   *Let's Make Love* (dir. George Cukor, USA, 1960).

52   In her essay 'The Pornographic Imagination', Susan Sontag makes a distinction between sexual acts and their representation (in books, films, and so on), and argues that acts themselves can never be pornographic, only their representations (see Sontag, *Pornographic Imagination*, p. 49). The only problem with this distinction is that perverse acts are always representative acts – the 'porno' is thus in itself always 'graphic'. Pierre Klossowski clearly recognized this when he argued that eroticism should be grasped as a form of representation. See Pierre Klossowski, *Origines cultuelles et mythiques d'un certain comportement des dames romaines* (Montpellier: Fata Morgana, 1986), p. 15.

address each other with pseudonyms or titles. Even acting (as is often the case in Sade or Bataille) as if they are re-enacting a narrated sexual act is enough to allow for this dimension of play, and the 'sacred seriousness' of perversion resulting from ambivalence. All forms of distortion and costuming fulfil the function of the negation symbol that is imperative for this. Moreover, a second method is also possible, as in obsessional neurosis. In addition to the principle of the 'costume', the principle of the 'stage' can also be employed to generate the symbol of negation, and to awaken the perverse impression that one is dealing only with the representation and not with what is represented. Thus, just as the real Elvis on stage in a look-alike contest seems like an imitation, real physical intimacy on the public stage seems to be a *mise-en-scène* taking place to entertain onlookers, and is structured exclusively on the basis of applicable criteria. This strategy of fictionalizing one's own sexuality is practised, for instance, by American artist Natacha Merritt who, so she says, practises all sexual acts holding a small digital camera in her hands.[53] She distributes the photographs on the Internet and in book form.[54] The same pleasure principle of fictionalizing one's own sexuality through public performance could also be at work in the similarly fictive sexual acts of the container-inhabitants of reality TV shows such as *Big Brother* or *Survivor*.[55]

---

53   See Roger Willemsen, 'Du bist nicht allein. Mein Sex soll auch deiner sein: Der moderne Voyeur als Lustsklave der Bilder', in *Süddeutsche Zeitung*, 27 April 2000.

54   See Natacha Merritt, *Digital Diaries* (Cologne: Taschen, 2000). This example clearly shows that there can be such a thing as sexual fetishism without fetishes. For the fetish is not just a penis symbol but, more generally, a symbol of negation, which constitutes denial. And this symbol of negation does not necessarily have to be an element of masquerade, a costume or camouflage. The fetishization as fictionalization can also take place by integrating the gaze of the public. In this sense not just the 'mask' but also the 'stage' brings forth fetishism.

55   But one should not forget what cultural conditions must exist for people to be willing to reveal their intimacy on a TV set, or to display it on shows like *Oprah Winfrey*. That this is for many people the last and only way to fictionalize their own lives, and thus to access the pleasure principle in culture, means that their lives must be lacking any other such possibilities. In an intact culture that offers enough public space, and thus the possibilities for a *mise-en-scène* of self, such forms of entertainment would hardly find a market. Only the destruction of public space that is taking place under neoliberal conditions robs large parts of the population of these possibilities. To cite an example of this: the coffeehouse of European vintage is a fictive space. An elegantly dressed waiter brings the cup on a silver tray and serves the guest fictions of etiquette.

In all of these examples, the condition of the game is on a par with the perverse idea of duty explained above. It, too, gives perversion the 'non' with which it can imagine even an x as a non-x. The 1:1 scale thus remains completely intact in perversion.[56] The notion of regression, which always ascribes a material transformation of the drive structure to perversion, thus seems inadequate. It should be replaced by the notion of displacement.[57] For displacement designates not only the material changes (which do not take place in some cases) but also the symbolic operations (which always take place) through which perversion attains its objects and acts.

If symbolic spaces have been delineated by a threshold, perversion can arbitrarily move objects and acts that are to be ascribed to these spaces back and forth. The forbidden acts and objects remain possible and accessible to perverts as long as they are located only in the space where they are not forbidden. Thresholds here prove to be thresholds that facilitate something. While places are fixed through thresholds, *objects and acts* can be brought into motion by displacement.

The importance of such threshold-setting operations for the emergence of perverse sexuality can be further illustrated through two examples. Referring to porn films, Žižek has noted that precisely this genre stands out for its peculiar characteristic of self-distancing:

The guest can feel like royalty for a while. There is yet another pact with the guest, who pays only at the end of his or her stay. The paper-cup coffeehouse in the American style presently making inroads all over Europe does not offer all of these features. Employees wearing T-shirts hand cups to the customers, who pay right away. They can stay at the coffeehouse, but nobody takes any interest in them. The seats at the tables are thus always zones of extreme neglect, where the best service one can get is when the mess made by the previous customer is cleaned up.

56 This is something Elizabeth Grosz also shows with regard to lesbian fetishism in which a woman is brought into the position of the fetish. Grosz, 'Lesbian Fetishism?', in Emily Apter and William Pietz, eds, *Fetishism as Cultural Discourse* (Ithaca: Cornell University Press, 1993), p. 114.

57 In this way one would also take into account the identity of the structures of perversion and obsessional neurosis recognized by Freud (see, for instance, Freud, 'Fetishism'). Displacement represents the semiotic mechanism of both. For perversion, however, we have discovered two criteria at once with disavowal and displacement. This can be explained by the fact that these two concepts correspond to two different aspects. Disavowal refers to a *defence mechanism* relating to the drive conflict, while displacement stands for the semiotic *distortion mechanism* that is crucial for locating symptoms. If it is true that every perversion is a game, then disavowal has the effect *that* something is played. Displacement, by contrast, shows *what* must be played.

[B]efore we pass to the sexual activity, we need a short introduction – normally, a stupid plot serving as pretext for the actors to begin copulation (the housewife calls in a plumber, a new secretary reports to the manager, etc.). The point is that even in the manner in which they enact this introductory plot, the actors divulge that this is for them only a stupid although necessary formality that has to be gotten over with as quickly as possible so as to begin tackling the 'real thing.'[58]

Why do the actors signal that they find the story of the film foolish? Should that (at least according to Laura Mulvey and her assumptions about visual pleasure[59]) not tear the onlookers out of their dreams and identifications, and destroy their pleasure? Is it not amazing that such a trivial genre as the porn film, that has so little to do with goals of political enlightenment, regularly evokes Brechtian 'estrangement-effects'?

An answer to this question seems possible only from the perspective of the threshold theory of perversion. Unlike in so-called normal sexuality, normality is strictly forbidden in perversion.[60] A lapse into normality would mean that a relation to an ideal ego is formed. One would thereby lose the increased amount of pleasure that perversion gains through the ambivalence based on a moment of (self-)contempt and the avoidance of ideals. For this reason, the prospect of lapsing into normal, socially recognized sexuality seems to be bound up with anxiety. This is why this possibility must be banished by means of the threshold – a symbol of negation offered by the game. So as not to frighten the porn audience, for whom the film is a game, with the thought that the depicted acts might be a faithfully accepted reality for the actors (with whom they perhaps identify), the actors, too, must show that they are just playing. This allows the depicted sexuality to retain the perverse status of belief/superstitious sexuality; only

---

58   Slavoj Žižek, *Looking Awry: An Introduction to Jacques Lacan through Popular Culture* (Cambridge, MA/London: MIT Press, 1992), p. 111.

59   See Laura Mulvey, 'Visual Pleasure and Narrative Cinema', in her *Visual and Other Pleasures* (New York: Palgrave Macmillan, 1989), first published in *Screen* 16: 3 (Autumn 1975), pp. 6–18.

60   See Lacan, 'Kant with Sade'. This, by the way, is a trait that cannot, it seems, be explained by the notion of regression. Whoever regresses simply does not have any desire for genital sexuality. By contrast, it is forbidden to whoever is perverse.

in this way can porn fans clearly see that everything is located at the level of an illusion without an owner. Otherwise, the depicted illusion would threaten to fall back first on the actors, and then on the viewers who identify with them.[61] But with this type of involuntary appropriation of the illusion, the pleasure of ambivalence would be lost.

If viewers of a porn film identify with its actors, then only with those who carry out their own 'dis-identification', who produce 'estrangement-effects', and retract thresholds of enhancement. Since perverts (for example, the porn fan) are necessarily players, they can only identify with an actor who is likewise a player, and therefore shows that he knows that it is all just a foolish game. A completely normal 'John/Jane Doe' does not lend himself or herself as a useful fantasy image for the pervert. (Whereas, by contrast, perverts lend themselves entirely as fantasy images for a 'normal' person who, in reality, does not wish to be perverse.)

In fact, it is not the actors in a porn film who show that they are playing. Instead, they represent *characters* who are playing. The pejorative treatment of the level of depiction as 'foolish game' represents part of the character not something beyond it. The contempt belongs to the image that the viewers can identify with, and is not an alienating commentary coming from outside the image. The goal of this method is not a cognitive, educational one (as with the Brechtian estrangement-effect), but instead an affective one. It is not about recognizing the boundary, but, rather, deriving pleasure from playing with it, from a gesture of distancing that is always, at the same time, a distancing from all ideals.[62]

The contempt for one's own ('foolish') game that the actors reveal is the threshold by means of which the heightened affect so typical of,

---

61   This would be just as uncomfortable as being found out in a Santa Claus costume by one's children (see Huizinga, *Homo Ludens*, pp. 22–3). The matter would thereby lose not only the naive believer, but also – worse yet – the structural location of a believing other.

62   This is also the origin of the strange 'intertextuality' of pornography – that often very clever game with parodistic or other references to different texts, as can be seen, for example, in Guillaume Apollinaire's *Les Onze Mille Verges, or, the Amorous Adventures of Prince Mony Vibescu* (Paris: Pauvert, 1973), or in Pierre Klossowski's 'Laws of Hospitality' (Paris: Gallimard, 1977). Susan Sontag has in this connection rightly emphasized that there is no 'meta-pornography' (only parodying pornography): 'Parody is one common form of pornographic writing' (Sontag, 'Pornographic Imagination', p. 51).

and sought in, perversion can be obtained. If what is represented was so unconditionally desirable, then the result would only be a simple positive affect. By means of contempt, an unconscious conflict can be generated between the pro and con. These two can then be added to an extremely greater amount of affect, which has the power playfully to rework everything that can be limitlessly affirmed. Even the actors thus show that they enjoy this 'foolish but still fantastic' thing. The viewers can take on this fixation presented to them by means of identification, and enjoy it by analogy.

In a different instance, the '1:1' of a heterosexuality that is even sanctioned by marriage can be observed in a perverse variant facilitated by a threshold. In the comedy *Casanova 70* (1965, dir. Mario Monicelli), Marcello Mastroianni plays a NATO officer who develops the idiosyncrasy of being potent only when making love is tied up with danger. The lion-trainer in the lion's cage, the young girl in the circle of family members seeking revenge for a dishonour, the pedicurist whose lovers seem to be burdened by a curse, the beloved with the madly jealous and dangerous spouse – all of these are thus particularly well-suited objects of his desire, while the impeccably beautiful lady from a good family who originally wanted to become a nun (played by Virna Lisi) seems to pose a problem.

At first glance this case appears to be an illustration of what Freud described in his study, 'On the Universal Tendency to Debasement in the Spheres of Love':[63] the differentiation between 'sensual' and 'tender' currents; undisturbed sexual functions in socially questionable or disreputable love affairs; impotence vis-à-vis the respected sexual object, and in the recognized relation of marriage. One could say that, for such a hero, certain objects must be eliminated as objects of desire from the outset. According to Freud, possible sexual objects have to fulfil the condition of 'debasement' in order not to risk mingling sensuality with disturbing tenderness.[64] Accordingly, the respected lady whom the hero has married must remain sexually inaccessible to him. Only affairs with the women deviating from this

63   Freud, 'On the Universal Tendency to Debasement'. SE XI, pp. 179–190.

64   Ibid., p. 183. With this description Freud has, in my view, provided an example of how genital heterosexuality can be perverse. The condition of 'debasement' seems to correspond exactly to what we have called contempt. The Freudian 'prostitute love' is dynamically based on the condition of ambivalence; topically, on the principle of evading every ideal ego.

ideal, or that show the trait of debasement (equivalent to regression), would be possible. What Freud identified as regression (as a deviation from 'normal' sexuality) for perversion, is debasement (as deviation from recognized forms of object choice) for psychic impotence.

However, the hero of *Casanova 70* has developed a mechanism that differs from the one described by Freud in one important respect. What he is looking for is not debasement but danger, not the disdainful affair but the life-threatening one. What, then, does danger mean in this context? Obviously, danger fulfils a similar function to debasement. It signals to the hero that he is pursuing his pleasure against the will of an outside power. While it is still rather clear in the case of debasement – of disreputable, 'debauched' affairs – that this power is society and the norms applying to it, in the case of danger it seems less clear. Revengeful Sicilians, a curse, threatening lions, and perfidious spouses create an ensemble of embodiments of danger that hardly fit into a pattern.

Altogether, this indicates that all of the real agents threatening the hero are only proxies of another (psychic) agency, whose objection he obviously seems to value highly in his amorous endeavours. Apparently it is important to him that some other (who remains vague) does not want him to enjoy something. The danger gives him this guarantee; as long as there is danger, the other is against him.[65]

This desire for the objection of the other describes the basic pattern of the neurotic stance. Neurotics refuse to enjoy when they believe that an indistinct other wants them to. They do everything in their might to deny such a triumph to others – a psychic agency, the legacy of earlier social agencies, such as parents, educators and the like.[66] Obviously the same structure must also be considered for

---

65 Compare Freud, 'Civilization and Its Discontents', p. 126: 'Fate is regarded as a substitute for parental agency. If a man is unfortunate it means that he is no longer loved by this highest power.'

66 See Fink, *Clinical Introduction to Lacanian Psychoanalysis*, p. 69: 'Every neurosis entails such a resentful stance towards the other's satisfaction.' In this general rule we seem to have found a formula deviating from Freud's oedipal explanation of the drifting apart of 'tender' and 'sensual' movement. This split appears when the approval of the other is to be evaded. (This then does not have an oedipal cause, but rather one that is brought on by the anal phase.)

Even in contexts that do not appear neurotic, this aspect of freedom from the approval of the other often plays a special role – for instance, in aesthetics. It is the reason why one and the same object meets with pleasure as long as it is seen as

perversion (as well as for its heterosexual-genital variant, psychological impotence). A telling sign of this can be found in *Casanova 70* in
a scene in which the young spouse tells the hero to come to her room
in the castle at night, adding that he need not worry about a stir being
made in the castle since her mother, who is also staying in the castle,
has already been informed. 'Mama is informed?' asks Mastroianni,
overcome by horror. He packs his bags and flees.

If there is no love without danger, then this condition is still
more promising than that of debasement. If debasement had invari-
ably implied a deviation in object choice, then danger represents a
more sophisticated condition that also allows a '1:1'. Danger represents a threshold that makes it possible to control the forbidden
object as long as this false object is shifted to the right position. Even
the recognized, respected wife becomes accessible to the cunning
Casanova, as long as she can be endowed with the negative sign of
danger embodying the objection of the other. In the last scene of the
film, we see the wife lying in the matrimonial bed, calling for the
hero, as he is just trying to make his way out of the high building by
climbing over the windowsill. This dangerous place represents for
him the threshold that enables him to shift the object into a favourable, desirable position. Balancing on a very narrow ledge, the hero
indulges in what we might now aptly describe as his 'freedom on the
threshold'.

THE GLAMOUR AND MISERY OF AMBIVALENCE: PLEASURE FROM PERVERSION AND OBSESSIONAL NEUROSIS

This chapter has so far dealt with the illusion of the other as culture's
sole and adequate pleasure principle. 'Religious' and 'sexual' variants
of the illusion without an owner – neuroses and perversions – seem
equally determined by this pleasure principle. For this reason, I have
repeatedly mentioned them both in one breath. Now, however, it is
necessary introduce modifications, under two aspects. The first

---

non-artistic. It is no longer pleasurable when it turns out to be an artwork. This also
explains the distinction that Kant made between the pleasure taken in hearing birdsong
and the displeasure found in the exact human imitation of it (see Kant, *Critique of
Judgment*, A 72). For the same reason, I once wrote: 'Reinforced concrete thresholds
[railway sleepers] are beautiful because they don't have to appeal to anyone' (Robert
Pfaller, '*Schwellen*', *Jahresbroschüre Experimentelle Visuelle Gestaltung* 1993–94, p. 29).

modification relates to the issue of pleasure's comparability. Are obsessional neuroses and perversions – owing to the effectiveness of the illusion of the other present in both – pleasurable?

Perversion's Aesthetic Morphology: Superstition and the Principle of Comedy

In relation to perversion, I want to affirm the following: contrary to an educated 'slacker' style of prudishness whereby people are all too happy to explain that 'no matter how hard they try' they cannot find anything to like about pornography because it is unfortunately all so boring and monotonous,[67] I uphold the theory that there is a specific type of perverse humour[68] that regularly spices up even the most lowly pornographic works – and sometimes even non-pornographic, acknowledged works of high culture.

Yet since perversion, as I have attempted to show, is not defined materially, but rather in topical terms – that is, it is not based on certain typical, deviant sexual practices, but emerges as a strategy of subverting the ideal ego – this perverse dimension of art and culture must be sought elsewhere than where it usually is: not in the content of cultural products, but in their form. The emergence of fetish-like objects, the thematization deviant practices,[69] or simply a conspicuous attachment to the Thing[70] (for example, to dolls or wax figures, or even to money) do not seem characteristic for fetishism or perversion in its role as a cultural force. Instead, the specifically perverse element (as also of art products that are far from sexual, and even far

---

67   See the views of Sade that Barthes lectured on and subjected to critique. Roland Barthes, *Sade Fourier Loyola*, trans. Richard Miller (Berkeley, CA: University of California Press, 1989), p. 36.

68   In accordance with the formal definition of perversion as a 'superstitious' sexuality resting on the principle of a suspended illusion, in what follows I will treat pornography and perversion as synonymous: perversion is always a 'pornographic' sexuality because it is a representative one. Not only must the neurotic symptoms therefore be understood as representations of (sexual) fantasies, but so must the perverse acts. Compare Sigmund Freud, 'My Views on the Part Played by Sexuality in the Aetiology of the Neuroses' (SE VII), p. 279.

69   On this approach, see Alfred Springer, 'Kunst und Fetischismus. Psychoanalytische Überlegungen zu einem Zusammenhang', in Karl Stockreiter, ed., *Schöner Wahnsinn. Beiträge zu Psychoanalyse und Kunst* (Vienna: Turia & Kant, 1998).

70   See Emily Apter, 'Introduction', in Apter and Pietz, *Fetishism as a Cultural Discourse*, p. 2.

from being object-oriented) is shown in a certain *relation to the ideal*: in the ambivalence proper to perversion, and in avoiding reference to an ideal ego.

This behaviour appears decisive for perverse morphology in art. It is the source, for example, of idiosyncratic, at times monotonous-seeming forms. Yet it is precisely these forms that often generate a certain abundance of good humour, which, I would like to suggest, are evident trace elements of a necessary component in the production of all 'normal' humour and jokes. The monotonous elements that perversion is accused of also form the aesthetic principles of a number of art projects, such as those by Andy Warhol, Hanne Darboven, Roman Opałka and On Kawara. It appears that the principle of symbolic defence,[71] which perversion practises in a sexual form, is also at work in non-sexual artistic works; it conditions the conspicuous repetitive forms, and apparently forms the special source of pleasure of such works. Whereas perversion is accused baldly of this sort of monotony, in art, as long as it is not manifestly sexual, it is usually considered a sign of high cultural earnest and successful sublimation, and is often even shifted to a position bordering on religious endeavour.

Although perversion is rightly accused of the notorious monotony, in other cases it is not objected to with the same vehemence, nor stripped of the specifically pleasurable element that it provides. Monotony, in the form of repetition, is also an irreplaceable factor in comedy.[72] In Chaplin's *The Great Dictator*,[73] for example, there is not only the dictator but also someone who looks like him. And at the end of Lubitsch's *To Be or Not To Be*,[74] just when the lover of the Hamlet-actor's

---

71   See Hal Foster, *The Return of the Real: The Avant-Garde at the End of the Century, An October Book* (Cambridge, MA: MIT Press, 1996); compare McDougall, *Theater of the Mind*. I will examine more closely the apotropaic moment of monotone repetition in art in Chapter 6, section 5, pp. 174ff, below.

72   Compare Bergson, *Laughter*, p. 31.

73   *The Great Dictator* (dir. Charlie Chaplin, USA, 1940). For the role of the double in comedy see Mladen Dolar, *Comedy and Its Double*, in Robert Pfaller (ed.), *Stop That Comedy! On the Subtle Hegemony of the Tragic in Our Culture* (Vienna. Sonderzahl, 2005), pp. 181–210.

74   *To Be or Not to Be* (dir. Ernst Lubitsch, USA, 1942). For a more detailed account of doubling and repetition in this film see Robert Pfaller, *The Familiar Unknown, the Uncanny, the Comic*, in Slavoj Žižek, ed., *Lacan. The Silent Partners* (London, New York: Verso, 2006), pp. 198–216.

wife seems somewhat pacified, someone else suspiciously gets up and leaves the room right at the beginning of Hamlet's monologue.

In comedy, repetition serves primarily to create confusion; conspicuously, we have the term 'comedy of errors' but not 'tragedy of errors'. Nonetheless, there are also certainly errors in tragedy – although they are tragic ones. Oedipus confuses his father with an aggressive driver and his mother with an unknown queen. Perhaps the difference between comic and tragic errors can be summarized as follows: in comedy, the error is that someone who has appeared by chance is confused with a given character – showing that, whoever a person is, they will be thought of as the person whose place they are taking. Tragedy, on the contrary, occurs the other way around. It lets a given character suffer the fate of being taken for just anybody. A considerable attraction of tragedy comes from the basic philosophical position that the characters would be justified in opposing the fate to which they mean nothing.

Comedy reduces the character to an effect of a structure: everyone is taken as being the person whose place they occupy. It thus thematizes the subjects' illusory 'over-determinedness': *you are much more exchangeable than you like to imagine.* To this extent, comedy is 'structuralist': it concedes the symbolic structure, the arrangement of places, with authority over the imaginary, the individual's self-image. Tragedy, on the contrary, upholds the thesis of 'under-determination': *in truth you are more than everyone believes.* Tragedy thereby clearly propagates an ideal ego – its heroes pursue it, and its lack of recognition by the environment makes their fate tragic. The pleasure that tragedy generates for its viewers, despite all of the adversity, is the pleasure in one's own ego. The pleasure of the comedy, on the contrary, consists in what I believe is a perverse 'laughing off' of those cathexis expenditures that are associated with the perpetuation of such a precious ego. Tragedy procures ego libido; comedy, on the contrary, object libido.[75]

By virtue of these opposing tendencies for misidentification, comedy and tragedy also operate with different forms of illusion. In

---

75 The reason for these different relationships to the ideal ego and to the possibility of identification seems to also harbour the reason that comedy, as Aristotle stated, aims at representing men as worse than and tragedy as better than in actual life. See *Aristotle's Poetics*, trans. S. H. Butcher, introduced by Francis Ferguson (New York: Hill & Wang, 2000), p. 52.

tragedy, the viewers sympathize with unrecognized heroes and reject the environment's misjudgement of their ideal ego. Through this sympathy with the hero's ideal ego, tragedy situates itself on the side of one's own illusion, of faith. In comedy, on the contrary, viewers sympathize with the misjudgement that the environment carries out on the characters: 'Doesn't the real dictator actually look like his double?' or 'I know quite well that that is the true dictator, but still he looks to me like an imposter': these and similar humorous statements are possible through comedy.[76] It therefore always moves to the side of the illusion of the other.

This seems to be the reason that comedy accommodates Mannoni's theory about the illusion of the other much better than tragedy. In my opinion, Mannoni was quite right to entitle his essay about the theatre 'L'illusion comique', although in the course of the text he does not establish any structural differences between comedy and other genres.[77] The basic principle that Mannoni recognizes – that the actors depict characters, and that the audience, which possesses the same better knowledge, upholds the illusion – seems to be valid for all genres of theatre. Comedy, however, immediately doubles this principle: not only does the actor represent a character, but because of the misidentification, this character, for its part, immediately represents another character. Moreover, that naive observer against whom, as Mannoni writes, the audience and actor 'are in cahoots'[78] is thereby redoubled – whereas formerly only an absent principle, now this observer appears visibly, in the form of characters on the stage. The comedy is, to this extent, always a play within a play: it performs its own principle on the stage. This sort of comedic repetition and doubling causes a Brechtian 'estrangement-effect', which serves to reinforce the audience's certainty of their being distanced observers

---

76 See the excellent analysis of this and further points in Lubitsch's film in Alenka Zupančič, 'On Love as Comedy', in her *The Shortest Shadow: Nietzsche's Philosophy of the Two* (Cambridge, MA/London: MIT Press), pp. 164–81. For a systematic account of the philosophy of comedy, see Alenka Zupančič, *The Odd One In: On Comedy*, (Cambridge, MA: MIT press, 2008).

77 Mannoni writes: 'Ce n'est pas pourtant que ces questions (illusion, identification, personnages) se posent d'une façon différente essentiellenment dans les autres genres, elles y sont seulement moins ouvertes', Mannoni, *Clefs pour l'Imaginaire*, p. 161.

78 Ibid., p. 164.

of a 'silly game'.[79] In psychoanalytic terms, it serves to release the identification of the audience with an ideal ego, and instead strengthens their ambivalence, their 'sacred seriousness', their fetishistic pleasure, through the contemptuous 'better knowledge'. Emphasis on this 'anti-subjective' tendency of comedy – and thus its perverse technique of gaining pleasure by aiming at ambivalence and 'underselling' the ideal ego, in contrast to tragedy, which operates through respect, ideal egos, and identification – seems important with respect to the following sections, in which I will deal in greater detail with pleasure and its loss.

From the Disreputable Pleasure of Perversion to the Displeasure of Obsessional Neurosis

In this short sketch I have attempted to relate perverse forms to several 'normal models' in art to indicate that perversion opens pleasurable, even excessively joyous experiences that in less manifestly sexual cultural genres can also be profoundly appreciated by a broad public. Thus, the recently popular claim of being bored by perverse cultural products, rather than professing a blatantly moralizing rejection of them, does not seem to provide enough of an objection to the thesis that the illusion of the other found in perversion, in which it operates, leads to boundless pleasure. With this theory, I do not want to deny clinical experience showing that perversion is a difficult business, and that it sometimes leads its adherents into hopeless dead ends of desire.[80] But the fact that a practice sometimes runs into difficulty does not negate the possibility that it is capable of functioning adequately and pleasurably for long periods of time, or that its structure even represents a general principle for all pleasurable activity.

In order to answer the question of whether the illusion of the other always evokes such pleasurable effects, since it succeeds in doing for (at least most) perverse practices, we have to look at the obsessional neuroses, too. The obsessional neuroses, as Freud pointed

---

79   I have further elaborated on these structural features of comedy and their connection with the philosophy of materialism in my essay 'Materialism's Comedy', in *Bedeutung Magazine: Philosophy – Current Affairs – Art – Literature – Review – Analysis.* Vol. 1 (London: Bedeutung Publishing Ltd., 2008), pp. 20–8.

80   See the contribution by M. Masud R. Kahn, 'Le fétichisme comme négation de soi', in Pontalis, *Objets du fétichisme*, pp. 77–111.

out, also deploy an illusion of the other; their ceremonies are consistently depictions, even if they might seem senseless to the actors themselves. They, too, are 'export goods': whereas the actors 'know' that their actions are nonsense, it is nonetheless felt to be wonderful that they obviously mean something for someone else. As I have shown, the compulsion to perform these actions is linked with this foreign illusion. Everything that is part of one's own imagination is easier to refrain from or defer than that which is the object of a foreign illusion.

Obsessional neurosis thus seems to share the following features with perversion: there are actions involving excess detail; there is 'superstition', which means that there are illusions that the actors 'do not feel at one with'; there is 'better knowledge', which causes contempt for the illusions and the seemingly senseless actions. It seems that we can pursue these correspondences right through to the fine details: perversion is not the only thing with 'sacred texts' that must be recited, magic words that produce the 'sacred seriousness'. Obsessional neurosis also evokes such formulae – for example, the abbreviated versions of prayers composed of combinations of letters developed by Freud's Rat Man.[81]

The only significant difference seems to be in terms of the experience of pleasure. Whereas perversion usually remains a peripheral phenomenon of the psychoanalytical clinic, because perverts apparently feel entirely comfortable in their passions for long periods, patients with obsessional neuroses seek the help of the analyst. The compulsion becomes destructive, grasping increasingly greater areas of their everyday life; some compulsions even drive the patients to suicidal states. In the case of obsessional neurosis, 'sacred seriousness' reveals its extremely unpleasurable side.

Freud's theory that neurosis forms the negative of perversion[82] seems thereby to refer to the ability to experience pleasure. We can depict the positive, point by point, in a negative version – to use the metaphor of photography – for perversion and obsessional neurosis, for the entire series of traits mentioned above: the fundamental ambivalence, the dominant process of displacement, and the formations that both neurosis and perversion produce. One and the same

81   See Freud, 'Notes upon a Case of Obsessional Neurosis', pp. 225, 242.
82   See Freud, 'Three Essays', pp. 165, 231, 238.

form can take a pleasurable coloration in the one case and an unpleasurable one in the other.[83]

It is necessary to recognize that the illusion of the other does not always lead to the triumphs that Mannoni and Huizinga identified. In which case, under what conditions does the illusion of the other, apparently without changing its nature, generate an intensive affect that is experienced as unpleasurable? It seems that at least the beginnings of an answer can be derived from a specification of the Freudian theory (although a complete answer must be left to the psychoanalytical clinic). The statement that neurosis is the negative of perversion applies in a special way to obsessional neuroses – whereas it seems far less characteristic of the other main variant of neurosis, hysteria, whose clinical picture comprises conditions rather than actions. Only obsessional neurosis can be matched point for point in its appearance, as sketched out above, with the forms of perversion.[84]

Yet this strict correspondence between obsessional neurosis and perversion, apart from the difference with regard to pleasure, seems to run contrary to another precept of psychoanalytic theory – namely, that each of the three main categories of the psychoanalytical clinic – neurosis, perversion, and psychosis – is founded and characterized by

---

83 With this interpretation of Freudian theory, I contradict another, widespread exegesis – presented, for example, in Grosz, *Fetishism as Cultural Discourse*, p. 103: '[Perversions and neuroses] are positive and negative sides of the same coin. The perversions avoid the repression that characterizes the neuroses. The pervert expresses precisely what it is that the neurotic represses. That is, the pervert does what the neurotic subject would like to do but is unable to because the expression of a perverse impulse yields more unpleasure than pleasure.' Thus, the pervert would do what the neurotic avoids. In contrast, I believe that neurotics, especially obsessional neurotics, also act: particularly through defence mechanisms, as Freud showed, they provide themselves with the return of a repressed pleasure. The neurotic symptoms *are the sexual activity* of the ill person (see Freud, 'Three Essays', p. 163). Neurotics and perverts thus do nearly the same things: their actions are precisely similar; only the experiences of pleasure are in opposition. Freud's photography metaphor seems to confirm this version: the negative is, ultimately, not that picture on which we cannot see what the positive shows. Instead, it is one on which the same thing can be seen, but always has the opposite coloration.

84 Freud even addresses a case of obsessional neurosis in his essay on fetishism, in which there is a juxtaposition of attitudes 'which fitted in with the wish' and 'which fitted with reality' (see Freud, 'Fetishism', p. 156); Freud's remarks on the conspicuous superstition of the Rat Man also point to the effectiveness of splitting the ego in obsessional neurosis (see Freud, 'Notes upon a Case of Obsessional Neurosis', pp. 229–30).

a specific defence mechanism: neurosis through repression, perversion through disavowal, and psychosis through foreclosure.[85] But how can there be such strong similarities between obsessional neuroses and perversion if they are founded on entirely different mechanisms? This new problem seems to offer a solution to the old one. If obsessional neurosis reveals such specific correspondences with perversion; if, like perversion, it is identified by the characteristic of superstition; and if superstition, as Mannoni showed, rests on the principle of disavowal, then the conclusion seems obvious that obsessional neuroses also arise (unlike hysteria) initially through disavowal. The difference with perversion – and the reason why the illusion of the other is experienced in a pleasurable way in one case and not in the other – must be that the pleasure that comes about through disavowal is repressed in the case of the obsessional neurotic. Repression causes the pleasure to be transformed into displeasure (I will explore this in more detail below). Initially, perversion and obsessional neurosis share a pleasure gained from disavowal, but the obsessional neurotic alone subsequently transforms this pleasure into displeasure.[86]

Starting from this outline for a solution, and supported by the formal conditions of the concept of perversion suggested above, in what follows I will identify all of those practices that are characterized by self-contempt and displeasure as obsessional neurotic, and all of those that are marked by pleasurable self-contempt as perverse. Even parasexual practices, such as pornography-hunting, would fall on the side of the obsessional neurotic, due to their manifestly unpleasurable character. On the contrary, unlike to classical psychoanalytic theory, I will classify on the side of perversion a series of pleasurable superstition practices, such as reading one's horoscope or watching soap operas such as, for example, *Beverly Hills, 90210*. I will also classify as perverse seemingly non-sexual pleasures in which one is oblivious to everything (including oneself), such as obsessively watching sport on television, or aimlessly driving around – the subject of the road movie – since this deals with the pleasurable effects of an illusion of the

---

85 See Evans, *Introductory Dictionary*, pp. 43–4; Nasio, *Enseignement de 7 concepts*, pp. 128–9.

86 That would mean that the forms of defence of the obsessional neurosis are aimed against an already perverse pleasure. The example of the obsessional neurotic anti-pornography activist, who presents the 'negative' of the perverse pornography fan, seems to confirm this thought.

other. And I do not want to withhold perversion's pleasure-promising title from even sophisticated pleasures, such as the joy of reading novels – which is something that, according to Jonathan Culler, rests on a splitting of the ego.

Self-Contempt and Sense of Duty

In addition to the comparability of obsessional neuroses and perversion, there is one other aspect of this theory of the illusion of the other as the pleasure principle in culture that must at least be considered. The theory of the contempt that is at work in the illusion of the other, which enables the excess affect of 'sacred seriousness', has led to the conclusion that the illusion of the other avoids all correspondences with an ideal ego. The pleasurable part of this illusion entails subverting any possible ideal ego.

In the previous section, however, with the help of the metaphor of 'facilitating thresholds', two forms emerged that approach the construction of this type of ideal. Where displacement does not produce a miniaturization, but instead allows the respective denigrated act concerned (murder, or heterosexual genital sex, and so on) in its original dimensions with the help of a negation symbol as a counter-act, a duty arises. The anti-abortionist who is intent on murder, the anti-pornography activist, and the 'incestuous' sadist libertine operate with an attitude strangely resembling that of Kantian morality. But, along with duty, it seems that an ideal ego is present. It is this correspondence with an ideal ego that ultimately grants a dutiful person (in the Kantian sense) the feeling of moral 'perfection'.

If the assumption was correct that the pleasure characteristic of the illusion of the other springs from subverting all possible ideal egos, then it is necessary to explain whether it is possible to be motivated by duty without referring to an ideal ego. If a sense of pleasure is arrived at, can we say that this pleasure springs from a subversion of all possible ideal egos? Or, on the contrary, do we have to declare that pleasure has already been attained here through the achievement of such an ideal? Might it be that here the illusion of the other is transformed into one's own illusion?

I would like to illuminate the theoretical background of this issue in the next chapter, and thereby enable the formulation of an answer to the question. In any case, the displacement that a duty produces, thereby approaching the construction of an ideal ego, seems to present an interesting intermediary stage in a possible 'dialectic of superstition'. It marks that point – like the 'reform thrusts' that Freud mentions – at which a transition from the self-contempt of superstition to the self-respect of faith might possibly take place.

WITHOUT AN IDEA AND STILL IN ILLUSION: SELF-FORGETFULNESS AS A SOURCE OF PLEASURE IN ART AND IDEOLOGY

At the beginning of this chapter I formulated the thesis that the 'fetishistic' principle of suspended illusion acts as the general pleasure principle in culture. This thesis might seem daring with reference to practices that appear to have nothing to do with illusions, or even with ideas: situations of pure motor activity – sport, for example – or letting random songs play in the background. Do these cases not constitute counter-evidence to my thesis?[87] Do they not mean that the assumption about illusion being the pivot of each and every game must be called into question? If illusion can be found in the theatre (for example, the illusion that the man in the sheet is indeed Julius Caesar), where, then, can illusion be found at a football match or horse race? Are these things not much more about naked truth, about quantifiable or measurable results? Is this not the precise theoretical location of the objection that the Shah of Persia, for example, was said to have made when he replied to his British host's invitation to watch a horse race by saying that he was already aware of the fact that one horse runs faster than the others?[88]

Does the boredom experienced by some people watching sport not arise from its utter lack of stimulation for imagination and fantasy? But how, then, can the compulsion for games be explained? Why must

---

87 Thorsten Veblen observed that sport is not only based on physical drive, but also holds massively pleasurable moments of illusion: 'It is noticeable, for example, that even well-meaning and sober hunters carry a large amount of weapons and equipment around, in order to convince themselves of the earnestness of their undertaking' (Veblen quoted in Volker Caysa, ed., *Sportphilosophie* [Leipzig: Reclam, 1997], p. 15). Adorno recognized this 'make believe' moment of illusion as ideological (see Adorno, in Caysa, ibid., p. 43). Yet neither theorist reflected any further on the unusual form of these illusions. What remains entirely unasked is *who* is meant to believe in the described act.

88 See also Huizinga, *Homo Ludens*, p. 49.

Formula 1 Grand Prix racing fans gather punctually every two weeks in front of the television? Should even this compulsion be a product of ambivalence, the question nevertheless arises: Can this ambivalence be maintained without the slightest illusion whatsoever?

To what extent do such matters legitimize the associations that I have constructed above? Now it is necessary to turn our attention to those things that are 'left running'. *Dromenon*,[89] a word coined by Huizinga, describes all that runs because we have left it running. Our theory of the beauty of all things left running or kept going in the background will thus be the theory of the *dromenon*.

To Keep Going: The Theory of the Dromenon

'It can be helpful to keep going no matter what',[90] wrote Jenny Holzer in one of her 'truisms' - one of the sentences that she displays in running neon text, as if the sentences themselves were also *something/anything* (regardless of what) that can help if it is only allowed to keep going.

Apart from the fact that this sentence very precisely defines and summarizes the aesthetic programme of Jenny Holzer's installations - which are all things left running, *dromena* - it nevertheless still seems to contain a paradox. For, why can something/anything help? Where does the indeterminacy come from - the indifference about what is kept going in the aesthetic process of keeping it going? Is it not characteristic of aesthetics that everything must be precisely so, and not otherwise? For example, a line must be drawn in one way and not in another, images must be hung in a certain way, photos cannot be printed in the reverse, and so on? Do artists not constantly irritate people with their pedantic ways? Why, then, can Jenny Holzer simply let just anything keep going? Why can it not be just this one sentence, for example, that says it?

What, then, is the pleasure principle that lends the excitement, the 'helping' power, to something that runs incessantly? The answer to this question would resolve not only the paradox formulated by Jenny Holzer - it would also help make understandable other artistic endeavours striving for the principle of keeping going, or letting something run, such as the technique of repetition and *ostinato*, the

---

89   Ibid., p. 14.
90   Holzer, *Truisms and Essays*, p. 3.

'minimalist music' of Steve Reich and Philipp Glass, or the avant-garde folk music of Attwenger; or the mechanical sluggishness of Laurie Anderson; the redundancy, or tautology ('what you see is what you see'[91]), or naked factuality, with traces of obsessive charm, in the fine arts, such as in works by Roman Opałka, Hanne Darboven and On Kawara. This argument is also useful, even in matters beyond art, for explaining everyday *dromenon* practices, such as playing sport, watching water flow, doodling while on the telephone, letting the television run in the background, or the relaxing, pointless racing around of cars.

A similar example from the field of art might possibly add a piece to this puzzle: Gertrude Stein's well-known, often misquoted, and for many readers enigmatic line, 'Rose is a rose is a rose'.[92] The riddle of this line is usually answered with an interpretation such as Harald Szeemann's:

A rose is a rose is a rose is a linguistic diversion in order to constitute in us the image of the rose, its appearance, its colour, its scent, its blooming, and its withering. The length of the tautology gives us time to go beyond the intriguing word and to create a more comprehensive image than that which we communicate and abbreviate with the familiar four letters, r-o-s-e.[93]

Repetition, therefore, serves to imprint, so to speak, the colour of the rose on the readers, in the same way that school children are made to write out a hundred times: 'I won't fidget during class'. The more the linguistic signs appear and are understood by readers, the more 'comprehensive' is the 'inner image' that they make of the described object – just as school children, according to an authoritarian pedagogy, form a clearer image of the forbidden fidgeting, or of its

91   For this sentence by Frank Stella, programmatic for minimal art, see Georges Didi-Huberman, *Ce que nous voyons, ce qui nous regarde* (Paris: Minuit, 1992), pp. 32ff.

92   Gertrude Stein, *The World Is Round: Pictures by Clement Hurd* (New York: Young Scott, 1967); compare J. M. Brinnin, *The Third Rose: Gertrude Stein and Her World* (Reading, MA: Addison-Wesley, 1987). The famous line – 'Rose is a rose is a rose' – appeared for the first time in Stein's 1913 poem 'Sacred Emily' (published 1922 in the book *Geography and Plays*, reprinted 1968 by Something Else Press, New York).

93   Harald Szeemann, *Museum der Obsessionen. von/über/zu/mit Harald Szeemann* (Berlin: Merve, 1981), p. 38.

consequences, through repetitive writing. According to such inter-pretations, the use of symbols and their repetition serve a magic of conjuring, of making manifest: the more a symbol is repeated, even if it is far from the thing described, the closer one would be (at least through the 'inner image') to the thing described. The source of pleas-ure in repetition would thus consist in acquisition of an image.

But the line from Gertrude Stein can be interpreted in a completely different way – in fact, in the opposite way. The repeti-tion of symbols can also cause one to have as little as possible to do with these symbols and the things they describe, and to revoke any possibility of creating a 'more comprehensive image' of them. Refer-ring to the Tibetan prayer wheel, Žižek states that the repetition of symbols through mechanical rotation can also allow one to think of completely different (and even obscene) things, or even of nothing at all: 'The beauty of it is that in my psychological interior I can think about whatever I want'.[94] This becomes possible by the fact that, ultimately, through the apparatus that keeps going, one is 'objectively' praying. Even an activity such as praying, which is meant to be utterly intimate, can apparently be carried out without forming an 'inner image' – what matters is that there is an outer, 'objective' image produced through the repetition of symbols. Furthermore, in direct opposition to Szeemann's interpretation, dealing with symbols here apparently serves to avoid the very crea-tion of and approximation to such inner images. This appears to be the main reason why certain religions have always found it neces-sary to fight against and forbid their own rituals and artistic religious production: the prohibition of rituals or images appears to be moti-vated by the assumption – as in Žižek's thesis – that rituals and images are self-perpetuating phenomena (*dromena*), which do not encourage people's personal religiosity, but, on the contrary, func-tion perfectly well without it.

These processes suggest that there is a second source of pleasure in dealing with 'inner images' – namely, that of avoiding such images. This in turn poses the question of what the pleasure is in this avoid-ance. What is the 'beauty' addressed by Žižek? One comes closer to a conclusion by understanding this avoidance as defence. The mechan-ical tampering with symbols does not serve to conjure up, but rather

---

94   Žižek, *Sublime Object of Ideology*, p. 34.

to banish, to magically pulverize and keep away, the denoted objects. Machines can also be implemented for this, such as Tibetan prayer wheels. And these machines can even run in their operator's absence, which is a decisive characteristic of their function; they include prayer wheels that are turned by the wind,[95] or Japanese prayer flags, or Christian devotional candles – or even Jenny Holzer's installations.

Gertrude Stein's puzzling line also takes its form from this kind of machine – a very simple prayer wheel indeed – namely a tree, into which a young woman by the name of Rose carved a sentence about herself: 'and then she saw a lovely tree and she thought yes it is round but all around I am going to cut Rose is a Rose is a Rose and so it is there and not anywhere can I hear anything which will give me a scare'.[96] After carving the text, it is 'simply there', endlessly, because, thanks to the round form of the tree, it goes on forever. That the tree is round, like the world, produces the effect of the text being endless, even if the writer – Rose – is long gone. Like Žižek or his Tibetans, she can meanwhile devote herself to obscene thoughts, to sleep, or to something else, and need have no fear as long as her text 'objectively' – that is, for someone else who can read it – runs as a *dromenon* around the tree.

Rose no longer has anything to fear at night, neither loud noises nor silence. Her tree keeps the carved sentence current; it 'mumbles' Rose's text, quasi-constantly. This symbol machine, kept running by virtue of its roundness, creates an *appearance*, and thereby allows Rose to achieve both a spatial and a psychological *disappearance*.[97] Rose need not be present, and when she is present she need not think of what has been written. What is kept going is simply there, and acts as a protective shield behind which Rose can hide her self, or even her absence. The symbol machine plays Rose's life, presence, and attention, for someone else – even if Rose has meanwhile devoted herself to a narcissistic, quasi-psychotic retreat into sleep, obscene fantasies, or even a complete mental void. Practically nothing can happen to Rose, even if she dies or completely forgets herself, because her symbol

---

95   See ibid.

96   Stein, *The World is Round*, pp. 75–6.

97   Compare Paul Virilio on the *dromenon* practice of driving and the phenomenon of psychological absence derived from the concept of disappearance. Paul Virilio, *Speed and Politics: An Essay on Dromology* (New York: Semiotext(e), 1986), *The Aesthetics of Disappearance* (New York: Semiotext(e)/Foreign Agents, 2009).

keeps her going, so that someone else remembers and thinks that she is alive.[98] It is not her actual death, but surely her death in the eyes of another that Rose effectively avoids by keeping something running.

In the same way that one speaks of 'playing dead', one could say here: *Rose is playing alive*. The benefits of playing alive are based on a strange fantasy – on the idea that what is horrifying about death is not actually being dead, but being considered dead. Rose's installation is meant to work against this. We can thus ascribe to it a certain psychological defence mechanism. According to a differentiation made by Jacques Lacan, hysteria and obsessive-compulsive neurosis are both based on a typical question. The question behind hysteria is: 'What role do I play in the desire of another?' and the question of obsessive-compulsive neurosis: 'Am I alive or dead?'[99] The text installation that Rose develops clearly answers the second question. It is an 'obsessive-compulsive' artwork. This can also be seen when one reads Rose's *dromenon* in a slightly different way than it would be read otherwise. If one 'punctuates' the endless sentence differently,[100] the text states (over and over again): 'A Rose is.' What is of concern here, then, is not an attributive judgment – crediting something with a particular characteristic – but, rather, an existential judgment, in which the existence of a thing (in this case the person of Rose) would be affirmed.[101] It thus says: 'Rose lives.'

That Rose wants to see this sentence endlessly signified by keeping it running suggests that someone else should continuously acknowledge the content of this existential determination. Otherwise,

---

98 It appears to be characteristic that repetitive rites, such as mumbling endless litanies or lighting 'everlasting flames', appear especially in connection with death cults and at moments of deathly fear. That this concerns a life-representing person substituting for the real, dead person (or one whose life is endangered) appears to confirm a comment by Huizinga, who noticed this 'interpassive' dimension in sporting duels and with regard to the ritual in general: 'The fact that it can be executed through hired fighters is itself an indication of its ritual character, for a ritual act will allow of performance by a substitute' (Huizinga, *Homo Ludens*, p. 93).

99 See also Fink, *Clinical Introduction to Lacanian Psychoanalysis*, pp. 160ff.

100 On the process of punctuation as a technique of psychoanalysis, see ibid., pp. 14–15.

101 Moreover, the tautology ('Rose is a Rose'), in which nothing more is attributed to a subject than that which is inherent in its concept, is much closer to an existential judgment than a predicate judgment. The tautology 'God is God', for example, at least wants to say: God exists, even if nothing can be accurately claimed about God.

one might believe that Rose were dead.[102] If, however, the other believes this, then Rose might find herself in the uncomfortable situation of being 'between two deaths': in fact still alive; but symbolically, in the estimation of another, already dead.[103] If, however, the other believes in Rose's aliveness, then her life is symbolically covered, so to speak. In fact not just her life, but even her death: as long as another is convinced of Rose's life, Rose can *rest in peace* (i.e. be dead).[104]

Rose wants her peace, and her *dromenon* thus protects her by running permanently. That the content of Rose's manifestation plays hardly a role, and turns out to be lacking in information (quasi-tautological[105]), can be explained by this protective function. In the end, the text says nothing more than what the running of the text already says: the running of the text alone already communicates the message that Rose lives. The text that says this (or something similar) is therefore an empty message, so to speak. It adds nothing new to the medium. The content is a mere placeholder. It is not important in itself; rather, what is important is that something else cannot or must not be present as long as it is present, due to its continued running. The text from Rose is kept running, like Woody Allen's often incessant talking in some of his films – he does not speak because he wants to say something in particular, but only because he is afraid that something else could be said instead, or because he is afraid that an embarrassing silence might descend.

What is kept running is a double placeholder, holding both Rose's place – because she herself would otherwise have to be there, where she could be threatened – and also the place of something else,

---

102   Contrary to Descartes, who was convinced that he existed only when he thought he did, Rose's 'partner in the discussion' is convinced that Rose exists when told she does.

103   On the difference between the 'two deaths', see Žižek, *Sublime Object of Ideology*, pp. 131ff.

104   This is similar to the assumption that interpassivity generally presents a manifestation of the death drive (if such a thing exists at all): it is based on the desire to be dead, without the death being noticed by another.

105   Due to its multiple meanings, this sentence is clearly not pure tautology. It says, among other things, that the girl Rose is a flower of the same name. But, through the further repetition, what had hitherto been a *predicate* (name of the flower) becomes the *subject* of a new sentence (name of the girl). The girl thereby disappears in a tautology of flowers, by which it is never clear that the girl Rose was ever meant. The usually incorrect quotations of the passage fall into the girl Rose's trap.

something foreign, alien, because this might otherwise be there, threatening Rose. Quite different from an art that is concerned with obtaining something beautiful, and therefore must consider the specific form of things considered beautiful – as in the myth of Pygmalion or even in Szeemann's interpretation of Stein – Rose's or Stein's art has to do with avoiding something; also unimportant is the protective device that she holds up 'apotropaically' in order to keep away the other thing.[106]

For this reason, everything that runs is a means of protection; every *dromenon* is an *apotropaion*, because it holds something up to ward off something else. What is being used for this purpose is irrelevant. It helps, as Jenny Holzer rightly says, simply by the fact that it keeps going and wards off something else. For example, the greater beauty afforded by music playing in the background as compared with a running motorcycle is – as Torberg's Tante Jolesch would have said[107] – pure luxury; music's decisive assisting function, on the other hand, is shown through whistling in a dark forest.

All that is kept running – and thus all that protects – is therefore a 'cool' medium, to use Marshall McLuhan's term. What is important with this type of medium is the medium itself – its running, and not its content. The content of such a medium is, as McLuhan says, 'like the juicy piece of meat carried by the burglar to distract the watchdog of the mind'.[108] In addition to the apathy of the cool medium towards its own particular content, McLuhan also emphasizes its protective, apotropaic function.

The reason for the apathy of the running forms with regard to the specific content – correctly identified by Jenny Holzer – can be found in the fact that letting something run fulfils a protective function. The running *dromena* occupy a place that otherwise might have been assumed by something threatening. They thus protect those who let the

---

106   With Lacan's differentiation between hysteria and obsessional neurosis (through the both questions quoted above) it becomes possible to relate the form-caring, 'protropaic' art to hysteria and, on the contrary, the apotropaic, 'regardless', 'no matter what' art to obsessional neurosis.. This would build a supplement to Freud's alignment between hysteria and art (See Freud, 'Totem and Taboo', pp. 73–4).

107   This famous character introduced by the Austrian writer Friedrich Torberg in his novel *Die Tante Jolesch oder Der Untergang des Abendlandes in Anekdoten* (Vienna, Tosa-Verlag, 1995) once states that 'everything which is more beautiful in a man than in a monkey is pure luxury'.

108   McLuhan, *Understanding Media*, p. 18.

dromena run: they cover their retreat into self-forgetfulness. If self-forgetfulness is something beautiful (for example, because it assumes security), then the beauty of this self-abandon is thus also attained by letting something foreign run. The things and people that have been left running make it possible for the resting ones to let themselves go.

Self-Forgetfulness: Movement and Imagination Without an Image

Processes that appear to be completely mindless, in which one thing or another is kept running, ultimately create an illusion. They perform 'life' for someone. And maintaining this illusion by the running of things affords those who let them run a certain amount of pleasure. This pleasure is thus due to self-forgetfulness. Not only the acquisition of 'inner images', but also the total loss of such images and the related submersion in self-forgetfulness, therefore function as sources of pleasure.

The pleasure of self-abandon is not only an aesthetic principle constituting the appeal of artworks, such as those previously analyzed; it is also an ideological principle. To achieve self-forgetfulness, numerous ideological practices are carried out, fulfilling an important social function. I will elaborate on this below – contradicting all those theories that claim that socializing, ideological practices are always identity-forming practices. At the same time, I want to show the extent to which self-forgetfulness is created through the use of symbolic practices, contradicting those theories claiming that the occurrence of self-forgetfulness allows us to conclude that, in such contexts, only the body and not ideology is significant.

Sport is among the most important practices producing the socializing principle of self-abandon in today's industrial and (financialized) service societies. In 1969, Louis Althusser stated in his typically laconic way, in his study 'Ideology and Ideological State Apparatuses',[109] that a sports club is an ideological apparatus. This observation, however, presupposes Althusser's unusual concept of ideology. For Althusser – as for McLuhan – ideology is not based on ideas.[110] This definition offers the only conceivable possibility for

---

109   See Althusser, 'Ideology and Ideological State Apparatuses'.
110   See ibid., p. 169: 'Disappeared: the term *ideas*.' Althusser's concept of the 'ideological state apparatus' corresponds exactly with McLuhan's idea of the 'medium'.

viewing a practice (such as sport) that contains hardly any ideas as an ideological practice. For Althusser, sport is an ideological practice because it provides the reproduction of the conditions of production (of the labour force and social relationships of production). Sport, especially under its current media observation, largely ensures that people will work in the same way tomorrow as they do today – and that they will integrate into society (in particular, as superior or inferior to other people), or that they will do both in a completely different, perhaps even more productive way. Sport thus contributes to the reproduction of the conditions of production, either simple or expanded. What is also astounding about this reproduction through ideological practices, according to Althusser, is that everyone 'starts acting' by themselves 'without having to have their own police officer at their heels'.[111] This readiness to act spontaneously cannot be achieved through violent means; violence and repression serve, at best, to make people passive. According to Althusser, the fact that people are active without being coerced is an outcome of ideology.

The fact that this reproductive function can be fulfilled without necessary recourse to ideas led Michel Foucault to the conclusion that not only the concept of *ideas* (as in Althusser), but also the concept of *ideology* (in contrast to Althusser), should be rejected. Since ideas are not important, what is decisive in explaining the phenomenon of 'power' is more knowledge of the *body*, rather than of ideology.[112] Thus, Foucault's theory of power is developed almost exclusively from a series of concepts focusing on physicality, such as 'conditioning', 'dressage', 'disciplining', 'gymnastics', 'stimulation', and so on.[113] The reference to the body allows Foucault's theory to seem especially appropriate, at first, in explaining the social function of sport. In the attempt to exclude the concept of ideology from his theory of power, however, Foucault does not easily escape a largely negative, merely limiting formulation of power, which he criticizes vehemently,

---

111   My translation of Louis Althusser, *Sur la Reproduction* (Paris: PUF, 1995), p. 212: '[L]'idéologie "fait agir tout seuls" les individus sans qu'il soit besoin de leur mettre à chacun un gendarme individuel au cul'.

112   See also Michel Foucault, *Power/Knowledge: Selected Interviews and Other Writings, 1972–1977*, ed. Colin Gordon (Brighton: Harvester Press, 1980), p. 58: 'Indeed I wonder whether, before one poses the question of ideology, it wouldn't be more materialist to study first the question of the body and the effects of power on it.'

113   See ibid., pp. 125, 141, 59, 56, 57.

although not always entirely successfully.[114] Nevertheless, Foucault defines this form of power as a *dromenon* due to its lack of reference to ideas. He describes power as something that 'traverses and . . . runs through the whole social body'.[115]

Foucault's conclusion – the complete rejection of the concept of ideology and, due to the absence of ideas in these kinds of reproduction processes, an exclusive reliance on the concept of the body – was nevertheless premature. This can be seen in a particular form of social sport, which to a large extent – if not decisively – guarantees the reproduction of the labour force and relations of production: sport on television. Joggers, aerobic dancers, gym members, players in soccer clubs, and so on, do not make up the bulk of the social presence of sport. Instead, this is constituted by the 'couch potatoes' – those who follow televised soccer games, car races, skiing, ice dancing, and so on, from the sofa. They remain motionless – with the possible exception of small mimetic gestures that are copied from or pre-empt the actors shown (in that the audience shows the actors how they should perform), or short, intensive explosions of emotion, such as joy, disappointment, or swearing at some of the players. A massive amount of social power is condensed in this area, without ever having touched the bodies of those who have been taken in by it. The reproduction of the labour force and of relations of production is realized primarily in front of the television, regardless of how the viewer relates to it. Although the protagonists shown on television perform outstanding physical feats – thanks to their discipline, training, stimulation, and so on – it is not they, but rather the physically unbothered television viewers who are taken in by the effects of power. We are therefore dealing with power in the absence of a trained body: this means that the social effectiveness of this process cannot be explained by a physiological theory of the body or of 'political anatomy'.[116] Instead, this

---

114   See also Thomas Lemke, who notes that Foucault, 'until he wrote "The History of Sexuality volume 1: An Introduction" works implicitly with a concept of repression, from which he thought he had already parted theoretically'. Thomas Lemke, *Eine Kritik der politischen Vernunft. Foucaults Analyse der modernen Gouvernementalität* (Berlin/Hamburg: Argument, 1997), p. 93n. (my translation). With the concept of 'stimulation', Foucault finds a quick solution to this difficulty. He risks, on the other hand, leaving the field of the merely corporeal and enters the problematic terrain of the imaginary – and thus of ideology.

115   Foucault, *Power/Knowledge*, p. 119.

116   On this concept, see Lemke, *Eine Kritik der politischen Vernunft*, p. 68.

effectiveness must be examined at the level of imagination, as Althusser postulated when using the concept of ideology in relation to sport. For if, contrary to Foucault's assumption, 'stimulation' is successful without influencing the bodies of the stimulated, the only explanation for this seems to be that the level of imagination has been successfully influenced. If there is no *real* connection between the active athletic bodies and the passive viewing bodies caught up in the reproductive effect, then there must be an *imagined* connection that explains this effect.

What fantasies, then, does sport supply to television viewers, and why are they prepared, after several hours of watching sport on television, to resume working and to integrate 'by themselves' into social hierarchies? How does television sport perform its ideological task of reproduction? The traditional theories of sport have apparently sought the answer to this question primarily in one area. They have tried to explain the fascinating power that sport exerts over the imagination by claiming that sport is useful in building identity because it provides viewers with idols.[117] The moving bodies on television influence the unmoving bodies (or the psychic apparatuses associated with them) in front of the screen by stimulating identification with them. The fantasy would therefore consist in the fact that inactive bodies, at least for a short time, empathize with active bodies and consider themselves identical with them – perhaps in order later even to imitate them.[118] Accordingly, the desire to watch sport on television would involve gaining identity through identification. It would be justifiable to use the concept of *ideology* with regard to television sport because, although there are no *ideas*, there are certainly *idols* that one can look up to as a spectator.

117　See also – all in Caysa, *Sportphilosophie* – Volker Caysa, *Vorwort*, p. 9; Wolfgang Kaschuba, *Sportivität: Die Karriere eines neuen Leitwertes*, pp. 238ff; Gunter Gebauer, *Die Mythen-Maschine*, pp. 290ff; Kurt Weis, *Die Priester der Muskelkraft*, p. 325. Compare Eilert Herms, *Sport. Partner der Kirche und Thema der Theologie* (Hannover: Lutherisches Verlagshaus, 1993), p. 69. In general, theories of identity appear to involve primarily the question of how people manage to 'construct' or 'develop' an identity (or multiple identities) – compare, for example, Heiner Keupp, *Identitätskonstruktionen. Das Patchwork der Identitäten in der Postmoderne* (Reinbek: Rowohlt, 1999), esp. pp. 60ff – and not the perhaps equally relevant, contrary question, through what practices they have brought about a temporary suspension of their identities (without negotiating a new identity).

118　See Karl Jaspers, *Masse und Sport*, in Caysa, *Sportphilosophie*, pp. 32–3.

But does this assumption really hold up when measured against the facts of television sport? Does identification with idols really take place during every live broadcast? And is the possibility for identification actually the decisive moment in the fascination with televised sport? Does television supply people with images – not only at a visual level, but also at the level of their identifications, the level of the imaginary? Is this the crucial source of pleasure?

Let us consider what happens when the (generally male) sports fan sits in front of the television. First, he must follow the live broadcast. When, for example, Formula 1 racing is on, he immediately stops all everyday activities; all encounters with other people are abruptly terminated. Then, when he is sitting on the sofa in front of the screen, the power of the programme continues in such a way that he cannot be disturbed. A kind of 'sacred seriousness' has taken over. Whereas during another type of television show or feature film it would be possible to direct a question to the person watching, or even to get them on the phone for a short time, during a live televised sporting event this is impossible. It even seems like sacrilege. Freud's observation (of the 'prohibition against interruption' in neurotic rituals and the 'isolation from all other actions')[119] is particularly applicable here.[120]

The separation of the sexes – which in totemic tribal cultures meant that only men were allowed access to sacredness and women were excluded from it[121] – appears to have carried over into televi-

---

119   See also Freud 'Obsessive Actions', pp. 119–20.

120   See also Siemes, 'Sieg ohne Tor', p. 41, which refers to a passage by G. Gebauer: 'There's the community of fans who, from its position in the stadium or before the television, is sealed off from the profane and receives its saints (the stars on the field) placing them into a "mythical meta-realm" where they cannot be criticized . . . In the belief in the star, the belief in the integrity of the person is still intact. In the participation in the game, people increase the "intensity of their social existence" and become more than normal citizens – as members of a community. Analogous to this self-elevation of the individual, society as a whole is elevated: in the game, society attains the ideal of itself. And because that is fairly simple and transported non-verbally as pure spectacle, soccer becomes the only world religion.' (My translation). Siemes consequently and justifiably reports his doubt about the sacredness that Gebauer claims of the soccer idols who, like tricksters, tend towards maliciousness. Due to their low level of morals, the idols are not suitable for idealization and identification. As I try to show in what follows, we can conclude from this that the pleasure gain and the ideological function of this practice are found in something other than identification.

121   See also Durkheim, Elementary Forms, pp. 107ff.

sion society. There is a gender-specific division here, too; televised sport inserts a definite wedge between the sexes, and relegates women to the realm of the profane with its reasonable, realistic goals, while it shifts men into a strange, unrealistic sphere of 'sacred seriousness'. Incidentally, in this realm it is not exactly clear what the object of this seriousness is, or how it is commanded. A woman's thoroughly logical incapacity to understand this behaviour is countered in turn by the man's incomprehension: the slightest intervention by a woman is answered with a curt defence. Even later, it still hardly seems possible to ask the men what they have actually seen and why it was so important. The event seems to have absorbed their attention to such a great extent that they are barely aware of it themselves. Men's sport-orientated, quasi-religious secrets appear to remain secret even to the men themselves.

In any case, in this process, the medium dominates over the message, as McLuhan would have said:[122] everything related to content and what can be discussed – manoeuvres, tricks, strategies, tactical or technical finesse, plays, and so on – could also be recorded on video. What captivates the men is, primarily, something other than the content; it is much more the medium of the live broadcast itself. It provides a sense of participation in an event, similar to that of holy communion, which belongs to a cycle of events – similar to religious systems of holidays, fasting days, and so on – that structures men's time in a circular progression – between the Grand Prix in Monaco in late spring and Silverstone in summer, until the final in Suzuka in autumn; from the qualifying games to the final round of the football World Cup every four years; and so on. Just as racing cars drive on a circular path, car races and all other sporting events move circularly though time.

Being at the games' festivities thus signifies that one has participated in the ritual, and has integrated into the cycle of the sporting event.[123] The delineation of borders (constitutive for all religions) between the profane and the sacred[124] – or from the slack, profane state of waiting, and the sacred, festive events, through to the

---

122   See McLuhan, *Understanding Media*, pp. 7ff.

123   On the cyclical moments of 'television liturgies', see Thomas, *Medien – Ritual – Religion*, pp. 472ff. The *dromenon* character of this cycle is captured well by Thomas's formulation: 'The liturgical current can only be assumed' (p. 473).

124   See Durkheim, *Elementary Forms*, p. 36.

corresponding feelings of boredom, of anticipation, of excitement, and finally the sleeping-off of the post-sport result – seems to be complete.[125] Accordingly, there is no content capable of being described in a narrative, no image, but rather a structure that is experienced; nothing that is meaningful, but at most a certain order, which is itself senseless.

For that reason, the 'sacred seriousness' in which the viewers of television sport immerse themselves constitutes a *sinking without depth*. Disturbing the viewers is forbidden, but it is not because they are about to receive a large amount of meaningful material that they run the risk of missing due to the disturbance. Instead, it is the opposite: they cannot be disturbed because they have entered a structure without sense and – like sleepwalkers – find themselves in a precarious state of self-abandon where every intervention would mean a painful reminder for them that they are, in fact, someone in particular. That is why they are later incapable of recounting what they have seen or where they have been: because they have been somewhere where they were not present.

Integrating into the cycle has helped them to forget themselves. The cycle is a *dromenon*: it is something that could run just as well without them. They had to integrate into it so that the cycle, which could also continue without them, also runs *for them* – so that it runs *instead of them*. It is the running of the cycle into which they have integrated, and which they have let run for themselves, that enables them to perform being aware and alive for someone else, even if they are, in the meantime, lacking in awareness, lifeless, and quasi-dead.

The fantasy that underlies this process is not theirs. They have, to a much greater extent, provided an image for someone else; they have kept an invisible observer assured that they were 'with it', conscious and alive. The *dromenon* is an act for these invisible observers who, unlike the actors themselves, are taken in, promptly and necessarily, by the illusion being presented. The actors do not even have to be aware of it; the illusion and the image behind this process were not theirs. Without an image of any kind, they still maintained an illusion – one that they even 'objectively' offered; that is, offered to someone else.

Using this illusion, which they have constructed for a foreign agency, they were able to master the task of reproduction. This is why

---

125   Compare Thomas, *Medien – Ritual – Religion*, p. 252.

sport is an ideological practice: based on the principle of illusions for others, the *dromenon* of sport reproduces the labour force and production relations. The pleasure gained through temporary self-forgetfulness under the protection of a *dromenon*, like the function of sleep, allows people to enter into a conscious state in which there is no self-awareness. The possibility of temporarily giving up their identity is a necessary condition for building it back up on the next working day, and maintaining it by the power of this identity, in accordance with the image that has been demonstrated to them, to 'act' entirely 'by themselves', naturally. Self-abandon chiefly enables the naturalness of self-certainty, the effect of creating the subject: 'It really is me, I am here, a worker, a boss or a soldier!'[126]

It is often possible to see that these people were temporarily without an image. After watching televised sport, they do not always come forward with a proudly inflated chest, with a stronger sense of awareness of who or what they are. They are also not proud of what they have done while sitting in front of the television. More often they appear somewhat ashamed, as if they had been caught in a shady affair. The feelings of shame and the disdain for the time spent watching television television, as irresistible as they were, are also manifest in the regret with which they admit the compulsion for this practice – for example, when they say: '*Unfortunately* I have to go and watch television now.'

The decisive element on which the reproduction and attraction of televised sport is based is thus the *medium* of televised sport as a *dromenon*; here, content is secondary. For its viewers, televised sport is primarily an *illusion without an image*, serving solely to deliver an image and to hide the viewers' own absence behind this image – to hide the immersion-without-depth into which they have entered. If televised sport appears, however, to have content after all, and, through the *images* delivered by the television, to serve as a role model for the viewers' identification, then this identity gain enabled by televised sport is only a further cover – another protective shield, as it were – that serves to hide the more fundamental fact of self-abandon behind the pretext of an identity gain. The viewers act as if they are dealing with idols, but this functions merely to disguise the fact that, in truth, they have set a *dromenon* in motion, which allows them to abandon their self-image for a while.

---

126 See Althusser, 'Ideology and Ideological State Apparatuses', p. 178.

The same thing can also be observed in the current phenomenon of dance. Dance, too, is clearly a *dromenon*. In this function, it also helps to solve a problem in theatre. It is common knowledge that ancient Greek drama, as familiar as it may seem in some respects, poses performative and theoretical problems chiefly with regard to one characteristic: the presence of the chorus.[127] The fact that a strange collective acts on the stage, alongside the individual characters, appears inexplicable in a contemporary understanding of theatre. It was Friedrich Nietzsche who was first able to solve this mystery. The chorus, according to Nietzsche, forms the navel of the theatre. It developed from the inebriate processions of the Dionysus cult. Only gradually did individual forms emerge from these collective and chaotic processions, which, as characters and heroes, embodied our familiar principle of individuation in the – now, less transient – theatre. The chorus and the processions represent the anti-individual, *Dionysian* principle of 'intoxication' – the 'non-visual' principle of music. The individual characteristics correspond, on the other hand, to the individualistic, *Apollonian* principle of the 'dream' – the visual arts.[128]

Recently, this declaration by Nietzsche has been visually elucidated in some Western metropolises: the dance events of the 'free parades' and 'love parades' have given the Dionysian principle renewed significance in youth culture, which otherwise seldom shows discernible interest in theatre. The processions of the 'revellers' are collective and without subjects, like those of the Bacchantes. In them 'Dionysian impulses' can be recognized, and 'as they grow in intensity', as Nietzsche writes, 'everything subjective vanishes into complete self-forgetfulness.'[129] At the parades there is hardly a sepa-

---

127   Both Jacques Lacan and Slavoj Žižek – who compares Greek tragedy with the canned laughter of modern television sitcoms – have described the chorus as a medium that carries for the viewers and in their place the feelings of fear and empathy, thus acting as an interpassive medium, a *dromenon*. See also Žižek, *Sublime Object of Ideology*, pp. 34–5.

128   See Friedrich Nietzsche, *Die Geburt der Tragödie aus dem Geiste der Musik = Die Geburt der Tragödie. Oder: Griechenthum und Pessimismus (The Birth of Tragedy and The Case of Wagner)*, trans. with commentary by Walter Kaufmann (New York: Vintage Books, 1967 [1872]), pp. 33, 38. Nietzsche's differentiation between dreams and intoxication/ecstasies corresponds to what I describe here as the differentiation of pleasure practices into the acquisition of and resistance to inner images.

129   Ibid., pp. 36–7. Nietzsche continues: 'In the German Middle Ages, too,

ration between the performers and the observers. This is exactly what makes the parade a *dromenon*: it presents a picture that is not meant for an audience that is present, but rather for all those naive observers for whom the *dromenon* performance is staged. Only in few cases do individuals stand out as stars on the parade trucks and, through their professional dancing, render themselves performers and turn the people on the streets below into observers. They thereby produce the separation between performer and viewer to some extent, and introduce a transition that leads away from music and dance, and towards theatre. These Apollonian individuals, meant to serve as idols for the rest of the viewers, add to the principle of 'intoxication' (according to Nietzsche's terminology) that of the 'image'. They thereby create a decisive veil masking the effectiveness of the process, which is necessary for it to function. By acting as if they were concerned with images, idols and identifications, performing and imitating, they permit 'one' – whom exactly, we don't really know – to forget that the parades are much more concerned with letting people dance and run, and with the pleasure of self-forgetfulness.

In this discussion of *dromena* that appear to function without ideas, I hope to have shown that my theory also applies according to which all cultural pleasure is based on the principle of the suspended illusion – and also the desire for self-forgetfulness. The following chapter investigates the extent to which the universally pleasure-providing function of suspended illusions can be combined with other, less pleasurable functions – and explores the political consequences.

---

singing and dancing crowds, ever increasing in number, whirled themselves from place to place under this same Dionysian impulse. In these dancers of St John and St Vitus, we rediscover the Bacchic choruses of the Greeks, with their prehistory in Asia Minor, as far back as Babylon and the orgiastic Sacaea. There are some who, from obtuseness or lack of experience, turn away from such phenomena as from "folk diseases" with contempt or pity born of the consciousness of their own "healthy-mindedness." But of course such poor wretches have no idea how corpselike and ghostly their so-called "healthy-mindedness" looks when the glowing life of the Dionysian revelers roars past them.'

Asceticism: Ascetic Ideals and Reactionary Masses – On the Organization of the Libido in Belief and Faith

Mannoni's distinction between two types of conviction – belief and faith – and Huizinga's assumption about the cultural meaning of play have allowed us to establish how much the feelings of pleasure that a culture creates for its adherents rest on the principle of belief, on illusions without owners. All cultural pleasure is 'fetishistic', which means that it comes about through suspended illusion. Belief, the illusion of the other, is culture's pleasure principle.

In some cultures, perhaps because of an intrinsic dialectic, faith is cast over belief. Consequently, the culture's pleasure principle is also covered over, which is the central theme that I will explore in what follows: unrecognized belief corresponds with a failure to recognize pleasure; a culture that can no longer admit to its beliefs is also incapable of admitting to its experiences of pleasure. It experiences its pleasure as unpleasurable, and can only draw pleasure from its displeasure. For that reason, the failure to recognize belief – obscured as it is by faith – is equivalent to the incursion of ascetic ideals into these cultures.

A society's ability to experience pleasure is thus determined by the reigning social form of illusion. Belief cultures are highly capable of pleasure, whereas faith cultures can create only secretive, unacknowledged feelings of pleasure through manifest experiences of displeasure. In the present age, phenomena that have a problematic relationship with pleasure seem to be advancing rapidly in popular culture and art. We are apparently witnessing a new push for reform, in which the 'faith' form of conviction covers over that of belief bit by bit, thereby generating ever more pleasure in displeasure.[1]

---

1 Richard Sennett, *The Fall of Public Man* (New York: Knopf, 1978) also establishes that the Western societies 'are moving from something like an other-directed condition to an inner-directed condition' (p. 5). Sennett also precisely recognizes the incapacity for pleasure that this generates (pp. 6ff).

A definitive effect of this change in the organizational forms of conviction and pleasure is the emergence of ascetic affects. These affects shape those ideological conditions under which people not only accept, but actively affirm politics that harm them. The most obvious phenomena resulting from the current, ascetic affective organization of the masses is the joy in 'rational' appreciation of supposedly necessary 'austerity measures', and the affected persons' active compliance in the neoliberal attacks on their own most immediate interests – such as social security, pension plans, education, infrastructure, and so on. The example of the reactionary masses will thus be used here to discuss the dual libido-economical problems of the inability to experience pleasure and, likewise, the desire for displeasure. I will begin, however, by focusing on the incursion of ascetic ideals as an ideological precondition for the masses' willingness to make – at times seemingly incomprehensible – political sacrifices.

UN-AMERICAN ACTIVITIES

At the moment, we can observe the massive encroachment of ascetic tendencies in hegemonic US popular culture – a relatively recent development.[2] Until the early 1980s, US cultural output seemed to be more or less official propaganda for 'sex and drugs and rock 'n' roll'. Only since then has it lapsed into a series of strange passions:[3] cosmetic surgery; fanaticism with regard to orderly teeth, hair and clothing; meticulous tanning and bleaching; body-building; the epidemic of jogging; scrupulously administered, discriminatory smoking bans; and petty regulations, for example, specifying that alcohol can be transported in the boot but not the passenger section of a car. Small children who are caught playing doctor are carried away in handcuffs.[4] Not even the president's intimate sphere is protected from the diligence of special investigators who report their

---

2   Compare the analysis in Sergio Benvenuto, 'Der amerikanische Cocktail', *Lettre International* 50: III (2000).

3   Hughes, *Culture of Complaint* (New York, et al: Oxford University Press, 1993), also recognized this change: 'Even the [US] popular culture, once celebrated and admired throughout the entire world for good reason, is now only a lousy imitation of its former self' (p. 16).

4   See, for example, the case of Raoul Wüthrich.

discoveries to an increasingly bored audience (causing a sensation for who knows whom). Prudery and fundamentalist Christianity seem to be advancing in a forward march that knows no limits.[5]

For Europeans, especially, this transformation in American culture appears as an obvious and abrupt upheaval: after all, following World War II, Americans taught us how to be cool and dress in T-shirts and jeans, sport bizarre haircuts, drink cola, listen to loud music, take drugs, fight in back alleys, read comics, chew gum, love freely, and race aimlessly through the countryside in our cars and on our motorcycles. Now, on the contrary, in their films they show us only interiors furnished by Ikea, and peopled by characters in business suits and ties who become excessively agitated upon catching wind of the slightest breach of what are rather narrowly defined conventions. The former emphatically liberal attitude of the West now appears as no more than a propaganda tool designed exclusively for the cold war, now dispensable.

FROM PROHIBITIONS TO SAD PASSIONS

At first glance it may seem as though American culture at the turn of the millennium has become a world of limitations and prohibitions. At second glance, however, it quickly becomes clear that these measures not only prevent things but also always produce things. They release an overwhelming abundance of affects, lending them their particular form. These affects, and not merely the restrictions and barriers, contribute to shaping this culture's specific asceticism.

For example, not only is there a ban on smoking, but this also provides the opportunity for people to become incredibly irritated and agitated when they see someone smoking, even if they are at a distance – for example, at the other end of an open-air train station. Disgust, resentment, accusations and guilt then initiate a chain of intense emotional experiences. What is remarkable about such experiences is that they are experienced as unpleasurable, although they

---

5   Compare Stuart Hall, 'Das Kapital will Sex', interview by Matthias Dusini, in *Falter* 12: 1 (2001), who remarks that 'there is more fundamentalism in the West than in the Third World and in Islam. We should talk about how American capitalism found its most secure cover in the fundamentalist Protestant religion. Mr Bush, as a white Baptist, comes from this exact constellation. He wants to cleanse the screen of obscenities; at the same time, he advances neo-liberalism' (pp. 70–1; my translation).

are expressed with a passion so great and apparently so indispensable that it seems as though, in some way or another, they would convey happiness.

But how is this possible? Might there be a pleasure that is not experienced as pleasurable by those who feel it? Might there be some sense in saying to someone: 'You really are enjoying that, you just don't realize it'? Or does this statement deal with an absurd paradox (as though one were saying, for example: 'In truth, you are not at all in pain, only you don't realize it and that's why you are shouting)? There is a philosophy that deals explicitly with the paradox of a pleasure that is not experienced as such: Spinoza's *Ethics*. In his final proposition, he writes: 'Blessedness is not the reward of virtue, but virtue itself; neither do we rejoice therein, because we control our lusts, but contrariwise, because we rejoice therein, we are able to control our lusts.'[6]

According to Spinoza, the virtue that helps 'control our lusts' is identical with bliss. Nonetheless, it seems necessary to emphasize that there is apparently a regularly occurring deception pertaining to this matter. The virtuous seem to believe that they are not yet happy, and that happiness arrives only later, as reward for the long period of abstinence, during which there is only virtuousness.

The virtuous who curb their pleasures (control their lusts) are already happy without realizing it. They fool themselves about their happiness. Because of this deception, they also fail to recognize the causal relations. In truth, it is their already-existing happiness that enables them to forgo other pleasures. They believe, on the contrary, that through forgoing other pleasures they are able to achieve happiness. But it is not the absence or omission of pleasures that leads to the pleasure of happiness – there is absolutely no guarantee of that. Instead, the reverse is true: the presence of the one pleasure makes it possible to omit others. If one forgoes pleasure, that gives an indication that another, greater pleasure must already be present.[7]

Based on the example of the virtuous ascetic, Spinoza shows that it is possible to be happy without realizing it. The problem of unhappiness is consequently (at least in these cases) not 'ontological', but

---

6   Spinoza, 'Ethics V', Proposition 42, in *On the Improvement of the Understanding*, p. 270.

7   Since, as Spinoza established, a finite thing can only 'be limited by another thing of the same nature' (see Spinoza, 'Ethics I', Definition 2, in ibid., p. 45).

rather 'epistemological.' The difficulty is not that happiness is missing and we now have to state where it can be found (and whether it can even be found at all). It might possibly be the case instead that happiness is always present, but that those who bear it sometimes do not perceive it as pleasure.[8] And according to Spinoza, this is precisely what characterizes unhappiness: unhappiness is a happiness that is not experienced as such by those who have it.

Nonetheless, happiness that is not felt as such is in no way ignored by those who bear it. Instead, a reversal takes place. They experience their happiness as extremely unpleasurable: they feel loathing, disgust and guilt, or they become furious at someone whom they suspect is happy – altogether uncomfortable feelings, to an extent that seems to correspond with or even surpass the mistaken happiness. The unhappiness is always at least as great as the unrecognized happiness. It is recognizable as the reverse of it in that it contains the same amount of affect, sometimes even amplified with additional affect.

Spinoza's concept of unhappiness or sadness (*tristitia*) as a reversed experience of happiness corresponds with Freud's concept of 'neurotic unpleasure.' Like Spinoza, Freud envisaged this kind of reversal. According to Freud, neurotic unpleasure arises as a product of a repression-based transformation of pleasure into unpleasure: 'The details of the process by which repression turns a possibility of pleasure into a source of unpleasure are not yet clearly understood or cannot be clearly represented; but there is no doubt that all neurotic unpleasure is of that kind – pleasure that cannot be felt as such.'[9]

Emotions such as disgust, fear, guilt, nausea, unpleasure, aggression, envy, jealousy, and so on, can consequently be understood as the reversed, negative form of a pleasure.[10] In his commentary on Spinoza, Gilles Deleuze identified such affects as *sad passions*.[11] Sad

---

8   Spinoza's theory can be found in psychoanalytic theory: see Fink, *Clinical Introduction to Lacanian Psychoanalysis*, p. 216: 'The question of satisfaction was always foremost in Freud's mind, and Lacan summarizes Freud's position by saying that "the subject is always happy" in some respect, always getting off on something, even if it is on his or her own dissatisfaction.'

9   Freud, 'Beyond the Pleasure Principle', p. 11.

10   This thought is also at the base of Freud's theory of the ability to depict neuroses as the 'negative' side of perversions. See Sigmund Freud, 'Three Contributions to the Theory of Sex', trans. A. A. Brill (SE VII), p. 165.

11   See Gilles Deleuze, *Spinoza: Practical Philosophy*, trans. Robert Hurley (San Francisco: City Lights, 1988), p. 25. Deleuze seems to base this fortunate discovery of a

passions arise through the reversal of pleasure in the experience of it. They are thereby perceived as unpleasurable or 'sad'. At the same time, they contain something of their original character of being pleasurable – and those who bear them therefore continue to pursue them as though they were pleasurable. To this extent, they are passions.

According to Freud, repression is the condition necessary for sad passions to arise. It causes the unpleasurable distortion: a pleasure that is not permissible is able to break through in that it is lived out and experienced as unpleasure. Because people experience such emotions as unpleasure, they suffer; but because this unpleasure is based on pleasure, they can nonetheless not do without it.

SAD PASSIONS AND REACTIONARY MASSES

Unhappiness is, as Spinoza and Freud agree in unison, not merely the absence of happiness, but instead a passion that the afflicted actively carry out.[12] Accordingly, unhappy people can also hardly free themselves from their unhappiness. Instead, they defend their misery against attempts at comfort or healing, as though it were a precious treasure. There is also happiness in unhappiness, a gain in forgoing pleasure, a satisfaction waiting in the darkest, most passionate asceticism.[13]

This passionate dimension of forgoing pleasure deserves special attention because it appears in more than just personal life: it is also a constant factor in politics. A blatant characteristic of right-wing politics is its perpetual success in turning disadvantages into advantages, leading precisely those who are damaged by it to become its most fanatical followers. That is possible because there is happiness in unhappiness – because the negative effects produced by right-wing politics engender sad passions that are able to cull from them additional, sorrowfully experienced pleasure.

---

concept on Spinoza's establishment of 'tristitia' as a 'passio'. See also Spinoza, *On the Improvement of the Understanding*, pp. 138–9 ('Ethics III', Proposition 11, n.).

12   Compare also the one-liner that Freud used to analyze another 'sad passion': '*Eifersucht* [jealousy] is a *Leidenschaft* [passion], which *mit Eifer sucht* [with eagerness seeks], *what Leiden schafft* [causes pain].' See Freud, 'Jokes and Their Relation to the Unconscious', p. 35.

13   The relationship between happiness and unhappiness has to be understood in strict analogy to that which Freud, in his essay 'The Uncanny', establishes between the German words *heimlich* und *unheimlich*. According to Freud, the preposition 'un' has to be read as 'the mark of repression' (See Freud, 'The Uncanny', p. 244).

For that reason, oppression is often not only accepted, but even desired. Gilles Deleuze and Félix Guattari emphasize this in *Anti-Oedipus*, pointing out that a theory of sad passions forms the key to understanding the success of reactionary politics: 'That is why the fundamental problem of political philosophy is still precisely the one that Spinoza saw so clearly, and that Wilhelm Reich rediscovered: "Why do men fight for their servitude as stubbornly as though it were their salvation?" How can people possibly reach the point of shouting: "More taxes! Less bread!" '[14]

Spinoza, one of the first modern philosophers to behold reactionary masses,[15] posed this question in the foreword to his 'theological-political treatise'.[16] Wilhelm Reich studied the same reversal mechanism in emerging national socialism: as Reich determined, there is a regularly appearing *reverse relationship* between economic conditions and the emotional state of those affected. Reich identifies this paradox – that the agreement of those injured increases proportionately to the damage that is done to them – as 'cleavage'.[17]

We can observe this paradoxical dynamic not only in royalist or fascist dictatorships, but also in the current phenomena of neoliberal politics. In Austria, for example, social cutbacks, given the trivializing name of 'savings package' (austerity measures), and enforced from 1987 onwards by the (then) so-called 'majority coalition' between the Social Democrats (SPÖ) and the Christian-Conservative People's Party (ÖVP), showed that the population had been seized by a paradoxical will to make sacrifices (a newspaper headline announcing the third 'austerity package' in December 1995 stated, roughly: 'All Austrians Want to Be Austere'). This served, so to speak, to train society in an affect that the right wing would later be able to deploy much more broadly for their own purposes.

---

14   Deleuze and Guattari, *Anti-Oedipus*, p. 29.

15   During the royalist coup in the Netherlands 1672. See also Deleuze, *Spinoza*, pp. 9ff; Étienne Balibar, *Spinoza et la politique* (Paris: P. U. F., 1985), p. 26; Yirmiyahu Yovel, *Spinoza. Das Abenteuer der Immanenz* (Göttingen: Steidl, 1994), p. 220.

16   See Benedict de Spinoza, *Theological-Political Treatise: Cambridge Texts in the History of Philosophy*, ed. by Jonathan Israel, Michael Silverthorne (Cambridge: Cambridge University Press, 2007), p. 7.

17   See Wilhelm Reich, *The Mass Psychology of Fascism*, trans. Vincent Carfagno (New York: Farrar, Straus & Giroux, 1970), p. 8.

Such affects appeared with greater vehemence concerning the government formed between the Christian-Conservative ÖVP and the German nationalist, right-populist Freedom Party (FPÖ) in February 2000. The essayist Franz Schuh noted, in light of this phenomenon, that the Austrian population in the past several years had transformed 'into a mob'[18] – as they seemed so incited by rage, envy, hatred, fear, and so on, and thus receptive to populist politics pandering to such emotions.

What is noticeable in these affects – which allowed, among other things, for this government to come to power – is not their strength, but chiefly their orientation: it is to be expected that a population sensing an existential threat from multinational capital's increasingly rapid and destructive movements under neoliberal conditions would direct its anger against this capital and against these conditions. But instead, this population directed its anger mainly at the migration of labour brought about by these conditions, and often against those who attempted to criticize the conditions and change them – against intellectuals, artists and political activists.

One might expect a population to demand better – that is, to demand from the state, unions or others protection from the destruction wreaked by multinational capital. Instead, we observe this population turning to embrace precisely those who make the most blatant promises to remove the remaining institutions that might possibly offer such protection.

In the end, it seems that this population – rather than calling out (like Mayakovsky), 'Give us the good life!' – favours the very parties that announce a *kassasturz* (general budgetary control), a 'budget reorganization', or, even more clearly, a 'loss of comfort' (as the Austrian finance minister, Grasser, called it in his first budget speech in 2000). The population favours this rather than the argument of the 'reverse Robin Hoods' – that is, it favours those who agitated the population before the government takeover and then proceeded to take money from public funds and redistribute it from the bottom to the top.

In right-wing politics, arduousness is transformed into an attractive feature. Weaknesses become strengths, disadvantages become

---

18   See Franz Schuh, 'Das Leben ist hart genug', interview by A. Thurnher and K. Nüchtern, in *Falter* 41 (1999).

advantages. And the population seems to act 'beyond the pleasure principle', as it were. It is not the case that nothing agitates them: agitation regularly turns into its opposite. The population revolts – and its revolt reaches the anticipated proportions – not against the causes of their oppression, but instead against that which could eliminate these causes. The anger reverses and becomes enthusiasm, or it remains as anger and is aimed at the wrong people.

This reversal constitutes the characteristic trait of what I would like to identify as 'reactionary affects'. Affects are reactionary when they surface quantitatively to a degree that corresponds with certain interests, but when qualitatively, in their orientation, they turn against these interests.

FOUCAULT AND REICH: DISADVANTAGES AND BENEFITS OF THE REPRESSION HYPOTHESIS

What is necessary to explain the emergence of reactionary affects – for example, to understand why one can desire one's own oppression – is an understanding of ascetics and the concept of sad passions. Deleuze and Guattari recognized this, and thereby also offered a (pre-emptory) implicit rehabilitation of Wilhelm Reich's theory, in light of the critique that it would later be subjected to by Michel Foucault.

As is well known, Foucault subjected to critique a 'negative conception' of power, which he saw at work, for example, in Reich's theory.[19] For Foucault, the term 'repression', in particular, referred to the idea of power that is simply negative, forbidding, and hindering. Foucault emphasized, on the contrary, that power's efficiency does not rest on prohibiting and hindering alone, but instead on producing activity and steering it in such a way that it evokes joy and an affirmative involvement on the part of the oppressed individuals:

> If power were never anything but repressive, if it never did anything but to say no, do you really think one would be brought to obey it? What makes power hold good, what makes it accepted, is simply the fact that it doesn't only weigh on us as a force that says no, but that it

---

19   See Foucault, *Power/Knowledge*, p. 91: '[T]he mechanisms of power are those of repression. For convenience sake, I shall term this Reich's hypothesis.'

traverses and produces things, it induces pleasure, forms knowledge, produces discourse.[20]

This remark applies particularly to theories on the relationship between power and sexuality.

Critique of the term 'repression' should help avoid the presupposition of a positive 'purity of desire' underlying a negative, violent power – a sexual prohibition.[17] Thus, just as repression cannot be understood as merely negative, it is also misleading to conceive of a liberating, pure, unspoiled sexuality that is not already saturated by productive power.

Foucault's objections appear entirely accurate: what is questionable, however, is whether they in fact apply to Reich's theory accurately, or have perhaps overlooked a decisive point – an element that Reich's theory developed, and the absence of which presents a weakness in Foucault's theory.[21] Reich's theory in no way states that an intact sexuality can be found beyond a political oppression that is entirely extrinsic to sexuality. On the contrary: what Reich formulates – in connection with Freud's rebellious 1908 essay[22] – is the thesis that individuals respond to societal sexual oppression with repression or regression.[23]

---

20   Ibid., p. 119

21   The weakness in Foucault's theory is probably caused by his superficial knowledge of psychoanalysis. The results can be read in passages such as: 'I would also distinguish myself from para-Marxists like Marcuse who give the notion of repression an exaggerated role – because power would be a fragile thing if its only function were to repress, if it worked only through the mode of censorship, exclusion, blockage and repression, in the manner of a great Superego, exercising itself only in a negative way. If, on the contrary, power is strong this is because, as we are beginning to realize, it produces effects at the level of desire – and also at the level of knowledge' (ibid., p. 59).

Here, Foucault mistakenly equates the political term 'oppression' with the psychoanalytical term 'repression'. The superego that Foucault quotes for illustration is not a merely negative or 'repressive' agency. That is shown, for example, in the paradox Freud discovered whereby the more one obeys the superego, the stricter it becomes (see Freud, 'Civilization and Its Discontents', p. 125; compare Chapter 9, section 2, on p. 238 below).

22   See Freud, ' "Civilized" Sexual Morality', pp. 177–204.

23   Perhaps English translations of Foucault have added to this misunderstanding: the psychoanalytical term 'repression' (German 'Verdrängung'), as well as the political term 'oppression' (German 'Unterdrückung') are both rendered in English by the term 'repression'. Foucault uses the term in the political sense; Reich, on the contrary uses it in the psychoanalytic sense. It seems likely that Foucault's critique of the concept of repression applies more to a conception of power that he himself once

Power corrupts sexuality: if a society upholds unrealizable standards for sexual morality, then people become either neurotic or perverse. In keeping with Reich, they thereby enact a transformation of displeasure into pleasure, and begin to desire their own oppression.[24]

Reich thereby drafts a thoroughly positive, productive concept of power: as he shows, societal sexual oppression not only prevents something, but also produces something – namely, a desire for oppression. And sexuality in no way remains hidden, untouched by power; instead, it changes by virtue of that power and becomes manifest – as a reactionary force. To this extent, Reich's theory seems entirely in accordance with Foucault's strictures.[25]

With this theory, Reich also accomplishes something that Foucault's theory lacks – namely, a criterion to distinguish a reactionary 'production' of power from a non-reactionary one. In his effort to avoid a negative conception of power, Foucault, as several critics have remarked, was only able to juxtapose various positive types.[26] In this, he seems unable to draw a fundamental distinction between a 'positive' production of fascist power and a likewise 'positive' production of, for example, democratic power. This problem arises from the solution to the previous one. For, as long as one has a negative conception of power, a simple criterion for criticism is available: there are people who suffer manifestly under power because they want something that the power denies them. Criticism can rely on them. If power, on the contrary, is positive or productive, corrupting desires and generating affirmative joy, then power theory must bring along its own criterion

upheld, rather than to Wilhelm Reich's (see Lemke, *Eine Kritik der politischen Vernunft*, p. 93, n. 47).

24 'Sexual inhibition alters the structure of the economically suppressed individual in such a manner that he thinks, feels and acts against his own material interests' (Reich, *Mass Psychology of Fascism*, p. 32).

25 Compare ibid., p. 41: '[S]exual repression strengthens political reaction and makes the individual in the masses passive and nonpolitical; it creates a secondary force in man's structure – an artificial interest, which actively supports the authoritarian order'. With his thesis of the (neurotic or perverse) sexualizing of power relations, Reich seems to evade the critique of Geuter and Schrauth, who maintain that 'Reich tends to assume human sexuality as a natural fact. He sees history's effect as mainly a hindering of it.' Ulfried Geuter and Norbert Schrauth, 'Wilhelm Reich, der Körper und die Psychotherapie', in Karl Fallend and Bernd Nitzschke, eds, *Der 'Fall' Wilhelm Reich. Beiträge zum Verhältnis von Psychoanalyse und Politik* (Frankfurt: Suhrkamp, 1997), p. 196, n. 11 (my translation).

26 See Lemke, *Eine Kritik der politischen Vernunft*, pp. 15ff.

and must then even contradict the – often entirely positive – feelings of those damaged by power.

In contrast to Foucault, Reich has such a criterion to hand. Reich's criterion for differentiation is, like Freud's,[27] the question of repression: Has repression taken place? That is, has pleasure that is manifest, and can be experienced, been transformed into manifest displeasure, or not? And now, because of this, is that which brings displeasure experienced as pleasurable? Do people fight for their oppression as though it were their happiness? Or do they fight instead for something that, when obtained, they too can experience manifestly as happiness? In other words, do they need their displeasure, or are they capable of bearing happiness?

THE ASCETIC ECONOMY: LOSS OF
HAPPINESS, GAIN OF SELF-ESTEEM

With the help of Spinoza and Reich, we have discovered the effectiveness of reactionary affects that lies behind the success of reactionary politics. But how can we explain the paradox of reactionary affects? How do the sad passions work? Why is pleasure manifestly experienced as displeasure? And why is displeasure sought as though it were joy?

In his 1914 essay on narcissism, Freud introduced a differentiation that allows an explanation of this: the differentiation between the narcissistic libido – or ego-libido – and the object-libido. Decisive here is the permeability between the two that Freud postulated, which occurs while maintaining the same total amount. When a certain amount of sexual energy is drawn from an object – for example, because the object has been lost – then this same amount of libido can be stored in another entirely different object, namely the ego. Object-libido can be transformed into ego-libido (and vice versa).[28] In the transformation of object-libido into ego-libido, however, the manner in which pleasure is experienced is transformed. To put it in plainer terms, we could say that *joy turns into self-esteem*. Every ascetic forgoes food, sexual satisfaction, comfortable society, and so on, but

---

27   See also the previously cited passage from Freud, 'Beyond the Pleasure Principle', p. 11.
28   See Freud, 'On Narcissism', pp. 74ff.

by doing so gains a considerable amount of respect for his or her own self.

What is crucial for self-esteem, however, is to conceal its origins in happiness. Self-esteem proudly considers itself something different, something more precious than joy (for example, in the words of Kant, it considers itself 'disinterested pleasure', or even as something done out of 'duty' rather than 'inclination'). In principle, self-esteem must hide from itself as much as from others the realization that psychoanalysis has reached: that one and the same libidinal substance circulates between happiness and self-esteem, that both are formed from the same material. Self-esteem's strength and its inability to achieve happiness are equal products of this concealment: self-esteem not only finds it difficult to feel its happiness as happiness; in addition, it is often even incapable of acknowledging itself as self-esteem. For that reason, as Spinoza noted,[29] the pride of self-esteem often capsizes into dejection or envy.

It is possible that self-esteem represents a happiness that is even greater than simple happiness, just as the ascetics claim. That could be the reason that self-esteem is often preferred to happiness. Self-esteem would thereby even quantitatively surpass the 'sacred seriousness' of happiness, which itself is formed from ambivalence and thereby represents an adding together of emotions. Ego-libido, in contrast to object-libido, would thus reveal an aptitude for accumulation. Freud even developed this type of thought in his 'mass psychology', when he stated that the aim-inhibited instincts create 'permanent ties', while those instincts that are directly sexual incur 'a loss of energy each time they are satisfied'.[30] The aim-inhibited instincts, those of the ego-libido, are suited to permanence, whereas the ones whose aims are not inhibited are subject to expenditure.[31]

Nonetheless, this type of increase in happiness through displacement to the side of the ego-libido leads to the problem that it destroys the ability to experience happiness.[32] The 'ontological'

---

29   See Spinoza, 'Ethics IV', Proposition 57, n. (pp. 224ff).

30   Sigmund Freud, 'Group Psychology and the Analysis of the Ego' (SE XVIII), p. 139.

31   See also Freud, 'Civilization and Its Discontents', p. 252: 'since, as is well known, temptations are merely increased by constant frustration, whereas an occasional satisfaction of them causes them to diminish, at least for the time being'.

32   Jacques Lacan found a very precise formulation for this principle. In his

advantage brings with it an 'epistemological' disadvantage: *the greater the happiness becomes through ascetic denial, the less it is capable of being experienced as pleasurable.*[33] For that reason, ascetics must project their own happiness outwards, and either locate it in a distant future (as the virtuous do in Spinoza's example) or find it in other people – preferably strangers or foreigners, who are hated and envied for it.[34]

THE ART OF BEARING HAPPINESS

Bertolt Brecht recognized quite precisely that, under certain conditions, happiness owing to the ego-libido that is experienced as displeasure can be greater than manifest, object-libidinal happiness, and that it therefore presents an enticing danger. In his poem, 'Do not let them fool you!', he says:

> Don't let them lure you
> Into exhaustion and duress![35]

Seminar II, he writes: 'In La Rochefoucauld, what is scandalous is not so much that for him self-love is the basis of all human behaviour, but rather, that it is deceiving, inauthentic. There is a hedonism specific to the ego, and which is precisely what lures us, that is, which at one and the same time frustrates us of our immediate pleasure and of the satisfactions which we can draw from our superiority with respect to this pleasure.' Jacques Lacan, *The Ego in Freud's Theory and in the Technique of Psychoanalysis, 1954–1955 (Book II) (The Seminar of Jacques Lacan)*, ed. Jacques-Alain Miller, trans. Sylvana Tomaselli (Cambridge: CUP, 1988), p. 10. See also Sennett, *Fall of Public Man*, p. 8.

33   Lacan's term for this increased desire that is nonetheless experienced as displeasure is 'jouissance', 'enjoyment' – see Jacques Lacan, *The Seminar, Book VII, The Ethics of Psychoanalysis, 1959–60* (London: Routledge, 1992), p. 184. Jouissance lies beyond the symbolic order's pleasure principle. 'Beyond this limit, pleasure becomes pain, and this "painful pleasure" is what Lacan calls jouissance; "jouissance is suffering"', Evans *Introductory Dictionary of Lacanian Psychoanalysis*, p. 92.

34   See also Dolar, who establishes that the basic principle of all racism is: 'The other enjoys at our expense', Mladen Dolar, 'Blut und Boden auf Slowenisch?', interview in *Falter* 30: 91 (1991), p. 18. Compare Jacques-Alain Miller, 'Extimité' in *Lacanian Theory of Discourse*, ed. Mark Bracher, Marshall W. Alcorn, Jr., Ronald J. Corthell and Françoise Massardier-Kenney (New York/London: New York University Press, 1994 (my translation), pp. 79–80.

35   Bertolt Brecht, *Manual of Piety*, trans. Eric Bentley, notes by Hugo Schmidt (New York: Grove Press, 1966), p. 233.

The concept of temptation developed by Brecht in these two lines presents a crucial theoretical discovery. It is the miniature version of an entire theory about happiness, which contrasts a series of common philosophical assumptions. When one is 'tempted' in the sense of this term, one does not give in – as is commonly understood – to a manifest desire or something pleasurable, such as in straying from the path on the way home from school even though your parents have told you not to, when some friendly-seeming stranger appears with candy. According to Brecht, this type of temptation, that of 'becoming weak', would not be nearly as dangerous or damaging in a political sense.

With the type of seduction identified by Brecht, one succumbs to quite different, more powerful forces: a sense of duty, discipline, self-esteem, and so on – the powers of morality, which with the help of ego-libidinal rewards cause people to abandon their pleasure and prefer manifest displeasure (exhaustion and duress). The seduction does not have to do with becoming weak, but with becoming strong.

If people can be seduced into becoming strong, as Brecht sees it, then an immediate conclusion can be drawn from that: there is no direct 'pursuit of happiness'. People do not aspire directly to a gain in pleasure, meaning that they are first inspired by the arduous efforts of culture to direct their activities to a 'higher' aim or social purpose. Instead, the exact opposite is the case: people strive directly for their unhappiness. The most primitive instincts are those orientated on the supposedly 'highest' aims. They are not at all egotistical instincts of self-preservation, but instead strivings dedicated to one's own ideal-ego – precisely those instincts that generously look beyond the actual, real person for the benefit of the ideal, that even willingly go 'over their dead body' for this ideal.

Brecht's theory of seduction thereby concurs with Freud's second drive theory developed in his narcissism essay. The 'ego drives', as Freud remarked, sharply contrast with the self-preservation drives. In that people follow their ego drives, they are not only asocial – *they are not even egotistical* in doing so. The ego drives cause people, as Pascal remarked, to find joy in losing their life, as long as people talk about it.[36]

---

36   See Blaise Pascal, *Pensées* (London/New York: Penguin Books, 1995), pp. 208–9 (§628). Compare Alain, *On Happiness* (New York: Frederick Ungar), p. 126.

For this reason, from 1920 onwards, Freud classified the ego drive as a death drive.[37]

For Brecht, these idealistic, ascetic, and ultimately suicidal strivings are what is actually primitive, barbaric. People follow them directly; it takes arduous cultural efforts to sway people to be pleased with their happiness and bear it – to be happy. The 'being fooled' that Brecht speaks of causes people to fall behind this level worked out by culture, and direct all of their energy towards their ideal ego, as though their happiness were found there. Barbaric 'regression' is evident in the striving for ideals.

Brecht tried to use the weapons of culture against this barbarism present in all idealism. His insistence on the theme of happiness in literature corresponds with the logic that also brought philosophers, such as Spinoza, to declare happiness philosophy's main issue. An art of happiness, as formulated in a great number of Brecht's poems, is therefore a theoretical undertaking, just like the ethics of Spinoza,[38] which necessarily opposes all idealism and all morality. The art of happiness, like ethics, helps to resist 'being fooled' in the Brechtian sense: it is the compilation of efforts necessary to bear happiness.

THE NON-PLEASURABLE SEXUALITY OF THE FAITHFUL: FROM FREUD AND REICH TO FOUCAULT

Building on Freud's theory of the behaviour of the ego-libido and object-libido – as well as on Reich's subsequent theory of the unconscious, neurotic pleasure in reactionary emotions – it is possible to bridge the gap to Foucault's theory of the history of sexuality. The opposition that Foucault saw in his own theories to those of Wilhelm Reich thus dissolves: when Reich's position is understood as more than simply the violent *Unterdrückung* ('forceful oppression') of sexuality, and instead as a theory of its *Verdrängung* (psychic 'repression'),[39] then it is possible to develop from it precisely those theses that Foucault used to criticize it.

---

37   See Freud, 'Beyond the Pleasure Principle', pp. 44, 52–3.

38   See also Deleuze, *Spinoza*, pp. 27ff.

39   Freud himself distinguishes between 'oppression' (*Unterdrückung*) and 'repression' (*Verdrängung*) even with regard to psychic life. Compare Freud, 'Psychoanalysis and Telepathy' (SE XVIII).

Foucault's position consisted in showing that sexuality (particularly in post-1968 Western societies) in no way met with violent repression, but instead with a fashion of general talkativeness, an 'incitement to discourse'.[40] Rather than violence aimed at sexuality, the means that turned sexuality into a field occupied by power was speaking about it. This, too, can be derived from Reich's theory. Reich's claimed shift from object-libido to ego-libido generated by the reactionary ideologies causes exactly the same thing that Foucault sees. When the ego-libido becomes the definitive good, privileged over the object-libido, then desire arises not only to have sex, but also to be *the subject of one's own sexuality*. There is then a transition from a sexuality organized according to the form of belief to one that reveals the form of faith. In the same way people suddenly have to declare themselves the owners of their illusions due to the changes in the reigning form of ideology, they also suddenly have to *confess to their sexuality*. This transition from belief sexuality to faith sexuality causes the general modus of discourse that Foucault detected. Nonetheless (and Foucault's analysis of this was not precise enough), it has a very definite way of speaking: namely, the confession.

And it is this certain way of speaking about sexuality that turns the pleasure of the confessor into something that is unconscious and not pleasurable. As Foucault correctly determined, faith sexuality, in which everyone has to profess what they are and what they want, proves to be joyless – because the confession form does not allow for any conscious pleasure. However, it is not the omnipresent, imposed talk about sex as such, and also not the discourse form of knowledge about sex, that lead, as Foucault believed, to an unappealing heteronomy and inflation,[41] but, instead, the fact that the general talk here (especially prevalent in prudish cultures[42]) is of quite a specific type – namely, a confessional one: a language game in which, contrary to

---

40   See Foucault, *The History of Sexuality, Vol. 1: An Introduction* (New York: Vintage, 1990), pp. 17ff.

41   Greek antiquity was not shamefully silent about these matters – as Foucault's own examples show – and still did not bring about any compulsions to sexual confession.

42   Benvenuto quite precisely describes and analyzes the compulsive, immediate declaration of one's sexual orientation, which is widespread in the US, and the subsequent exclusive life in the appropriate, corresponding ghetto. See his 'Der amerikanische Cocktail'.

many other forms of speaking, subjects are generated and ego-libido accumulated. Confession puts sexuality into a relationship with an ego ideal.[43] The libido-economy is also thereby reorientated so that the latent desire for displeasure becomes the only possible and sought-after experience of desire/pleasure.

It thus seems that, just as belief presents the criterion for the excessive, manifest pleasure of perversions, faith is the criterion for the even more excessive, but latent pleasure of neuroses. Illusions without owners generate cultural desire; the appropriation of illusions through confession, on the contrary, generates the 'gain from illness'[44] of neurotic displeasure.

Ultimately, that is also the mechanism through which political power uses sexuality for its own purposes: as Reich showed, only in a faith-based sexuality are individuals sexually susceptible to the unpleasurable measures of repression, limitation and denial. Only then do they allow themselves to 'be fooled' in a Brechtian sense; only under these conditions are they inclined to barbarism – to preferring self-esteem over pleasure.

---

43   Hughes, quite correctly, recognizes this when he writes: 'The self is now the sacred cow of American culture, self-esteem is sacrosanct' (Hughes, *Culture of Complaint*, p. 7).

44   See Freud, 'The Ego and the Id' (SE XIX); and 'The Economic Problem of Masochism' (SE XIX), p. 166.

CHAPTER EIGHT

Happiness: Happiness and Its Obstacles – One's Own Illusions

Sigmund Freud's second drive theory, formulated in 1914, differentiates between object-libido and ego-libido, and assumes permeability between the two. This seems like an appropriate instrument for understanding the paradoxical phenomenon of the masses agreeing to politics that aggrieve them. Freud's theory allows us to understand those apparently unpleasurable experiences of anger, hatred, jealousy, fear, shame, disgust, and so on, which seize reactionary masses as 'neurotic unpleasure', and show that there is concealed, repressed pleasure to be found in them.

People thus gain something from these apparent losses: and just as there is (according to Freud) a 'gain from illness', there is also a 'gain from subjugation'. The experiences of displeasure, which neurotics as well as reactionaries affirm and support, provide latent pleasure. The manifest displeasure that is experienced is therefore of a neurotic sort – a pleasure that appears in the guise of its opposite. In this repressed pleasure, we are able to recognize why people welcome manifest experiences of displeasure, desire their oppression, and – like analysands at a certain stage of analysis – protect their misery from every attempt to free them from it. The unconsciously experienced pleasure is defended as a treasure, but experienced manifestly as displeasure.

This incapacity for happiness found in reactionaries and neurotics can be explained by the specific way that it is accommodated (or stored). Pleasure that is manifestly experienced as displeasure is stored as ego-libido. It is therefore orientated towards self-esteem and not towards delight in objects. This storing of libido in the ego has a decisive advantage: there, libido grows, whereas with the love of objects it is regularly decathected – that is, depleted. The fact that a certain amount of libido is invested in one's own ideal-ego and not in objects means, however, that it loses its ability to be consciously experienced as pleasure. Whenever a surplus is present, it is no longer possible to experience all of the pleasure as pleasurable.

This conception of drives or instincts laid out by Freud seems suitable for explaining the paradox of the willingly victimized, reactionary masses. From 1920 onwards – impressed by the phenomena of trauma and compulsive repetition, which transgressed the homeostasis of the pleasure principle – Freud modified his theory in favour of a dualism of Eros and the death drive, yet the 1914 theory delivers decisive clues with regard to the phenomena that interest us, and we might also be able to use it to explain those phenomena that led Freud to assume the presence of a death drive.[1]

Through his discovery that we not only have thoughts that escape our awareness, but also feelings of pleasure that we experience as unpleasurable, and with the thesis that the storing (accommodation) of the feelings of pleasure in the object-ego is the reason for the loss of their ability to be experienced as pleasure, Freud established the prerequisites necessary for examining a theoretical topic that had eluded philosophy in a rather peculiar way for quite some time: happiness.

HAPPINESS: PHILOSOPHY'S FLEETING
TOPIC AND STEADFAST NON-TOPIC

A good part of philosophy begins with the question of happiness and the life that one must lead to experience it. Happiness thus often appears to be the only subject worthy of contemplation. Sextus Empiricus, for example, remarked: 'According to some people the Cyrenaics too endorsed the ethical branch of philosophy only, and dismissed the physical and logical branches as contributing nothing to a happy life.'[2] Nonetheless, philosophy quite abruptly lost sight of its main topic. Rather than *Seinsvergessenheit* ('oblivion of being'), from the end of the eighteenth century until long into the twentieth,

---

1   Especially since, as Freud remarked, the ego-libido also has effects that go beyond the pleasure principle. See, for example, Freud, 'Mourning and Melancholia' (SE XIV), pp. 246, 248, 257–8.

2   Sextus Empiricus, *Against the Professors*, 7, II – quoted from Voula Tsouna, *The Epistemology of the Cyrenaic School* (Cambridge: CUP, 1998), p. 156. See also Epicurus: 'Vain is the word of a philosopher which does not heal any suffering of man. For just as there is no profit in medicine if it does not expel the diseases of the body, so there is no profit in philosophy either, if it does not expel the suffering of the mind.' Epicurus, *The Extant Remains* (Oxford: Clarendon Press, 1926), p. 133 (*Fragments*, 54).

philosophy seems to have been shaped by *Glücksvergessenheit* ('oblivion of happiness').[3]

This remarkable loss of a previously central topic corresponds with blindness in relation to a certain concept – that of imagination. As I would like to show in what follows, this is no accidental connection. Appropriating imagination, making it one's own – that is, faith – builds up an obstacle against happiness. The loss of the concept of imagination subsequently makes it impossible to treat happiness theoretically. A philosophy incapable of posing the question of happiness is unable to do so because it no longer has a concept of imagination. And it no longer has one because philosophy has itself apparently become a part of its object – because it has begun to place itself at the service of imagination, as faith.

IMAGINATION: A FACULTY OF COGNITION AND
SOURCE OF NARCISSISTIC PLEASURE

Remarkably, for quite some time the concept of imagination seemed relevant only in connection with cognition, particularly in the philosophical tradition of the German-speaking realm. Imagination is, accordingly, the 'form of all possible knowledge'; it is that which constitutes, a priori, the formal knowledge of all objects,[4] serving as an expansion and systematic ordering of scientific knowledge, or what is produced when (thanks to the reproductive quality of imagination) ideas are brought together repeatedly and in new combinations.[5]

Imagination is thus the repetition of a past idea, the expansion of a current one, or the invention, through a new combination of existing elements, of an idea that had not been present before. The

---

3   We can quickly round up the few authors who, in the first half of the twentieth century, present an exception to this rule: Alain, Ludwig Marcuse, Sigmund Freud and Bertolt Brecht. A return to active philosophical research in this area has appeared only recently. See Holmer Steinfath, ed., *Was ist ein gutes Leben? Philosophische Reflexionen* (Frankfurt: Suhrkamp, 1998); Ursula Wolf, *Die Philosophie und die Frage nach dem guten Leben* (Reinbek: Rowohlt, 1999); Fulvia de Luise and Giuseppe Farinetti, *Storia della felicità. Gli antichi e i moderni* (Turin: Einaudi, 2001).

4   See Immanuel Kant, *Critique of Pure Reason*, A 124.

5   See J. H. Trede and K. Homann 'Einbildung, Einbildungskraft', in J. Ritter, ed., *Historisches Wörterbuch der Philosophie* (Basel/Stuttgart: Schwabe & Co., 1972); compare Jean Starobinski, 'Grundlinien für eine Geschichte des Begriffs der Einbildungskraft', in *Psychoanalyse und Literatur* (Frankfurt: Suhrkamp, 1990).

ingeniousness at work here fulfils exclusively those functions that serve the knowledge of the world: at most, perhaps, it exaggerates a bit, carries it to excess, feigns a little too heavily, and thus makes sure that we – in accordance with Engels's formulation – imagine all possible things and some others as well.[6]

But this understanding does not examine the concept of whether imagination does more than simply supplement the possible *objects*. The question is never posed of whether it might also add something on the side of the knowing *subject*, and whether this subject expansion might not possibly be its decisive, driving function. Imagination would, accordingly, not only be the idea of an object, where in truth another object, none, or too little of one is available. It would, most of all, also be the idea of a subject where in truth a different one, none, or too little of one is available. This idea of a subject, according to our terminology, would be imagination in the form of one's own illusion – an illusion with a subject, a faith.

That is the precise meaning of the term 'imagination' in certain earlier philosophical traditions – for example, for Spinoza, Blaise Pascal, or the ancient philosophers of happiness. For them, the question of the imagination has an entirely different meaning that is no longer restricted to the area of epistemology. An imagination that adds not only to the idea of the object, but also to that of the subject, fulfils not only a theoretical, but predominantly a practical function. Imagination in the form of one's own illusion is a source of pleasure. Since the completion it achieves refers to an ideal of the ego, and thereby to the accumulation of ego-libido, the pleasure that it produces is primarily a pleasure experienced as displeasure.

Imagination produces the idea of freedom, for example, where knowledge of the real causes of freedom is missing.[7] It thereby not only supplements an object – for example, the process of causality in the external world – but at the same time allows an image of a subject to emerge, which evokes favour thanks to an alleged autonomy. This idea of autonomy and its libidinal power of attraction initiate what La

---

6   See Friedrich Engels, *Herrn Eugen Dührings Umwälzung der Wissenschaft*, (Moskau: Verlag für fremdsprachige Literatur, 1946), p. 407. See also Friedrich Nietzsche, 'Jenseits von Gut und Böse. Vorspiel einer Philosophie der Zukunft', in id., *Werke, Bd. III* (Frankfurt/Berlin/Wien: Ullstein, 1984 [1885]), p. 96.

7   See Spinoza, 'Ethics II', Proposition 35, n., pp. 108–9: 'Their idea of freedom, therefore, is simply their ignorance of any cause for their actions.'

Rochefoucauld and Pascal identify as 'self-esteem' (*amour-propre*),[8] and Pascal and Spinoza as 'pride' (French: *superbe*, Latin: *superbia*).[9] Imagination as the completion of the idea of the subject generates an excess of subject experience that is connected with strong, ego-libidinal affects.

But these affects – self-esteem and pride – lead to 'sad passions', to displeasure in the form of anger, fervour, fear, ambition, guilt, obstinacy, and the like. For the sake of its supposedly most intimate self, the subject undertakes a series of activities that in truth are entirely heteronomous activities associated with such strong and unpleasurable affects. The subject becomes furious (with the illusion of freedom), speaks without wanting to (with the illusion of freedom), or joins the army to 'show' those who mean well.[10] The less a subject acts from the necessity of his or her own nature, the more bitterly he or she holds on to the illusion of self-determination and pursues his or her own heteronomy simply for the sake of 'proving' it to be autonomy.

The ancient philosophies of happiness also saw the reason for unhappiness in an imagination that leads to an upleasurable experience of pleasure. The Cyrenian school, as well as the Cynical, Stoical, and Epicurean schools and the school of philosophical Scepticism (Pyrrhonism), were concerned with developing techniques – 'techniques of living' or 'expertise in living'[11] – to help fight and avoid those experiences of displeasure that arise because of an ego-libidinal imagination. This imagination must be fought to prevent the transformation that it causes – of pleasure into displeasure. These techniques should help, not necessarily to prevent every emotion, but to prevent

---

8   See François de la Rochefoucauld, *Réfléxions ou Sentences et maximes morales* (Paris: Garnier, 1954), p. 43 (CCXXXV); Pascal, *Pensées* (trans. Krailsheimer), p. 324: 'The nature of self-love and of this human self is to love only self and consider only self.' Like Lacan, Pascal identifies the term 'moi' with that of the 'deliberate self-delusion' (ibid.).

9   See Pascal, *Pensées*, p. 63; Spinoza, 'Ethics IV', Proposition 57, pp. 225–6.

10   See Spinoza 'Ethics IV', Appendix 13, p. 239: '[B]oys or youths, who cannot peaceably endure the chidings of their parents, will enlist as soldiers and choose the hardships of war and the despotic discipline in preference to the comforts of home and the admonitions of their father: suffering any burden to be put upon them, so long as they might spite their parents.'

11   See Sextus Empiricus, *Outlines of Scepticism* (Cambridge et al.: Cambridge University Press, 2000), p. 213 (section 270); compare Hossenfelder, *Antike Glückslehren*, p. 353. Freud, too, used this term in 'Civilization and Its Discontents', p. 82.

imagination's transformation of pleasure into displeasure. It is therefore a misunderstanding in the interpretation of these philosophies of happiness to characterize them as ascetic schools, or to interpret their hedonism as merely a defensive manoeuvre to avoid displeasure.[12]

For the ancient school, the problem of pleasure is an 'epistemological' one and not an 'ontological' one, just as it is for Spinoza.[13] Pleasure is always there;[14] the question is simply that of *whether one succeeds in experiencing it as pleasurable*. The 'prevention' of displeasure therefore does not lead to a passive, ascetic zero state. The Epicurean and Pyrrhonian 'ataraxy' (imperturbedness), the Pyrrhonian 'epoche' (reservation, suspension of judgment), and the Cynical and Stoical 'apathy' (freedom from affect)[15] are not the unfortunate results of an eradication of the sensual and emotional, which has killed off all pleasure along with every displeasure and renders the best of life as a sort of premature rigor mortis.[16]

---

12   On the characteristic of 'negative hedonism', see Herbert Marcuse 'Hedonism' (1938), in *Negations: Essays in Critical Theory*, trans. Jeremy J. Shapiro (Boston: Beacon Press, 1968), p. 138; Hossenfelder, *Antike Glückslehren*, p. 165.

13   See the discussion on Spinoza 'Ethics V', Proposition 42 in Chapter 7, above.

14   See also, for example, the Epicurean thesis of the permanent availability of pleasure (Hossenfelder, *Antike Glückslehren*, p. 170). Only in this way is it comprehensible that Epicurus can exclude a zero state and is able to advocate the thesis that the lack of unpleasure is pleasure (Epicurus, *Letter to Menoceus*, 128, in Epicurus, *The Extant Remains*, p. 87). Because pleasure is always there, and because it can only be experienced in one way (pleasurable) or the other (unpleasurable), this zero state does not exist.

15   See Hossenfelder, *Antike Glückslehren*, p. xix; Georg Luck, *Die Weisheit der Hunde: Texte der antiken Kyniker in deutscher Übersetzung mit Erläuterungen* (Stuttgart: Kröner 1997), p. 20.

16   This should also be held against the assertions, capable of being misunderstood, that are made by the cynical and stoical epigones themselves – for example, against Seneca, who remarks: 'It has often been disputed, whether it were better to have moderate affections, or none at all. We *Stoics* are for discarding them entirely; the *Peripatetics* are satisfied with moderating or governing them.' Seneca, Epist. CXVI, See Hossenfelder, *Antike Glückslehren*, p. 80. The much later successor, Alain, seems to be far closer to the ideas of the founder when he writes: 'The famous stoics have perhaps been misunderstood, as if they had taught us only how to resist a tyrant and how to face torture bravely' (Alain, *On Happiness*, p. 178). For that reason, Alain constantly insists on the Stoical principle, 'Suppress false ideas, and you suppress evil' (ibid., pp. 175, 190). Against Herbert Marcuse's theory of Epicurus's negative hedonism, see Ludwig Marcuse, who states that Epicurus never renounced happiness, but only renounced things for the sake of happiness. Ludwig Marcuse, *Philosophie des Glücks. Von Hiob bis Freud* (Zürich: Diogenes, 1972), p. 62: 'Epikur ist groß gewesen im

The ancient philosophies of happiness did not want simply to avoid displeasure, but instead to convert it back into pleasure. For this reason, the avoidance of displeasure, according to this school, includes all of the active measures that serve to transform the unpleasurable experience of pleasure into a pleasurable one. And the reason why pleasure is experienced as displeasure is found in imagination. Thus, it is necessary to dismantle imagination to transform displeasure back into pleasure. For that reason, the theoretical efforts of the ancient philosophies aiming at the development of theories and techniques to create happiness were dedicated to dissolving imagination.

Thus, according to the ancient philosophies of happiness, imagination is the main problem associated with displeasure – the only cause of displeasure worthy of the name. Natural misfortune seems marginal and easily endurable in comparison with that artificial unhappiness that captures people because they fabricate an imagination of natural misfortune. In any case, however, regardless of the extent of unhappiness that they cause, these two types of causes of unhappiness – the natural and the imagined – must be neatly separated from one another, because their effects overlap and might possibly add together into a seemingly single, unavoidable overall affect. The physician and Pyrrhonian philosopher Sextus Empiricus must have known this, since he dealt with both forms of unhappiness, natural and imagined: 'For he who has no additional belief about pain being an evil is merely affected by the necessitated motion of the pain; but he who imagines in addition that the pain is objectionable only, that it is evil only, doubles by this belief the distress which results from its presence.'[17] The fact that the two forms of malaise might have separate causes is evident in that they occasionally appear separately. Sextus Empiricus has a beautiful and

---

Verzichten – und nie ein Verehrer des Verzichts. Er verzichtete nicht auf Glück – sondern um des Glücks willen.' It seems characteristic that the radical ascetics among the adherents of Cynicism and Stoicism primarily emerge in the later, Roman periods – at a time when these philosophies were already represented by emperors, such as Julian and Marcus Aurelius (see also Luck 1997, p. 20). The new, ascetic orientation was probably an effect of the social advancement of these philosophies.

17   Sextus Empiricus, 'Against the Ethicists', 158, in Sextus Empiricus, *Against the Physicists, Against the Ethicists*, with trans. by R. G. Bury (Cambridge, MA/London: Harvard University Press), p. 461.

clear example of this:

> For do we not observe frequently how, in the case of those who are being cut, the patient who is being cut manfully endures the torture of the cutting –
> His fair hue palling not, nor from his cheeks
> Wiping the tears away [Homer, Odyss. xi. 529 ff.] – because he is affected only by the motion due to the cutting; whereas the man who stands beside him, as soon as he sees a small flow of blood, at once grows pale, trembles, gets in a great sweat, feels faint, and finally falls down speechless, not because of the pain (for it is not present with him), but because of the belief he has about pain being an evil?[18]

Natural displeasure and the corresponding imagined displeasure can thus be found separately in two different people. At the same time, this example provides evidence that the person affected by the imagined displeasure will be much more strongly afflicted by the displeasure than the one who is simply exposed to natural displeasure.

Consequently, it is not pleasure that must be controlled and tamed, as is sometimes claimed.[19] The ancient philosophies of happiness are certainly efforts at moderation, but not primarily the moderation of pleasure. Instead, what must be controlled and moderated is imagination. Such an imagination might, in some cases, also be imagination of enjoyment or the possibility of its 'accumulation'.[20] But precisely then, imagination usually contradicts actual enjoyment: it tears away from enjoyment (under the pretence of a greater, future enjoyment), induces its deferral, and inadvertently develops – usually unnoticed – an enjoyment of the deferral.[21]

---

18   Sextus Empiricus, 'Against the Ethicists', 159–60, in ibid., p. 463. The quote within the text is from Homer's *Odyssey*, II, 529. On this passage, see also the beautiful illustration in Alain, *On Happiness*, p. 21.

19   Even appeals for the control of pleasure already present answers to a general dread of pleasure – for example, when Aristippus states that to be the master of pleasures means not to refrain from them but to enjoy them without being at their mercy, just as to be master of a ship or a horse does not mean to make no use of it but to guide it where one will. Compare William Keith Chambers Guthrie, *A History of Greek Philosophy, Vol. 3: The Fifth-Century Enlightenment* (Cambridge: CUP, 1969), p. 495; Hossenfelder, *Antike Glückslehren*, p. 50.

20   Aristippus, in Diogenes Laertius, *Lives of Eminent Philosophers*, book 2, chapter 8, section 90, quoted in Hossenfelder, *Antike Glückslehren*, p. 49.

21   For that reason, Aristippus privileged distinct pleasures over happiness

The philosophical call for moderation is thus not a call for the moderation of enjoyment, but often precisely for the moderation of relinquishment. Epicurus, for example, remarked: 'There is also a limit in simple living. He who fails to heed this limit falls into an error as great as that of the man who gives way to extravagance.'[22] The ancient philosophies of happiness thus regularly deliver a critique of imagination, a critique of those 'mere opinions, to which are due the greatest disturbance of the spirit.'[23] They work primarily on the control of such imagination and of these opinions with the help of 'techniques of living'. The *control* is aimed at the imagination; the *moderation*, just as much at renunciation as at enjoyment.

MISGUIDED 'CARE OF THE SELF': FOUCAULT'S MISUNDERSTANDING

It seems important to emphasize one point in order to avoid a grave misunderstanding. In his history of sexuality, Michel Foucault highlighted both the concept of mastery (*enkrateia*) and that of moderation, which implies soundness of mind and prudence (*sophrosyne*), as key concepts of the entire ancient ethical line of questioning.[24] Yet, as a result, Foucault interpreted these concepts, following a Platonic–Socratic tradition, as concepts of an ethics of self-mastery,[25] invoking an agonistic 'relationship' of the subject 'with oneself',[26] a ' "polemical" attitude with respect to oneself', which tended towards a result 'that was quite naturally expressed as victory',[27] and leads to the achievement of 'freedom'.[28]

Without making any differentiation – or even considering Epicureanism and Pyrrhonian Scepticism – Foucault assigns these figures taken from the Platonic–Socratic tradition to the

---

– that is, 'a number of particular pleasures'. See Diogenes Laertius, ibid., section 87, quoted in Hossenfelder, ibid., 48.

22   Epicurus, Vatican Sayings, 63, in Epicurus, *The Extant Remains*, p. 117.

23   Epicurus, Letter to Menoeceus, 132, in Epicurus, *The Extant Remains*, p. 89–91.

24   See Foucault, *History of Sexuality, Vol. 1*, p. 63.

25   See Plato, *Gorgias*, 491d; Michel Foucault, *The History of Sexuality, Vol. 2: The Use of Pleasure* (New York: Vintage, 1990), p. 68.

26   Foucault, *History of Sexuality, Vol. 1*, p. 67.

27   Ibid., pp. 69–70.

28   Ibid., p. 92.

argumentation of the Cyrenean school, Cynicism, and Stoicism. He
thereby comes to the final conclusion that there would have been a
long prehistory of 'care of the self' reaching back to classical antiquity. The later-emerging Christian forms of the 'relationship to the
self' would have been built upon this universal, ancient problem of
care of the self.[29] There would thus be no epistemological break
between the 'interiority of Christian morality' and the 'exteriority of
a pagan morality'. Foucault here disavows the difference between the
line of questioning of an external, quasi-medicinal 'ethics' and a
'morality' that argues in terms of inwardness, which Deleuze has
worked out so precisely.[30] Foucault writes: 'The evolution that
occurred – quite slowly at that – between paganism and Christianity
did not consist in an interiorization of rules, acts, and transgressions; rather it carried out a restructuration of the forms of
self-relationship and a transformation of the practices and techniques on which this relationship was based.'[31] It seems that Foucault
has failed here to recognize the meaning of the ancient line of
inquiry into happiness, as well as its stark differentiation from the
Christian (as well as possibly the Socratic or Platonic) problematic.

For the Cyreneans, Cynics, Stoics, Epicureans and Pyrrhonians,
the idea was never mastery of the self, but instead the control of imagination. If the term 'mastery' is understood as self-mastery, as Foucault
implies, and is related to two parts of the same soul – for example, in
accordance with Plato's picture of the chariot drawn by the two
dissimilar horses[32] – then this misses the way in which the crucial
question of a philosophy of happiness has to be approached; it even
leads to betting on the wrong horse. In no way do the philosophies of
happiness mean to say that the nobler horse must exercise control
over the unruly one. On the contrary, what must be fought against is
precisely the illusion that such a noble horse exists and deserves to be
supported in its claim to mastery.

For all imagination is, as we have seen, ultimately the illusion of
such a noble horse, an ideal ego. For this reason, in the view of the

29   See especially ibid., p. 84; compare Wilhelm Schmid, *Die Geburt der
Philosophie im Garten der Lüste. Michel Foucaults Archäologie des platonischen Eros*
(Frankfurt: Fischer, 1994), p. 29.

30   See Deleuze, *Spinoza*, pp. 27ff.

31   Foucault, *History of Sexuality*, Vol. 1, p. 63.

32   See Plato, *Phaedrus* 246a; and see Foucault, *History of Sexuality*, Vol. 1, p. 67.

ancient philosophies of happiness, it is necessary to proceed against imagination: for every imagination transforms pleasure into displeasure in that it subjects it to an ideal and attempts to accumulate it at this psychic location.[33] *Pace* Foucault, for the ancient philosophies of happiness, *control* never meant self-mastery, but instead always control over imagination – including mastery over the fabrication of fictions of oneself. And *moderation* is a tempering of the desire to be something better.

Through his disregard of the ancient confrontation with the problem of imagination and his partiality for the 'care of the self' and self-mastery, it seems that Foucault not only missed the goals of the argumentation of the ancient philosophies of happiness, but also – which is even worse – supported the aims of contemporary narcissism, which, as Richard Sennett remarked, drives major portions of Western society into a self-referentiality that makes it largely incapable of pleasure. For narcissism possesses 'the double quality of being a voracious absorption in self needs and the block to their fulfillment'.[34] Foucault's philosophy of care of the self thus appears as part of the imagination of which the ancient philosophies wanted to cure people.

The narcissistic ego-libidinal aspect, which is considered within the concept of imagination used by the ancient philosophies of happiness (and by early modern philosophers such as Spinoza, Pascal and La Rochefoucauld), must therefore be taken into consideration in order to understand why it is so necessary to combat imagination – and, along with it, the ideal ego – to arrive at happiness. This is the only way to dissolve the 'sad passions' caused by the accumulation of ego-libido. Only by combating self-enamoured imagination can displeasure again be turned back into pleasure. A passage from Alain about the Stoic Epictetus can perhaps demonstrate this. It shows that the Stoics – who like the Cynics were most liable to arouse suspicions of ascetic self-control and pleasure-killing philosophies – dedicated their attention instead to pleasure experienced unpleasurably as a result of imagination. Epictetus says to the passenger on a ship, frozen

---

33 Based in the economy of the libido, this is why the current fashionable practices of 'care of the self' are not only egotistical, but also ascetic despite all supposed hedonism: they are fixated on an ideal ego, thus transferring libido from objects to the ego and thereby transforming them into displeasure.

34 Sennett, *The Fall of Public Man*, p. 8.

by fear during a storm: 'You are afraid of this storm, as if you were going to have to swallow the whole vast sea; but, my dear sir, it would take only a quart of water to drown you.'[35]

A peculiar consolation, one might think. Nonetheless, this philosophical intervention might have shaken the seafarer out of his fear. Why do people go numb with fear, rendered incapable of doing anything but staring spellbound at the danger that threatens them? This imagination, too, which has indeed made several additions to the object from which the threat emanates,[36] has a subjective side. It also complements the subject: imagination makes the subject a tragic hero who, in line with his or her fate, is faced with the admirable task of drinking an entire ocean. The reason for staring at the stormy sea is not the exaggerated imagination of danger that emanates from an object, but rather the narcissistic pleasure – experienced as unpleasurable – that is associated with the tragic hero's self-image.[37] Cutting down this hero quite harshly to an entirely banal, pathetic, one-quart-drowned person would thus be an efficient means of tearing them out of their egotistical fascination, – thereby lifting the spell of anxiety and transforming it into ordinary fear.[38]

PASCAL'S ADVICE: HOW ONE'S OWN ILLUSION CAN BE CURED WITH THE HELP OF THE ILLUSION OF OTHERS

Imagination, as understood by the ancient philosophies of happiness, corresponds with what Octave Mannoni identified as *foi* ('faith'): it includes a reference to an ideal ego, and ego-libido is accumulated in it, which is why people cannot let go of it even if this illusion and its objects are experienced as utterly unpleasant. In an imagination grasped in this way, not only is an overblown object

---

35   Alain, *On Happiness*, p. 175.

36   See also ibid., p. 176: '[A]nd this fear is worse than the injury'.

37   Evidence for this interpretation is the fact that Epictetus's intervention, even if it is perhaps paradoxical and baffling, nevertheless seems funny. There is an effort of cathexis that is made redundant by the intervention, and can now be decathected through laughter. This effort of cathexis is the one tied with the maintenance of the illusion of the tragic ideal ego. Epictetus's paradoxical intervention can be compared with that of Joad in Racine's *Athalie*, who answers the terrors of reality with the even greater terror of a fear of God (see Section 3, on p. 84ff, above).

38   For the difference between anxiety and fear see Sigmund Freud, *Beyond the Pleasure Principle*, p. 12.

depicted, but also an exaggerated subject; imagination thereby fulfils more of a practical, subject-related function than a theoretical, object-related one – namely, that of enabling narcissistic self-esteem. Imagination generates 'pride' in the sense used by Spinoza and Pascal.

The opposite of imagination is what Mannoni identifies as *croyance*, and what I have described as 'belief', the 'illusion without an owner', or the 'illusion of the other'. This illusion of the other resists imagination (faith). It prevents the reference to an ideal ego, in that it undermines all possible ideals. It produces an illusion, but not without putting it at a distance through better knowledge, and does so to generate both contempt and self-contempt in its bearers. Self-contempt in the illusion of others resists the self-esteem that characterizes imagination.

For this reason, the illusion of the other forms the foundation for a series of techniques for happiness. With the help of the illusion of the other, it is possible to elude the unhappiness that is caused by imagination. Through techniques that rest on the principle of the suspended illusion, it is possible to oust unpleasurable states deriving from imagination and the reference to an ideal ego. The illusion of the other functions thereby as more than just an alternative ideological principle alongside that of belief: it is *the principle of dismantling* those unpleasurable tensions caused by imagination – the illusion in the form of faith.

Blaise Pascal, like the ancient philosophers of happiness, recognized such techniques of dismantling and techniques of living that rest on the illusion of the other, and often suggested them, in connection with religion, to the imaginary conversation partners in his texts. Here we can see that the 'care of the self' and the corresponding 'control of the self' were not the central themes of ancient ethics – nor were they always the dominant questions addressed by Christian thinkers, as Foucault believed. The Christian philosopher Pascal, like the Stoics in their theory of unhappiness, did not characterize the lack of self-control as the central problem, but instead exorbitant imagination (and the arrogance that it causes).

Similar to the way that the Stoic Epictetus acts vis-à-vis the seafarers frozen in fear, Pascal intervenes when confronted with a religious person who is numb with an unpleasurable lack of belief. Pascal attempts then to disperse the subject-oriented side of this imagination – the narcissistic pleasure of one's own ideal ego hidden within it.

Thus, in response to someone who complains of not being able to hold any religious belief, Pascal remarks, 'But at least realize that your inability to believe, since reason urges you to do so and yet you cannot, arises from your passions . . . So concentrate not on convincing yourself by increasing the number of proofs of God, but on diminishing your passions.'[39]

The goal, then, is 'diminishing' and not 'increasing'. The difficulty consists not in too little of something, but in too much. It is not found at the theoretical, cognitive level, as perhaps is believed by the agnostic that Pascal bemoans. The problem of the agnostic's lack of belief does not derive from a lack of 'proof'. Instead, it can be found at the practical, affective level, at that of the 'passions': it consists in an *excess* of 'passions'. Although he presumably has a great number of theoretical arguments to hand, the patient does not seem capable of believing. He draws a great deal of self-esteem precisely from the discord between his theological knowledge and his atheistic position. This forms the affective obstacle. Concealed there is the 'gain of illness', the unnoticed enjoyment. Because the agnostic is utterly pleased with himself in the pose of his being 'unfortunately-not-a-Christian-believer', he cannot believe.

Like the happiness-seekers in Brecht's verse,[40] the agnostic who looks for even better proof is also running in the wrong direction. For him, happiness seems to be somewhere 'ahead', in the direction of his search for proofs. Yet the proofs only help to strengthen his self-esteem and elevate that unacknowledged pleasure he finds in himself when, in defiance, he stands by his lack of belief and refuses to be comforted. The agnostic thus battles, as Pascal could say in Spinoza's words, for his religious unhappiness as though it were his happiness.

The fact that Pascal, unlike Spinoza, situated this happiness in religious belief might seem rather strange. Yet that should not obscure the fact that Pascal dealt with the entire issue of religion from the perspective of happiness, and therefore conceived of the relationship between happiness and unhappiness in quite an unusual and interesting way. Entirely contrary to the common, mainstream way of conceiving this relationship – not only in Christian philosophy, but

---

39   Pascal, *Pensées* (trans. Krailsheimer), p. 155.

40   'Denn alle rennen nach dem Glück / Das Glück rennt hinterher.' ('For all chase after happiness / It chases them everywhere.') Bertolt Brecht, *Die Gedichte von Bertolt Brecht in einem Band* (Frankfurt: Suhrkamp, 1984), p. 1,118.

also in the atheistic Enlightenment philosophy that followed (which was often just as much of an ego-strengthening philosophy as was Christian philosophy) – for Pascal, religious happiness did not lie 'ahead', in the direction of greater knowledge, more cogent proof, greater self-esteem, or more self-control. Instead, such happiness has long been running behind, chasing after those who seek it.

The solution is therefore found in the opposite direction: not in the direction of 'increasing', but in that of 'diminishing'; not in the direction of *knowledge accumulation* – for, along with knowledge, self-esteem always secretly increases, and cognitive improvement strengthens the affective obstacle – but, instead, in the *dismantling of self-esteem*, in measures against imagination. The pleasure that is not experienced as pleasurable, which has accumulated in the self-esteem of the unbelievers, must be worked on with measures that belong to the ranks of the *illusion of the others*. Pascal therefore suggests several – at first glance startlingly simple – measures:

> You want to find faith and do not know the way? You want to cure yourself of unbelief and you ask for the remedies? Learn from those who have been bound like you . . . Follow the way by which they began; by behaving just as if they believed, taking holy water, having masses said, etc. That will make you believe quite naturally, and will humiliate your understanding.[41]

Rather than suggesting a deepening of theological intensification, he suggests an exercise in superficiality. The candidate should simply act 'as though' he believes, and the problem – more precisely, his problem – will thereby be solved. A small, playful, theatrical performance of religious conviction will help to precipitate this conviction – whereas, on the contrary, convincing oneself by means of proof is seen as an impediment. Belief must be acted out for some undetermined other; as in other instances of the illusion of others, in this case, too, belief is dealt with as purely an export good. The question of one's own needs, on the other hand, does not play any role: Pascal does not touch upon whether the patient also 'really' believes, 'himself', and even considers such questions to be misleading.

This utterly paradoxical and practically heretical-seeming

---

41   Compare Pascal, *Pensées*, pp. 155–6.

'theatrical theory' on the formation of religious belief remains necessarily incomprehensible when not understood against the backdrop of an affective theory. The situation in which a spokes-person for religion carries out their duty by attempting to spread the advice to 'dumb-down' ('cela vous fera croire et vous abêtira'[42]), and express the 'humility of reason', must cause religious people to wonder and the non-religious to burst out laughing. Is this a hidden animosity towards religion coming from Pascal that voices itself here, claiming quite bluntly that, to be religious, one must be a bit more ignorant?

In order to understand Pascal's intervention, it is necessary to take into account that he judges thoughts according to their affective function – like Brecht, as I have already tried to show. What he notices in the unhappy unbeliever is that his thoughts are merely rationaliza-tions for a position that has already gained his favour, and that all further thoughts thus serve only to nurture this position. Rather than bravely looking straight into the eye of all sad truths (the lack of persuasiveness of all theological proof), the agnostic who is addicted to proof has already begun to love the sadness itself, and to draw unrecognized enjoyment from it. All of the rational effort is now simply at the service of the sad passion of pride. It is therefore to be expected that the agnostic's theoretical field is already entirely closed. It is well armed immediately to rebut, or even convert into a proof, anything that presents a counter-proof to the position that has come to be loved, or anything that might even cast doubt on it.

Since it is affect that closes thinking, and misconceives its own, heteronomous, affect-serving function, affect is the only thing that can reopen thought. The affect contained in pride must be released; the pleasure of self-esteem, which is experienced as displeasure, must be transformed into another form of pleasure that can be experi-enced pleasurably. That is possible through play – for example, through the game of 'acting as if one believes'. Because play is always a 'senseless', 'foolish' game, and because its practice contains a moment of self-contempt, it is a means of releasing an excess of 'sense' and self-esteem – while also inducing a 'dumbing-down' in the sense that Pascal implied.

A diverse range of games are suitable here. The passage quoted

---

42   Pascal, *Pensées* (ed. Chevalier), pp. 227–8 (§451).

from Pascal does not mean that an excess of rationalizing theological theory can be dismantled simply with the help of theatrical religious rituals. Pride is not supported by theory alone, and it is not ritual alone that removes it. Instead, there are also theoretical games – which, like the Pyrrhonian sceptical tropes, techniques of questioning constantly referred to by Pascal in his *Pensées*, can help resolve exaggerated certainties generated by imagination. Such a theoretical game is the infamous 'wager' that Pascal suggests.[43] Just before that, Pascal characterizes the Christian religion as unfounded and incapable of being grounded in proof, a 'folly' (*stultitia*)[44] comparable with a game. In response to the anticipated objection that this characterization simply removes blame from those who produce the Christian religion, but in no way from those who accept it,[45] Pascal answers: 'Let us therefore examine this point, and say: God is, or is not. But towards which side will we lean? Reason cannot decide anything. There is an infinite chaos separating us. At the far end of this infinite distance a game is being played and the coin will come down heads or tails.'[46]

God's existence becomes a matter of a toss-up, a flip of the coin: 'heads' (or 'cross' – *croix*) means God exists, 'tails' (*pile*) means that there is no God. Pascal thus assigns 'heads' with beatitude and the good, and 'tails' with knowledge and truth.[47] With a mathematical calculation that would honour any professional roulette player, he tries to prove in what follows that, with a fifty-fifty chance, it would be clever to go for the side that stands for wagering one life ('heads'), as Pascal says, which promises that you lose nothing and win all – not merely two or three times the wager (although, even in that case, the wager would be worth it), but instead, eternally (namely, eternal life and endless happiness).[48]

---

43 Also belonging to the logic of Pascal's theoretical game is the figure that the apparently false thoughts are preferable to the – perhaps much more deceptive – apparently true ones. See, for example, §513: 'To have no time for philosophy, is truly to philosophize'. Pascal, *Pensées*, p. 153.

44 See Pascal, *Pensées*, p. 153; *Pensées* (ed. Chevalier), p. 224.

45 Freud formulated exactly the same objection to the statement 'Credo quia absurdum': 'But this *Credo* is only of interest as a need, as a claim to power it need not be comprehended'. Sigmund Freud, 'The Future of an Illusion' (SE XXI), p. 28.

46 Pascal, *Pensées*, p. 153.

47 Ibid., p. 154

48 See Wilhelm Schmidt-Biggemann, *Blaise Pascal* (Munich: Beck, 1999),

Regardless of the accuracy of this calculation, what seems interesting is the fact that it is suggested at all. Does this 'frivolous' computation not contradict every ethical position?[49] Could a genuine religious subject be distinguished precisely by choosing his or her position and sticking by it 'against all odds'? Isn't this sheer opportunism, which even from a religious perspective makes every halfway upright atheist seem worlds more respectable?

We must recall in response to these plausible objections, however, that Pascal views religion from the perspective of happiness, and not that of morality. For Pascal, unhappiness and unbelief are one and the same, and they result from an assumed character. His suggestions for conversion are therefore not attempts to improve people's morals, but instead therapeutic advice – medicinal attempts, as it were, to heal them of their unhappiness and unbelief. And play fulfils just such a healing function. For that reason, he suggests a game and tries to prevent, through the game's own traits of uncertainty and ease, the inappropriate attitudes of assumed certainty and narrow-minded rigidity of character in the face of that which is uncertain.

With the help of ritual and theoretical games, Pascal attempts to remove unhappiness that is caused by pride. He does not battle pride on moral grounds, but because he sees the cause of all proud people's unhappiness in the internalization that characterizes pride.[50] Serving to dismantle this pride are externalities that reach inner certainties through the theatre of rituals, as well as theoretical jolts in the form of wagers and sceptical arguments. Pascal views scepticism as an instrument for happiness (or belief), on the basis of its function in dismantling the affective *amour propre* and pride, rather than its cognitive function of undermining all knowledge.

All of Pascal's suggestions are directed at a conversation partner whose unhappiness is caused by pride – and they are effective only for this sort of patient. They are therefore always attempts to minimize the subject's experience as a subject – to create for others the transition from a form of faith equipped with an ideal ego that creates self-esteem to a position that operates without an ideal ego. Pascal's

---

pp. 97–8.

49   Ibid., p. 95.

50   Pride, according to Pascal, consists in not wanting to attach the 'interior' to the 'exterior' of religion. See Pascal, *Pensées*, p. 300; *Pensées* (ed. Chevalier), p. 234.

suggestions are thereby, in Octave Mannoni's terms, attempts to transform a *foi* ('faith') into a *croyance* ('belief')[51]. What is unusual about Pascal's theological position is, first, that he distinguishes between two forms of conviction, and, second, that votes in favour of the form that is not usually considered but is usually held in contempt: Pascal locates the true Christian position – and, therefore, happiness – not in the narrow-minded, egotistic faith, but in the playful form of *croyance*, corresponding with the illusion of others.

---

51   The concept of superstition has a different meaning for Pascal than the terms *croyance* and 'supersitition' have in Mannoni's definition. Whereas the latter always refers to a 'je sais bien, mais quand même', to an illusion suspended by better knowledge, for Pascal, 'superstition' identifies an entirely uncritical, distanceless belief in formalities: 'It is superstitious to put one's hope in formalities, but arrogant to refuse to submit to them.' Pascal, *Pensées*, p. 107 (§364). One could reformulate Pascal's differentiation in psychoanalytical terms as follows: 'superstition', the 'blind' belief in formalities, corresponds with *psychosis*; 'être superbe', being proud, would be the attitude of the *neurotic*.

CHAPTER NINE

Appearance: The Invisible Other – Theory of the Naive Observer

As has been shown, illusions without owners structure a general, cultural pleasure principle. Operating with illusions without owners is, accordingly, a technique for gaining happiness. With the help of illusions that are suspended by knowing better, and are therefore contemptuously held at a distance, non-distanced illusions can be shed, as can all of that exaggerated self-esteem and accumulation of ego-libido that renders the experiencing of pleasure unpleasurable.

There is yet another technique (a secular one), functioning in much the same way as the techniques recommended by Pascal (performing religious rituals and the theological wager), for gaining happiness based on the principle of others' illusions: politeness. This secular technique is a symbolic practice of great, genuine transformative power. In this respect, it can be defined as everyday magic practised by civilized people. The philosopher Alain, like Kant before him, recognized the amazing, transformative power inherent in politeness, and analyzed it in terms of its function in generating happiness:

> Polite behavior can strongly influence our thoughts. And miming graciousness, kindness, and happiness is of considerable help in combating ill humor and even stomach aches; the movements involved – gracious gestures and smiles – do this much good: they exclude the possibility of the contrary movements, which express rage, defiance, and sadness. That is why social activities, visits, formal occasions, and parties are so well liked. It is a chance to imitate happiness; and this kind of comedy certainly frees us from tragedy – no small accomplishment.[1]

Alain expresses with great precision the nearly medicinal power of politeness, as well as its symbolic, playful nature, which rests on the principle of the illusion of the other. What also crops up is the

---

1   Alain, *On Happiness*, p. 45.

contemptuous, *comedic* moment of such suspended illusions that are based on knowing better – something that we came across when discussing culture's 'normal forms' of perversion.

The example of politeness is especially suitable for further clarifying the theme of illusions without owners, because in the case of politeness (in contrast to the case of religious rituals, theological wagers, perverse play, or superstitious behaviour) there is absolutely no one who can claim that they have never encountered it. Using this example, I will now attempt finally to explain whose illusions 'the others' illusions' are – that is, who owns illusions without owners. The theory of the naive observer will serve well to tackle this problem. Using such a theory, it will then be possible to clarify why symbolic actions have real effects.

THE INVISIBLE OTHER: THE THEORY
OF THE NAIVE OBSERVER

In the case of politeness, the fact that operating with suspended illusions has real effects might seem baffling and paradoxical. Two grown adults who both know 'not to take things seriously', and who are even perhaps enemies, nonetheless habitually engage in polite behaviour and then go their separate ways with a sense of relief, or even exhilaration. In certain circumstances, they even cease to be enemies. But what is it that changes so greatly through the exchange of pleasantries, such as, 'Hi, how are you?' and 'Fine, thanks' – through the performance of concern and well-being?

A related example can perhaps shed some light on the matter. Let us say that two company employees who despise one another are observed by an outsider, someone from another firm, and are asked about the office atmosphere in their firm. Even two staunch rivals would make an effort to treat their antagonism as an internal affair. They would attempt to conceal it from the outsider and express only positive things about the atmosphere in their firm. Yet this situation would affect the internal atmosphere in the office as soon as the outsider leaves. The fact that the two acted together to hide their antagonism from a third party made them accomplices for a moment. On this one matter, at least, the two enemies agreed: they stuck by one another for a brief moment. Preserving the illusion with respect to an outsider also changed the inner reality.

This sort of transforming, uninvolved third person is likewise at work in all other forms of politeness. Also in cases where only two people are present and exchange polite banter, the presence of a third party of this sort is implicit due to the way that politeness works. The polite actors are accomplices regarding this third party: in order to explain how politeness functions, it is necessary to assume the presence of this third person; after all, the two are relieved after their exchange of pleasantries, at times they are even exhilarated, as they have become accomplices with regard to this third person. The fact that they are relieved or even exhilarated, can be traced back to the fact that they have succeeded in producing common ground by building up an illusion and preserving it with respect to an uninvolved third party – a third person who in this case has the special characteristic of being invisible.[2]

In theory, the assumption of such an invisible, observing agency that is not embodied by an actual person is not unusual. It is a *topical* assumption: the result of a construction, which – like the schematic plan of a subway system – differentiates *sites*, and thereby examines solely their relationships to one another, without specifying the distances between the subway stations. In a similar way, calculations tap into the existence of psychic agencies based on their functions and achievements, and do so without any regard for actual material entities that might come into question as carriers of such agencies. Freud offered a similar explanation of the assumption of mental localities by comparing them with *virtual* pictures in a telescope and differentiating them from *real*, material parts – such as optical lenses.[3] Our invisible third person is comparable with such virtual images, and differs from real elements – and is thus a *virtual observer*.

Freud also conceived of virtual observers, and accepted their existence in the form of psychic agencies. In his 1914 essay on narcissism, 'Ego Ideal', he brought in a new psychic agency, the *ego ideal*, which watches over the correspondence between a real person and their ideal ego;[4] and in 1923 he introduced the *super-ego* in the text

---

2   To this extent, the two polite actors are 'under the same illusion', in the same way that Octave Mannoni claimed was true for theatrical actors and the audience (see Chapter 2, above).

3   See Freud, 'Interpretation of Dreams', p. 611.

4   See Freud, 'On Narcissism', pp. 94–5.

'The Ego and the Id'.[5] Our third person can be conceived of along these lines: as virtual observer and psychic agency.

Nevertheless, our invisible third party is in one way quite distinct from the agencies that Freud had in mind. Freud's observing agencies are, after all, if not all-knowing observers, at least capable of recognizing the thoughts – even the most intimate thoughts – of the people observed. Yet that does not apply at all to our invisible third person. Ours is just as oblivious of the secret thoughts and true feelings of our polite co-workers as is the outsider from another firm. Our third person's entire function in this affair consists of *not* being able to see behind the façade. For that reason, our invisible third person, in contrast to Freud's agencies, is a *naive observer*.

The naivety of the invisible observer leads to clear differences in its mode of action from that of Freud's omniscient, mind-reading observer. One of the most important differences concerns the issue of guilt. Under certain circumstances, all of the observing agencies, regardless of whether they are real or virtual, trigger a sense of guilt. Freud thereby developed the theory of virtual observing agencies by differentiating them from real observers in terms of the sense of guilt that they evoke.

Real observers always judge only what they see for themselves – which does not include all intentions, only those that are surmised, and not even all acts, but only those they are aware of. Thus, according to Freud, a sense of guilt with regard to real observers is a simple, corresponding *social angst*, a fear of a loss of love:

> At the beginning, therefore, what is bad is whatever causes one to be threatened with loss of love. For fear of that loss, one must avoid it. This, too, is the reason why it makes little difference whether one has already done the bad thing or only intends to do it. In either case the danger only sets in if and when the authority discovers it, and in either case the authority would behave in the same way.[6]

For a child, such fear of discovery most likely refers to the parents, and for adults, to a broader group of real people. Yet since both cases deal with real observers, the guilt that surfaces in the form of social

---

5   See Freud, 'The Ego and the Id', pp. 28ff; 'Future of an Illusion', p. 11; 'Civilization and Its Discontents', pp. 123–4.

6   Ibid., p. 124.

angst does not have to do with the 'bad' nature of intentions or deeds, but rather with the fact that they have been found out: 'Consequently, such people habitually allow themselves to do any bad thing which promises them enjoyment, so long as they are sure that the agency will not know anything about it or cannot blame them for it; they are afraid only of being found out.'[7]

Social angst becomes an actual 'bad conscience' only when the observing agency loses its *real* (and thereby *particular and limited*) nature.[8] *Virtualizing* the agency additionally removes all limitations that might be applied to the fear of discovery. The virtual agency discovers and punishes all bad deeds and intentions. The unpleasurable feeling of social angst thus transforms into a sense of guilt; fear concerning the *discovery* of one's intentions and deeds shifts to become a concern with the *quality* of these intentions and deeds. What is now considered negative about the intentions and acts is no longer that they are discovered, but that they are bad. As Freud realized, virtual observation is, to this extent, stricter than the observation carried out by real people.

Freud attributes the considerably greater severity of the virtual agencies (as compared to all real agencies) to the way in which they arise: one disposes of the real agency by internalizing it. This gain in autonomy occurs at the price of now being subjected to total control encompassing all deeds, as well as all intentions:

A great change takes place only when the authority is internalized through the establishment of a super-ego. The phenomena of conscience then reach a higher stage. Actually, it is not until now that we should speak of conscience or a sense of guilt. At this point, too, the fear of being found out comes to an end; the distinction, moreover, between doing something bad and wishing to do it disappears entirely, since nothing can be hidden from the super-ego, not even thoughts.[9]

Virtualizing the observing agency by means of internalization therefore leads to total surveillance. The internalized observer misses

---

7   Ibid., p. 125

8   'Social angst' thus relates to 'bad conscience' exactly the same way as – in Freudian terms – the 'fear' with regard to a particular object relates to objectless, undefined 'angst' or anxiety.

9   Ibid., p. 125

nothing, is privy to all secret intentions and all concealed misdemeanours.[10] It is nonetheless important to recognize a certain benefit in this. An agency that knows everything regarding a subject's deeds, more so than any real person, also helps subjects maintain their position against all real people. The others might perhaps misunderstand what I am doing, but as long as I am in agreement with my 'inner humanity', I am nonetheless able to do it without any necessary sense of guilt.[11] The super-ego permits a peculiar recklessness with regard to real people. When a subject's knowledge complies with the knowledge of their omniscient observing agency, then they can consider it better knowledge, and disregard the views of other people as mere error, as illusion unworthy of attention.

The social angst with regard to other, real observers, on the contrary, applies not only to discovered intentions and deeds, but also to misunderstood ones. Even when I have no bad intentions whatsoever and have not performed any bad deeds, I could still lose the love of others should it seem as though I have done so in the eyes of the other. Social angst thus leads one to forgo not only bad deeds in

---

10   As Freud observed, something changes in the 'economy' of guilty feelings when the observing authority is internalized. Whereas refraining from evil deeds spares one of guilty feelings (or social angst) with regard to real observers, it *heightens* the sense of guilt with regard to the virtual authority of the super-ego. 'For the more virtuous a man is, the more severe and distrustful is [the super-ego's] behaviour, so that ultimately it is precisely those people who have carried saintliness furthest who reproach themselves with the worst sinfulness. This means that virtue forfeits some part of its promised reward...' (ibid., pp. 125ff). As Freud subsequently showed, instinctual renunciation fortifies one's conscience: '[C]onscience is the result of instinctual renunciation...' (ibid., pp. 255, 129); compare Freud, 'The Ego and the Id', p. 54: '[T]he more a man controls his aggressiveness, the more intense becomes his ideal's inclination to aggressiveness against his ego.' We could formulate this paradox as follows, using the terms from Freud's second drive theory in order to make it understandable: when renouncing a drive, object-libido transforms into ego-libido. At the same time, this process changes pleasure into manifest unpleasure. The manifest unpleasure of the sense of guilt is thus the unrecognized enjoyment of renouncing the drive, and the corresponding gain in self-esteem.

11   Conscience always corresponds with a subject's cognition in a process of mutual legitimation. When cognition is aware of bad deeds, then conscience is justified in producing a sense of guilt. But when conscience does not produce any sense of guilt, then cognition is justified in feeling righteous even against the judgment of all other observers. In his theory of ideology, Louis Althusser identified this relationship, which serves as a mutual guarantee, as the recognition of subjects in the Subject. See Althusser, 'Ideology and Ideological State Apparatuses', p. 179.

danger of being discovered, but also those in danger of being misunderstood. Conscience, on the other hand, covers this caveat: if I know the way a deed should be understood, then my conscience knows, too. I do not have to pay any heed to appearances. At one with the humanity in me, I need not be concerned with the adequate legibility of my gestures in the eyes of real people. Internalizing the observing agency thereby means dropping theatrical efforts at clarification.

Our naive observer seems to occupy a peculiar, intermediate position between Freud's real observers who trigger social angst for fear of being found out and internal observers who trigger fear of one's own conscience. In one way, our naive observer responsible for the effectiveness of polite gestures is, as I have said, a virtual observer. This observer thus seems more closely aligned with the virtual observers of the super-ego and ego ideal, and also displays a similar power of discovery: the mere prevention of discovery by other people does absolutely no good. Neglected propriety is always found out – even when the impolite person is entirely alone.[12]

On the other hand, the invisible observer's powers of discovery apply only to performed acts. That which is secretly thought or felt remains hidden from this observer. In this regard, the naive observer differs clearly from virtual agencies, and even seems to outdo some real observers in terms of naivety. After all, real observers might possibly be able to see certain intentions behind pretend behaviour. The naive observer, on the other hand, judges solely on appearances.

This results in a peculiar disaccord between the subject and the naive observer: whereas the subject is in agreement with the conscience as an agency, in that they both always have the same knowledge available, the subject is not in agreement with the naive observer, who always knows a great deal less than the subject. Nonetheless, the naive observer's view of things is completely binding for the subject. As is true of the situation of real observers and the problem of avoiding a loss of their love, with regard to the invisible third person, what is intended or thought 'in truth' is not relevant; all that matters is how things are perceived by the invisible third person. The subject's better knowledge has the status of 'I know perfectly well . . . but still . . .' with regard to this invisible third person's naive but binding perspective.

---

12 See Alain, *On Happiness*, p. 221: 'An impolite man is impolite even when he is alone. . . .'

This perspective belongs to the class of unshakeable illusions that are maintained against better knowledge – the *croyances* in a Mannonian sense. In contrast to the knowledge that is formed through the superego, which corresponds with the knowledge of the subject, the conscience of the naive observer is *a conscience that opposes the subject's knowledge*.

For this reason, the naive observer is much more closely aligned with the real observer than with the virtual one, to such an extent that it is necessary to pay heed to the discoverability and legibility of salutary gestures: it does no good to have simply thought polite phrases in one's mind, or spoken them softly. The gestures must also be performed in a clear and explicit manner. Indications that are too subtle or that use a code unusual for a particular site raise problems with regard to the invisible third party. Just like real observers, the naive observer requires theatrical efforts at clarification.

THE GUILT OF APPEARANCES: THE NAIVE OBSERVER AND A SENSE OF GUILT

Coerced Games

Because the naive observer is a psychic agency capable of triggering a sense of guilt, and because the naive observer acts as a conscience on the basis of appearances, and does so even against the subject's better knowledge, this agency is well suited to the methodical generation of a sense of guilt. False appearances produced by means of acting can bring about a sense of guilt. This can also occur under coercion. When one forces people to act out their own guilt, they consequently feel guilty – regardless of whether they really are – and they even feel guilty in cases when they know for sure that they are not.

This is the basis for a series of special ideological practices, such as coerced games, examples of which can be found in myths, history and fiction. These examples likewise offer solid proof to counter the notion advanced by numerous game theorists that it is impossible to force people to play.[13] On the contrary, I would like to show that often

---

13   See also, for example, Kant, *Critique of the Power of Judgment*, B116; Schiller, *On the Aesthetic Education of Man*, p. 34; Huizinga, *Homo Ludens*, p. 7; Caillois, *Man, Play and Games*, p. 6

those in power coerce the less powerful into mandatory play, and that this coercion to play fulfils a precise and specific ideological function. A notorious example of this type of paradox is the so-called 'Frankenburger Würfelspiel', or Frankenburg Dice Game. After armed Protestant farmers chased away a Catholic priest in Frankenburg, Upper Austria, on 14 May 1625, the imperial governor, Adam von Herberstorff, sent a decree to the inhabitants of the Upper Austrian parishes involved. They were thereby summoned

> to appear on the following day by three p.m. at the latest, in Haush-
> amerfeld, an open area near Frankenburg. At the same time, all who
> heeded this call were promised pardon and mercy. It was mainly
> this promise that prompted the people to appear at the designated
> site following the fleeing of the actual perpetrators. The governor
> pulled together troops in a great rush and came to Frankenburg
> with three guns and a hangman. He demanded that the parishes'
> leaders stand aside, separately, and explained to the remainder of
> the crowd that they would be granted mercy if they stopped their
> resistance to the [counter-]Reformation. Since the main offenders
> had fled, the community leaders would be punished for allowing –
> through their passivity – the revolt to occur and for gravely
> neglecting their duties.[14]

Some aspects of these preliminary conditions already reveal a ludic character. All who show up are promised a feigned amnesty; yet in a breach of this promise, punishments are handed out – to be precise, representative punishments. The population is pardoned in a humili-ating ritual,[15] yet they have to watch as their leaders are punished in place of the escaped ringleaders – although not all of the community leaders are punished, only half. 'The governor explained to the digni-taries that he would let some of them live, out of mercy, but would hang the others'.[16] This punishment is, in the end, meted out once again in the form of a game:

---

14   Georg Heilingsetzer, *Der oberösterreichische Bauernkrieg 1626*, (Vienna: ÖBV, Militärhistorische Schriftenreihe 32, 1985), p. 7 (my translation).

15   See Willi Flicker, 'Der oberösterreichische Bauernkrieg von 1626 in seinem politischen, konfessionellen, sozialen und kulturellen Umfeld', (Innsbruck, Masters thesis, University of Innsbruck, 1991), p. 60.

16   Heilingsetzer, *Der oberösterreichische Bauernkrieg 1626*, p. 7 (my translation).

A black cloak was spread out under the linden tree on Haushamer field. Then the governor let the thirty-eight prisoners, in pairs, play dice for their lives. The losers were tied up by the hangman; it was possible to plead for the lives of two of them, and on the very same day, the others were hung on the linden tree and the church tower. Two days later, the corpses of the hanged men were stuck on spears near Vöcklabruck on Salzburger Straße, 'so that farmers, citizens, and wayfarers could see what the revolt had brought.'[17]

The 'mercy' of the governor consisted in killing only the losers of the dice games that he had forced them to play, rather than killing all of the prisoners.[18] These types of 'aleatory' process appear typical in the punishment of collectives when no individual perpetrators can be identified[19] – or, as in this case, as a substitute for the punishment of an escaped ringleader. In those cases where guilt cannot be clearly assigned to any one person, it is assigned with the help of chance – which ultimately also provides those in power with an excuse for having executed innocent people.

But these aspects of procedure and forgiveness included in such a solution to the question of guilt should not make us lose sight of the fundamental ideological function of coerced games. After all, the condition behind such 'mercy' and the corresponding forced game is that those in power are in a position to kill *all* of the powerless people. There must be some advantage in their carrying out a half-massacre and allowing some of their opponents to survive under the conditions of the game. A theory of the coerced game would have to explain this advantage.

---

17   Flicker, 'Der oberösterreichische Bauernkrieg', p. 61 (my translation).

18   On this point, the Frankenburg Dice Game differs clearly from the ball games of the Mayas and Aztecs in which, apparently, the *victorious team* was ritually murdered following the game. Also, the situation that the people in the Aztec festivals 'often voluntarily accepted death' (Erdheim, *Die gesellschaftliche Produktion von Unbewußtheit*, p. 229) and that they were 'declared to be gods' – before their murder – and treated to the appropriate amenities for an entire year of their life (ibid.) – are peculiar, and oppose simple attempts at explanation. Neither the theologically questionable concept of 'sacrifice' nor the economic calculation whereby it is necessary, 'to kill all prisoners of war' (ibid., p. 234) seem to coincide with these peculiarities. Genocides are, after all, usually carried out without the intricateness of declaring the victims to be gods for an entire year.

19   See Heilingsetzer, *Der oberösterreichische Bauernkrieg 1626*, p. 7.

The existence of such an advantage also seems likely because coerced games take place only in situations where a procedural solution is applied to an otherwise irresolvable question of guilt. The coerced games are, accordingly, not limited to games of chance or dice. They are therefore also not exclusively categorized as *alea*, according to Caillois's classification.[20] There are also forced games of 'competition' (*agôn*), in which people must battle either against one another in various ways or alone, against a set task. Yet the trait of an aleatory assignment of guilt to a few among many, which comes to the fore so strikingly in the Frankenburg Dice Game, is absent in cases where a person fights alone in an imposed task. The coerced games must therefore fulfil a different function that simply providing a direct punishment in cases where a direct assignment of guilt is impossible.

Johan Huizinga recognized the life-threatening and forced dimension of the guessing game (which, according to Caillois, belongs to the *agôn* genre) and identified it as a '*Halsrätsel*' or 'capital riddle'. This is a riddle contest in which at least one of the participants has been forced to participate, and in which his or her life is at stake. Common in Germanic mythology, as Huizinga points out, is the motif that someone, in order to save their (already forfeited) life, must solve a riddle posed by the king, or must present the king with a riddle that he is unable to solve. At a symbolic level, the riddle thus re-enacts the coercion present at a real level brought about by an asymmetrical relationship of power, forming the precondition of the game (which is not voluntary for one of the parties involved). Huizinga writes: 'The answer to an enigmatic question . . . comes quite literally as a sudden *solution* – a loosening of the tie by which the questioner holds you bound.'[21]

Huizinga succeeds in discovering these repressive preconditions of the game, even though they contradict the thesis that he explicitly supports previously whereby the game is, by nature, a free act. There are, indeed, coerced games with coerced stakes. Huizinga even supports the general notion that the riddle is 'a sacred thing full of secret power, hence a dangerous thing. In its mythological or ritual

---

20 On this category, as well as the entire four-part classification – competition (agôn)/chance (alea)/simulation (mimicry)/vertigo (ilinx) – see Caillois, *Man, Play and Games*, p. 12.

21 Huizinga, *Homo Ludens*, p. 110

context it is nearly always what German philologists know as the *Halsrätsel* or "capital riddle", which you either solve or forfeit your head. The player's life is at stake."[22]

Thus the riddle is not just occasionally a coerced game, or a game where one's life is at stake, but perhaps even inherently so. Perhaps in myths, the motif of forfeiting a life is a fictional, artistic device meant simply to heighten suspense, but there is historical evidence indicating the actual existence of such practices. Due to its perfidy, the example that Huizinga cites of Alexander the Great, who had Indian wise men answer riddles for their lives,[23] points more to an actual attempt at humiliation of a subordinated culture than an episode in which suspense has been heightened. The motif's wide distribution is also remarkable. Along with the numerous examples cited by Huizinga of Germanic 'neck-saving' riddles, as well as the confrontation between Oedipus and the Sphinx,[24] it is easy to find other similar cases – the story of the three prisoners[25] that Jacques Lacan evokes as a conceptual model, for example, is also within this genre. Here, too, the staging of coercion, of a situation of violent, despotic *Herrschaft*, is pre-eminent; the decisive ideological, control-securing function of the coerced game comes from partial annulment of that total coercion which exists as a precondition of this procedure.

In addition to *alea* and *agôn*, the other known genres of play are also suitable for the function of grand coercion. Depression-era marathon dance competitions, as depicted in the film *They Shoot Horses, Don't They?*,[26] straddle the border between *agôn* and *ilinx* ('vertigo'). In the end, *mimicry* (simulation) is also suitable for the coerced game. However, mimicry is not simply one form among others; instead, it seems to shape the entire genre of coerced play. In a previous section I formulated the thesis that games, even if they do not appear to depict anything, always contain a fiction.[27] This fictional dimension of all games means that they all must be subsumed under the category of mimicry. And the reason why the coercion to play

22   Ibid., p. 108

23   Ibid., p. 111

24   Ibid., p. 111.

25   See Jacques Lacan, 'Logical Time and the Assertion of Anticipated Certainty: A New Sophism' (1945), in *Newsletter of the Freudian Field* 2: 2 (Fall 1988).

26   *They Shoot Horses, Don't They?* (dir. Sydney Pollack, USA, 1969).

27   See Chapter 4, above.

practised by those in power presents an advantageous means of power can be found in this fictional dimension. Due to their fictional character, games convey an illusion; with the help of coerced games, these illusions can coerce others. In this way, power can partially change its methods from pure violence to illusion. Coerced games thereby enable a transition from a limited power of pure repression to an expanded, more effective type of power that is bolstered by both repression and ideology.

An example from the realm of fiction, Sergio Leone's Western *Once Upon a Time in the West*,[28] serves as an effective depiction of the ideological function fulfilled by coerced games. The evidence for the real, historical existence of coerced games has already been provided before. Yet the ideological mechanism functions the same way in fiction as in reality: otherwise, the causal connections depicted by the film would fail to form a comprehensible narrative. An additional, outstanding accomplishment of the so-called 'spaghetti western' was its development of an extremely sophisticated observation of such affairs. In the attempt to replace the black-and-white moral scheme of the classical American western by developing more elaborate ways of looking at a problem, the spaghetti western, like some later westerns, arrived at a series of motifs that reveal the complexity of social situations in which there is not only the 'good and the bad', but also, for example, 'the ugly',[29] and in which protagonists must confront opponents who are not only extremely violent but also utterly insidious. A characteristic of the insidiousness of these opponents is that they attempt – for example, by taking captives – to transform any resistance on the part of an opponent into complicity. Spaghetti westerns are therefore not merely the subject of theory, but also its ally. They can be seen as independent, informative theories 'in the practical state' (to quote this Althusserian formula),[30] for example, with regard to guilt.

In *Once Upon a Time in the West* there is a traumatic 'primal scene'. Gangsters have captured two men. They hang the older of the two by setting him with a noose around his neck on the shoulders of the

---

28   *Once Upon a Time in the West* (dir. Sergio Leone, USA, 1969).

29   See also, for example, Sergio Leone's western *The Good, the Bad, and the Ugly* (USA, 1966).

30   See Louis Althusser, 'From "Capital" to Marx's Philosophy', in Louis Althusser and Etienne Balibar, *Reading Capital* (London, New York: Verso, 2006), p. 32.

younger, a boy, whose arms are bound. The hanged man is condemned to die the moment that the boy can no longer bear his weight. The ringleader sticks a harmonica between the boy's lips. The moment the boy collapses, the harmonica screeches out a piercing sound. Charles Bronson plays the man who was once this boy, and apparently is compelled to spend his entire life searching for the gangsters. In the end, he shoots the ringleader (Henry Fonda). When the dying man asks who he is, he answers by pushing a harmonica into his mouth.

This is no ordinary tale of revenge. For 'Harmonica' (Bronson), witnessing his brother's murder is not the only horrible thing. The trauma comes, rather, from the gangsters' having depicted him as an accomplice through the procedure of the elaborate, theatrical staging of the murder in the form of an execution. In the end, his brother's life was on his own shoulders. If he had held out a bit longer, his brother would have lived longer, which fact apparently implicates him in the deed. He knew that he had absolutely no chance of saving his brother, *but it still seemed as though it was up to him.*

The gangsters succeeded in making the boy feel guilty in the form of 'I know well, but all the same. . . .'[31] He knows that he is not guilty, and his conscience is aware of that – but he is guilty in the eyes of a naive observer. The violent, coerced theatre has created appearances, and thereby awakened the observing agency that judges this appearance accordingly – and done so in a way that is even more horrendous, more 'sartorial', than any super-ego.[32] Whereas his conscience absolves him, the naive observer levies an objection (and not at all silently) against him. A notorious Kantian situation of 'Du kannst, denn Du sollst' ('You can, because you must') echoes throughout his life in the sound of the harmonica, immune to any rational clarification that saving the other was impossible. He knows it perfectly well, but he is not able to shake off the view of some other who finds him guilty.

The gangster's violence has psychically split the hero and made him into a fetishist: he is split between – in Freud's terms[33] – an

31   See Chapter 2, above, on Octave Mannoni's theory of disavowal.

32   See Joan Copjec's essay, 'The Sartorial Superego', in Joan Copjec, *Read My Desire: Lacan against the Historicists* (Cambridge, MA/London: MIT Press, 1994), pp. 65–116; compare also Nasio, *Enseignement de 7 concepts*, pp. 105–20.

33   See Freud, 'Fetishism', p. 156, where he distinguishes between an attitude that fits in with reality, and a wishful attitude.

approach from his knowledge, the 'attitude that fits in with reality' and an approach from his guilt, the 'attitude that *does not at all* fit in with the wish', but is instead, extremely 'undesirable' (and even unjust). The harmonica offers him a fetish that 'helps' him maintain this 'undesirable' approach. He can overcome the trauma of this 'guilt' only through an act of repetition, which is, once again, a theatrical act.[34] The goal of this act is to free oneself of the fetish.[35] This is only possible through a staging arranged for the naive observer. It is necessary to clarify to this agency that the guilty person is not Bronson, but Fonda – that is, that Fonda is the harmonica player. When Bronson silently sticks the instrument into the mouth of the dying Fonda, thus answering the question of who he is, it is consequently more than just an answer. It is a christening in which not only the object, the fetish, but also the name carried by Bronson throughout the film, 'Harmonica' – and thereby the guilt – change hands.

This example of forced theatrical play (mimicry, in Caillois's sense), displayed with virtuoso clarity in *Once Upon a Time in the West*, explains what coerced games are all about – what constitutes their ideological mechanism, and what advantage is brought to the ones in power by having the others play: *the coerced game depicts the player's complicity.* Whether they want to or not, those who win in the Frankenburg Dice Game become co-executioners of their peers. Since they have played dice for a wager, it looks as though they hoped for victory and hence for the death of the others. In the eyes of the naive observer, who is more naive than all of those present but whose views nonetheless remain formative for them, they are guilty in the deaths of their peers. The advantage for those in power can be found here: rather than producing more dead heroes, they kill fewer and in addition rob those killed of any possible honour in the circumstances of their deaths.[36] The potential dead heroes are reduced to mere losers at a game. Moreover, there are also a number of survivors who are likewise not heroes: instead, they are collaborators who have profited from the death of their peers.

---

34   On the necessity of repetition after coerced games, see Chapter 3 of Slavoj Žižek's *Enjoy Your Symptom! Jacques Lacan in Hollywood and Out*, 2nd edn (London/ New York: Routledge, 2001), pp. 69–112.

35   The motif of the 'battle' over this type of fetish also comes up in Alfred Hitchcock's *Strangers on a Train* and Jacques Tourneur's *Night of the Demon*.

36   See Stephen Greenblatt, *Learning to Curse: Essays in Early Modern Culture* (New York: Routledge, 1995), p. 50.

The same mechanism of generating guilt through a coerced game is evident when those in power pose an impossible choice for those at their mercy, such as the 'Your money or your life' type analyzed by Jacques Lacan.[37] These types of 'choice' are also mimicry, since 'choosing' is merely feigned; for those who have to make a choice, both possibilities are unacceptable. Žižek analyzed this using the example of William Styron's novel *Sophie's Choice* – the story of a Jewish mother whom the Nazis force to choose one of her children to die, or else they will kill both.[38] In this game, too, the depiction of a choice creates a sense that the mother has colluded in the murder of one of her children. And although this sense is obviously absurd for everyone involved, it produces guilt, which in the end can only be extinguished through repetition – in this case, through the mother's suicide.[39] Just as 'Harmonica' is able to pass the identity of the guilty person to the true perpetrator through his symbolic act in the western, the mother absolves herself of her guilt by choosing her own death and thereby putting herself in the place of the (other) victim – that is, the child whose death she chose.

The same mechanism of creating guilt by forcing an apparent choice is also found in a comedic form in the motif of the 'two-shirt mother'. Everyone knows that some mothers ensure an unchallenged position of power in their families by creating a sense of guilt in the other family members. For example, a mother gives her son two shirts for his birthday. When, on the next occasion, he wears one of them, as he should, she then exclaims, with deep disappointment, 'Ah, you didn't really like the other one.'[40]

Apart from the fact that it is possible to coerce people to play, what seems interesting in such – usually appalling – examples is that, *with the*

---

37   See Lacan, *Le séminaire III*, p. 212.

38   See Žižek, *Enjoy Your Symptom!*, pp. 69–80.

39   See Slavoj Žižek, '*Grimassen des Realen: Jacques Lacan oder die Monstrosität des Aktes* (Cologne: Kieenheuer & Witsch, 1993), p. 192, n. 32: 'A similar repetition of the coerced choice can be found in a series of Hollywood films, from *Now Voyager* through to *Deerhunter*: 'In a primordial scene, the hero is forced to choose, and this choice, although forced, marks his existence with a permanent brand of quilt which is erased when in a repeated scene of choice, he "chooses the impossible" via a gesture of suicidal renunciation.'

40   I thank Jennifer Friedlander of Pomona College, Claremont, CA, for this example.

help of games, it is possible to compel people to feel guilty. The coerced feelings of guilt thereby form a point of transition between raw violence and changing someone's attitude, between repression and ideology.[41] At a theoretical level, these cases show that an analysis exclusively focusing on the 'body' and 'power', as suggested by Michel Foucault,[42] is incapable of offering any valuable clues about the described mechanisms. For what is it that influences the (largely untroubled) body? In order to answer this, a theory of ideology appears necessary that allows for an understanding of the illusions of others as a powerful factor.[43]

Naive observers are the carriers of the others' illusions. Their existence and methods are recognized and used in the case of coerced games by the most real power, who is least suspicious of succumbing to philosophical speculation. The most real power recognizes that it can control things more effectively by forcing this type of fiction than by practising raw violence. Here, when it comes to violence, less is more. For maintaining power, it is more efficient to have fewer dead people, and thereby produce more symbolically destroyed victims.

The victims are destroyed by means of symbolic representation. The act of apparent collaboration generates a feeling of guilt. As in the everyday magic of politeness, symbols and set gestures also prove effective here. The feeling of guilt comes over the victim in the same way in which the comforting feeling of a shared moment washes over people acting politely – and in which the illusion of responsibility seizes those television viewers who act as though they might influence the course of a game when watching a sporting event. Thus, the controlling technique of coerced games is also an everyday magic practised by civilized people, which uses symbolization to produce what is symbolized.

---

41   For a discussion of the classical differentiation between repressive and ideological apparatuses, see Althusser, 'Ideology and Ideological State Apparatuses', p. 137.

42   See Michel Foucault, *BODY/POWER* (1976), interview with Michel Foucault by the editorial collective of *Quel Corps?*, available at generation-online.org.

43   For this reason, Althusser's ideology–theoretical analysis seems far superior to Foucault's body and power–theoretical approach. Commentators – for example, Warren Montag, in '"The Soul Is the Prison of the Body": Althusser and Foucault, 1970–1975', Yale French Studies, No. 88, *Depositions: Althusser, Balibar, Macherey, and the Labor of Reading* (New Haven: Yale University Press, 1995), and Horst Brühmann, in 'Bachelard mit Lacan und Spinoza', in *Riss* 43 (1998) – who have pointed out the extensive commonalities of the two theories, appear to shy away from pointing out the deficits that surface in Foucault's theory through the comparison.

Negative Fetishism

But why are the symbols effective in the case of coerced games? Why is it that the victims not only have to play, but must also internalize the 'objective' illusion – a perspective that is not necessarily the perpetrator's, but merely that of an imaginable naive observer? Why is it that they are compelled to feel – against their better knowledge – what some other person might possibly have thought ('You played against your comrades, and wished for their death')? These questions appear difficult to answer when viewed against the theoretical backdrop unrolled thus far. The coerced games, as cases of the other's illusion, seem to take a peculiar position among the hitherto examined techniques of happiness and unhappiness.

We traced back techniques for happiness to the illusion of the other. According to Pascal, in the ancient philosophies of happiness the relief presented by the production of an illusion of the other in comparison to maintaining one's own, conscience-filled illusion, appears to enable happiness, as it also does in Alain's theory of politeness. Through transition to the illusion of the other, it is possible to dismantle the ego-libido active in avowal (making every pleasure an experience of displeasure) and turn it back into object-libido. Arrogance and self-love, as causes of manifest displeasure, can be dismantled, and pleasurable experiences of one's own desire enabled.

Techniques of unhappiness, on the contrary, are techniques of ego-libido accumulation. They include leading unhappy people to fancy themselves in the role of the tragic hero – as Alain put it, to 'create a character' out of their unhappiness.[44] 'Subject effects', including feelings of autonomy and responsibility,[45] were disguised gains that could be reaped from reference to an ideal ego. These are expressed in the manifestly unpleasurable affects of obstinacy, sadness, anger, jealousy, fear, guilt, and so on.

The effects of coerced games seem to rest between these two categories. On the one hand, they are unpleasurable and associated with guilt. On the other, however, this sense of guilt does not

---

44   See Alain, *On Happiness*, p. 59.

45   For this concept see Althusser, 'Ideology and Ideological State Apparatuses' (Notes towards an Investigation)', in *On Ideology* (London, New York: Verso, 2008), p. 46; and Althusser, *Écrits sur la psychanalyse: Freud et Lacan* (Paris: Stock/IMEC, 1993), p. 131.

correspond with a 'subject effect'. The effects do not arise from a relation with an ideal ego, and are not evoked by a knowing, observing agency of the 'super-ego' or 'ego ideal' variety. For the victim of coerced games, the games remain 'dumb games', and their own guilt, in accordance with these games, remains a dumb fiction that contradicts their better knowledge. Unpleasurable and yet without ideal ego, the effects of the coerced games are most comparable with the symptoms of neuroses. We would like to identify them here as 'negative fetishism'.

But why is it that the involuntary players are incapable of anything other than accepting this illusion that has been violently forced upon them, and which contradicts what they know? Why have they actually convinced themselves of this sense of guilt that the violence of those in power has inflicted upon them? Why do they not simply consider themselves helpless victims of extreme violence? What libido economy is at work with regard to victims' subjective collaboration in what is inflicted upon them? Answering these questions would solve the general problem of 'remote control' (so aptly dubbed by David Signer): a problem that has long haunted psychoanalytic theory. It presents the question, namely, of why 'counter-transferences' take place on a regular basis and 'projective identifications' are triggered, and also occur in situations when there is absolutely no advantage for the remote-controlled person.[46]

The coerced games seem to play out 'beyond the pleasure principle'. Nonetheless, there must be something seductive about illusions that are forced upon victims. Something appears to go beyond mere violence and cause the acceptance of the illusion. Some sort of gain in pleasure must be associated here with the illusion of the other, and so closely tied to it that the victim is incapable of doing anything other than striving for it and accepting the displeasure of the guilty feelings.

The discovery that victims of coerced games uphold the illusion of their guilt, which they experience as unpleasurable, creates a challenge for psychoanalytic theory. The theory of disavowal and

---

46 If this question is not answered, then the term 'projective identification', in particular, runs the risk of being a word without a concept, which means feigning a solution to a problem simply by naming it. See Althusser and Balibar, *Reading Capital*, trans. Ben Brewster (London/New York: Verso, 1997), pp. 46–8. For this reason, Mannoni sharply criticized this term – see Octave Mannoni, 'La désidentification', in J. Dor, ed., *Le Moi et l'Autre* (Paris: Denoel, 1985).

ego-splitting is the psychoanalytic position with regard to such illusions of the other, as we have seen in relation to Octave Mannoni. Yet Freud interpreted the process of disavowal and ego-splitting as a *defence mechanism*. The defence mechanism is put into action to provide 'realistic' acknowledgement of a discovery that is considered extremely threatening, and at the same time keep a firm hold on the 'desirable' attitude falsified by this discovery. As a result, there is knowledge of the horrendous discovery as well as its denial – for example, the 'realistic' sense of 'castration' and the 'desirable' illusion of female penis ownership. The splitting of the ego between these two attitudes serves to maintain the desirable position. If it were not desirable, and hence pleasurable, there would be no reason to hold fast to this belief.

Yet this is precisely the case in the case of guilt generated by the coerced game: it is unpleasurable and is nonetheless maintained despite better knowledge (the knowledge of one's own hapless innocence). There is no obvious reason justified by the economy of the libido for the victim to hold fast to this illusion. And yet victims do so by undergoing an ego split, separating the illusion of their guilt from the realistic attitude. The victims of coerced games could say, in keeping with Mannoni's formulation, 'I know perfectly well that I am not guilty, but still, I can do nothing but feel guilty.'[47] The ego splits into two attitudes, both unpleasurable: 'realistic' helplessness and 'desirable' guilt. In contrast to 'positive' fetishism, in the 'negative' form, the benefit meant to come from this process remains open.[48]

For 'positive' fetishism, the benefit, as we have seen, is maintaining the desirable attitude despite the objection of experience. The

---

47   Just as in the examples analyzed by Mannoni, in this case, too, we have to assume that the 'better knowledge' constituting the realistic attitude does not play a neutral role, but instead acts to uphold the illusion (in this case, the imagined guilt), and also acts as reinforcement of the adherence to this illusion.

48   Freud himself mentioned cases of ego splitting that were not of a pleasurable, perverse nature, but rather an unpleasurable, obsessional-neurotic one. See, for example, Freud, 'Fetishism', p. 156. In addition, the Rat Man, superstitious against his better knowledge, was one of the obsessional-neurotic cases of ego splitting. See Freud, 'Notes upon a Case of Obsessional Neurosis', pp. 229–32. These cases are thus also ones of 'negative fetishists', to the extent that they adhere to a manifest unpleasurable, 'not desirable' attitude countering 'realistic' knowledge. Yet, as far as we can see, Freud did not take this as an occasion to undertake a new explanation of ego splitting in terms of the economy of the libido.

pleasurable content of the idea constitutes the gain. The process of ego-splitting is carried out for the benefit of this gain. The occurrence of this negative, unpleasurable fetishism seems, instead, to be a condition of its special *form*, which causes every attempt at defence to be transformed into a power beneficial to the illusion to be fended off. Because the denied attitude is unpleasurable, the victim ever more firmly reaffirms their better knowledge with regard to this attitude. But the more they do this, the more they confirm the unpleasurable, denied attitude. That is, precisely when they attempt to assert their better knowledge with regard to the illusion of the naive observer, they become ever more ensnared in the illusion of the other, which – as always – is bolstered by better knowledge. Even the attempt to adhere to the knowledge of one's own innocence with the help of better knowledge inevitably leads to the reproachful illusion of the other, which requires just such an alleged 'revolt' in order to be maintained.[49] This is what makes coerced games so compelling. They are able to transform even the resistance to them into a power working to their advantage.

In contrast to positive fetishism, with negative fetishism it is possible that there really is no libido-economic gain – unless the deception of having resisted the illusion of the other by means of one's own knowledge brings satisfaction. This negative fetishism takes into account that the illusion of guilt will evoke resistance, the effects of which benefit the fetishism. Thus, the attempt to avoid libido-economic loss ends up contributing to this very loss. This seems to offer an explanation for why 'remote control' works – why it so often succeeds in setting off counter-transferences. These counter-transferences are the result of the attempt to avoid them. Due to the specific relationship between knowledge and illusion, which marks the illusion of the other, the supposedly resistant adherence to better knowledge links up with the understood illusion.

In keeping with a 'cunning of unreason' typical of the illusion of the other, the dogged pursuit of one's own autonomous rationality

---

49   Slavoj Žižek, in 'Das rassistische Schibboleth', in Weibel and Žižek, eds, *Inklusion: Exklusion. Probleme des Postkolonialismus und der globalen Migration* (Vienna: Passagen, 1997), p. 158, illustrated this thesis using the example of the good soldier Schwejk, who overzealously carried out his superior's orders, showing that some ideological formations can only function across a distance, in the form of a dis-identification. In this context, unreserved identification, on the contrary, offered the possibility of subversion or escape.

leads one to become captive to the heteronomous illusion of the other. This 'cunning' is the reason why it is possible to force people not only to play, but also to recognize the fiction mediated by play. It is impossible for players to reject the fiction generated by play because play builds on the structure of disavowal, within which better knowledge provides a linchpin for the fiction.

If one were to abandon better knowledge – distance from the illusion of the other – and accept it as one's own illusion, this would help in breaking its power. Removing the linchpin of better knowledge downgrades the compulsive illusion of the other to one's own belief – that is, conviction. But for now we will have to leave open the question of whether it is possible to have such a 'psychotic' relationship to imaginary guilt whose affirmation occurs without any reserve from an antagonistic subjectivity – and, if so, at what price.

Why Magic Has to Be Performed Out Loud

Along with the phenomenon of politeness, from which we arrived with the help of Alain at the assumption of the naive observer, and the phenomenon of coerced games, there is yet another area where the power of the naive observer makes a vivid appearance: magic.

An imperceptible tension characterizes the psychoanalytic theory of magic developed by Freud in 1912–13. Freud's theory contains two different approaches: on the one hand, the 'philosophical' explanation of magic through the so-called 'omnipotence of thoughts', and, on the other hand, an 'art theory' approach, so to speak, that is related more to the material culture of magic.

Freud elevated the first explanation to an official one by integrating it into his newly published theory of narcissism in 1914. Nonetheless, he seems to have forgotten that his second explanation cannot be reconciled with the first. Instead, as will be shown in what follows, the 'art theory' explanation refutes the 'philosophical' one.

In his 'art theory' approach to magic, Freud achieves a theoretical breakthrough (albeit one of which he is largely unaware). This breakthrough has widespread consequences for psychoanalytic theory. Freud's art theory–related explanation of magic requires the assumption of a naive observer – an agency that differs greatly from the other observing agencies (ego ideal and super-ego) that Freud introduced into psychoanalytic theory, beginning with the narcissism essay in 1914.

Assuming the existence of this agency clearly invalidates Freud's assignment of magic to the narcissistic stage of childish libido development: it is not the magician, but quite the opposite – the supposedly enlightened ones rejecting the magic – who must be identified as narcissistic. This means that an escape from narcissism must be conceived differently from the way in which psychoanalysis has hitherto understood it. Following its basic oedipal presumptions, the way out of narcissism does not occur through the education of a super-ego (since this turns out to be a narcissistic formation), but instead through the dismantling of this super-ego for the benefit of the agency of a naive observer. In the terms of cultural theory, this realization would clear the way for the recognition of why the 'discontent of civilization' appears only in certain cultures, whereas others – as Freud also occasionally noticed – are able to remain free of it.

The entire problem can be seen as emanating from a single symptomatic point. The shibboleth that divides the 'philosophical' version from the 'art theory' one is the issue of why one has to speak out loud when performing magic.

FREUD'S 'PHILOSOPHICAL' EXPLANATION OF MAGIC

According to Freud, two ideas characterize the infantile view of the world: first, universal penis ownership (by men as well as by women) – a necessary condition for considering the sight of female genitals a 'castration experience' (and, viewing this as a 'realistic' attitude);[50] and, second, a similarly universal idea – that of the 'omnipotence of thoughts'.[51] Universal penis ownership and omnipotence of thoughts are analogous concepts of omnipotence, which are both soon subordinated in a similar and necessary way to 'castrating' objections coming from reality (or what might be considered reality). But both seem to have withstood these objections for the time being with the help of denial, and to have found a continued existence beyond the childish stage – as sexual fetishism in one case, and as the magic of everyday civilized life in the other. Perhaps sexual fetishism is limited to just a few perverse individuals, but, as Wittgenstein asserted, the magic of everyday life is a phenomenon to which all representatives of

---

50   See Nasio, *Enseignement de 7 concepts*, pp. 7ff.
51   On this term, see Freud, 'Totem and Taboo', p. 88.

civilized adulthood are subject. It does not seem as though anyone is entirely free of small, foolish habits – such as crossing fingers at a soccer game, speaking to a car, honking uselessly in traffic, or occasionally bursting into a rage at innocent objects.

When so-called 'civilized' people consider themselves free of magic, they tend to distort the interpretation of magic. A characteristic of classical ethnology's position is the opinion that in magic, an ideal relationship, is 'fallaciously' considered a real one. People have 'mistaken' the order of their ideas for the order of nature, and hence 'imagine' that the control they have, or seem to have, over their thoughts allows them to exercise a corresponding control over things.[52]

Freud made two adjustments to this common 'theoretical' characterization of magic as a mistake in judgment. First of all, according to Freud, magic is more about a wish than about a mistake.[53] It is not simply 'thoughts' (and not all of them) that are confused with reality, but in fact the most strongly affect-filled thoughts that are considered to be the most realistic.[54] Thus, just as the scientist sees the verification of his thoughts in empirical results, the everyday magician sees such verification in the affect contained in his thoughts.

Second, Freud says that magic is not merely a theory 'developed from speculative curiosity', but instead 'an instruction' arising from 'a practical need'. Magic is a 'technique'.[55] With these two modifications of the classical view of magic in terms of desire and technique, Freud led theory away from an understanding of magic that identifies it as a theory. Serving desire, not thought, magic seems no longer necessarily to be a theory, but instead a myth, or – as a 'technique' subordinate to 'need' (and with that, possibly also performed in spite of knowing better) – a ritual; consequently, what is at issue is an ideological form that fulfils a different function from that of cognition, and can exist relatively autonomously alongside it. What might possibly be thought in magic is not thought for the sake of cognition, and it seems that there might not be any thoughts at all. With that, Freud makes it at least imaginable that magic might be something other than a mistake or foolishness.

---

52   See the corresponding evidence from Tylor and Frazer in ibid., pp. 79, 82–3.
53   Ibid., p. 83.
54   Ibid., pp. 86–7.
55   Ibid., p. 78.

Despite these two modifications, however, Freud continued to maintain the position that magic is based, as it were, on a certain picture of the world – namely, an 'animistic' one that maintains the 'omnipotence of thoughts':

> A general overvaluation has thus come about of all mental processes . . . Things become less important than ideas of things: whatever is done to the latter will inevitably also occur to the former. Relations which hold between the ideas of things are assumed to hold equally between the things themselves . . . In the animistic epoch the reflection of the internal world is bound to blot out the other picture of the world . . . By way of summary, then, it may be said that the principle governing magic, the technique of the animistic mode of thinking, is the principle of the 'omnipotence of thoughts'.[56]

Freud subsequently categorizes this theory of the omnipotence of thoughts as a stage of childish sexual development – namely, that of (primary) narcissism.[57] In this stage, the child, whose sexual instincts are already bundled and compiled as a unit, before any libidinous relationship to an external object, takes his or her own formed ego as object. An ego, whose sole object is itself, must experience itself as the centre of this world, and must experience nothing other than itself, mirror-like, in this world, and thereby remain largely inaccessible to those experiences 'which could teach them man's true position in the universe'.[58] This sexual overvaluation of one's own ego, which (according to Freud) children and also 'uncivilized' people have not yet abandoned, and which neurotics, by contrast, arrive at secondarily along regressive paths, leads to the psychic consequence of 'intellectual narcissism' – that is, to 'omnipotence of thoughts'.

Animism – the omnipotence of thoughts – is thus the 'theory' of magic, while narcissism is its basis in human libido development. Magic thereby corresponds with a stage of sexual development in which ego-libido and object-libido are not yet separated from one

---

56   Ibid., p. 85
57   Ibid., pp. 88–9.
58   Ibid., p.89.

another.[59] Oedipalization has not yet taken place, no external object in the shape of the mother is desired, and the experience of 'castration' – limitation of the mother's availability to the child as imposed by the father – is still to come for the little, narcissistic, royal majesty. This makes clear that the introjection of a constrictive paternal authority cannot yet have taken place. The object ego is a *sexual object* for the little narcissist, and is thus an object of the *object-libido*, not the ideal ego that is aspired to by ego-libido by means of identification. Hence, there is also no observing super-ego or ego ideal, which (as an interjected parental agency) guards over the correspondence between ego and its ideal ego, and harshly punishes every non-correspondence with a sense of guilt. (The installation of such a psychic agency would signify the transition from narcissism to object love, and from magic to religion.[60]) Up to this point, the conclusion that Freud arrived at agrees completely with the one outlined above, supported by Octave Mannoni, regarding superstition and magic: superstition and magic, as contemptible practices considered 'senseless' by their own practitioners, undermine any possible relation to an ideal ego. In superstition and magic, there is no ideal psychic site, which is why there is no proud confessor.[61]

The conclusion that Freud drew from this finding, however, seems questionable: when the ego has only itself as a sexual object, and thus tends towards a massive overestimation of its own power, then, according to Freud, it overestimates its *thoughts*. Narcissistic omnipotence is an omnipotence of thoughts, which constitutes a sort of 'Berkeleyanism' or 'solipsism', as Freud affirms in quoting a formulation by R. R. Marett.[62] The little magician would thus be a philosopher who believes him- or herself to be equipped with an 'intellectus archtetypus' that necessarily evokes a corresponding reality with every thought. There is nothing to limit this power of thought; absent are not only the harsh, observing agencies of the super-ego and ego ideal, but also all types of observing agencies.

Part of this power is yielded only in a later stage, following magic – that is, the omnipotence of thoughts, or intellectual narcissism – in

59   Ibid., p. 89.
60   Ibid., p. 90.
61   Compare Mauss/Hubert 2001, p. 33: 'Nobody can become a magician at will.'
62   Freud, 'Totem and Taboo', p. 90, n. 1.

'sorcery'. Whereas magic is still omnipotent and 'abstains from spirits', sorcery, according to Freud, is 'the art of influencing spirits by treating them in the same way as one would treat men in like circumstances: appeasing them, making amends to them, propitiating them, intimidating them, robbing them of their power, subduing them to one's will – by the same methods that have proved effective with living men.'[63]

Spirits would thus be the first limitation to the omnipotence of thoughts, whether they are assessed as objects or as observing agencies. With spirits, thoughts make the first confrontation with the limits of their power. Freud correspondingly sees the first steps towards the transition to religion – and consequently to the creation of a super-ego or ego ideal – at this moment: 'Whereas magic still reserves omnipotence solely for thoughts, animism hands some of it over to spirits and so prepares the way for the construction of a religion.'[64]

Unlike in earlier texts,[65] Freud now differentiates between the omnipotence of thoughts and animism. He now reserves for magic what he judges as the more primitive omnipotence, and, on the contrary, assigns animism the higher-ranked sorcery. Only primitive magic consists of the omnipotence of thoughts, and consequently, narcissism; there are no limits to fantastical childish power, no foreign powers, and thereby also no observing agencies of any kind that measure the childish being against some sort of ideal – the narcissistic being is its own ideal.[66]

FREUD'S 'ART THEORY' EXPLANATION OF MAGIC

Nonetheless, Freud makes a comment that seems to counter his own proposal of defining magic as the omnipotence of thoughts – and consequently, the absence of all observing agencies. As Freud established, the practice of magic has a materiality. Magicians make

63   Ibid., p. 78
64   Ibid., pp. 91–2.
65   Ibid., pp. 85–6. Freud's indecision with regard to the position of omnipotence of thoughts and animism seems ultimately based in a problem in his definition of narcissism: the assumption that narcissism is a state 'lacking every intersubjective relationship' (Laplanche and Pontalis, *Language of Psychoanalysis*, pp. 255ff). Lacan's theory of the mirror stage contradicts this theory, as does Mannoni's theory of superstition.
66   See Freud, 'On Narcissism', p. 94.

artefacts with meticulous care, which they apparently require in order to practice their 'omnipotence':

> In only a single field of our civilization has the omnipotence of thoughts been retained, and that is in the field of art. Only in art does it still happen that a man who is consumed by desires performs something resembling the accomplishment of those desires and that what he does in play produces emotional effects – thanks to artistic illusion – just as though it were something real. People speak with justice of the 'magic of art' and compare artists to magicians. But the comparison is perhaps more significant than it claims to be. There can be no doubt that art did not begin as art for art's sake. It worked originally in the service of impulses which are for the most part extinct today. And among them we may suspect the presence of many magical purposes.[67]

In this type of art, 'psychic reality' is also taken to be 'factual'; the satisfaction of something similar to reality is experienced as something real that is satisfying. To this extent, an overestimation of thoughts in relation to reality occurs once again. But what is noticeable is that these thoughts cannot remain as thoughts if they are to be confused with reality. Instead, these thoughts require representation. It is not the conceived wishes that are experienced as fulfilled, but those that are produced in forms and materials. Thus, strictly speaking, art as a magical practice does not rest on the principle of the omnipotence of *thoughts*, but instead on the omnipotence of *represented thoughts*. *The magician is an artist rather than a philosopher* – or, to put it in terms of the myth, Pygmalion rather than Narcissus.

It is neither thinking nor wishing magically that change reality; instead, it is the *representation* of thinking or wishing – their expression, their pictorial or scenic formulation. For someone who apparently cannot read thoughts, wishes must thus be clarified. This shows that in magic, too, the so-called 'omnipotence' is already no longer in the hands of the magician; instead, it has been delegated to the naive observer. For that reason, too, it is necessary to speak out loud rather than simply think when performing magic:[68] the thoughts

67   Freud, 'Totem and Taboo', p. 90.
68   See Durkheim, *Elementary Forms*, p. 35: 'The formula to be pronounced.'

and wishes must be portrayed in order for the agency of the naive observer (who judges only on appearances) to perceive them. That which is simply thought or wished for would escape this agency. For that reason, magic requires material production, and cannot rest content with mere philosophical speculation.

But there remains a factor that points beyond the necessity of this depiction. Apparently, it is not only the represented thoughts and wishes that help in achieving their success. Instead, representation also seems to lead to 'success' entirely on its own, even when this success was not a thought or a wish. Mere depiction, by itself, causes the emergence of what is depicted, even without thoughts or wishes behind it. Freud provides evidence of these thoughts in a passage on obsessional neurotics: 'If one of [the neurotic patients] undergoes psycho-analytic treatment, which makes what is unconscious in him conscious, he will be unable to believe that thoughts are free and will constantly be afraid of expressing evil wishes, as though their expression would lead inevitably to their fulfilment.'[69]

Omnipotence is thus not dependent on thoughts or wishes. Instead, it is much more dependent on their *expression* – even if they are not the thoughts and wishes of the one who utters such statements. Instead, it acts in the same way as when guilt is depicted, without its corresponding to the thoughts or intentions of the one doing the depicting: it is as though a naive observer takes the mere depiction as occasion to make a reality of it. The naive observer does not consider the intentions of the actors at all, but instead takes them literally – that is, takes their depictions literally – often against their will. The omnipotence of thoughts is thus defined by a peculiar heteronomy. The (depicted) thoughts are, indeed, potent: they can, for example, kill. But they are not free: they kill not only when the one thinking them wants them to.

Magic does not correspond at all to a narcissistic fantasy of omnipotence. Instead, should a narcissistic ego ever be in possession

---

Compare Mauss/Hubert 2001, p. 29: 'And even if the magician has to work in public, he makes an attempt to dissemble: his gestures become furtive and his words indistinct.' The fact that it must be spoken and acted unclearly has to do with the necessity of the secret, which is founded in the libido economy – as I attempted to show in Chapter 4 – in the moment of contempt. Under these conditions it is even more remarkable that actions are visible and statements audible, instead of remaining as thoughts.

69   Freud, 'Totem and Taboo', p. 87.

of magic, a great share of this ego's power is ceded to someone else. And this someone else is not simply an assistant; he or she also acts against the ego. Not only does what I am thinking or wishing comes true – so does what I depict, regardless of whether I think or wish it. This is caused by an observer who takes the material depiction alone as occasion to become active and create a reality that corresponds with it. Just like the slightly simple fairy in the playful fairytale that Freud quotes about the three wishes and the sausage,[70] the naive observer makes real everything that he perceives as a wish – regardless of whether it was meant or not. In magic there is a 'dumb god', so to speak, who does everything that he thinks people want, becoming a nuisance for people.

As a result, magic is not horrible because it disappoints fantasies of omnipotence. It is not the fact that the presented omnipotence does not exist that is horrid, but, rather, the reverse: the awful thing is that the omnipotence does exist, yet not as the omnipotence of one's own thoughts, but instead as the omnipotence of a foreign, naive observer who fulfils every depicted wish. In magic, the narcissistic ego finds a limit to its own power in a foreign, naive observing agency that lends a meaning to the expressed thoughts that is different from the one intended by the ego.

Thus, the 'castration experience' with regard to magic is found not in the lack of omnipotence of thoughts, nor in magic's ineffectiveness, but, rather, the reverse: in the situation that magic is effective because the naive observer makes the depictions come true. The characteristic attitude of magic thus consists in knowing perfectly well that one cannot help reality through the use of signs, but nonetheless fearing that someone else who does not know that will make the meaning of the signs come true. Those who come into contact with magic also 'know perfectly well' (but still) – like the psychiatric patient in the joke that Žižek uses who knows that he is not a kernel of corn, but nonetheless is still afraid that there might be a chicken who doesn't

---

70   See Freud, 'The Uncanny', p. 246: 'In the story of the "Three Wishes", the woman is tempted by the savoury smell of a sausage to wish that she might have one too, and immediately it lies on the plate before her. In his annoyance at her forwardness her husband wishes it may hang on her nose. And there it is, dangling from her nose.' Finally both agree that the sausages should disappear again, and this third wish also gets fulfilled.

know that.[71] Plenty of people who emphatically claim not to believe in voodoo would nonetheless still refuse to gouge out an eye in a picture of their own mother.[72] All such everyday magicians are, in this sense, 'sorcerer's apprentices', as depicted by Goethe: they conjure up more than they want. Just like the Rat Man, who 'kills' the old spa patient through playful imprecations,[73] they have to say: 'I know perfectly well that it is nonsense, but it still seems to me to be horribly true.'

The 'castrating', disappointing finding with regard to the idea of the omnipotence of thoughts is that one must be careful when choosing signs. The practised, everyday magics of politeness and coerced games prove, through their real effects, that (against Freud's assumption) it is not they, but the idea of the freedom – that is, the ineffectiveness – of the expressed thoughts that represents an illusion, a bit of enduring childish narcissism. The everyday magician who exhibits caution in dealing with signs recognizes a foreign power: the 'enlightened person' who willingly perforates the photo does not.

The negative fetishism, which we can observe in coerced games, as well as the unpleasurable omnipotence appearing in the form of everyday magic – an omnipotence not of thoughts, but of performance – have informed us at the theoretical level about the fact that fetishism and magic cannot be regarded as narcissistic relicts. The illusions of guilt, as well as the possible effects of speaking or representing, are unpleasurable in these cases, and force themselves on the actors against their wills. The actors do not adhere narcissistically (against reality) to attitudes fitting in with their wishes, and neither do they narcissistically consider themselves to be omnipotent. Instead, they have gone through an initial form of castration: they accept not

---

71 See Žižek, *Sublime Object of Ideology*, p. 35.

72 An experiment by Howard Mounce shows that the fear of 'expressing evil desires' is not peculiar to obsessional neurotics: 'He asked his students to imagine that they had pierced the eyes in a drawing of their mothers and that they then discovered that she had gone blind. Would they think themselves responsible?'. Frank Cioffi, *Wittgenstein on Freud and Frazer* (Cambridge: CUP, 1998), p. 169.

73 See Freud, 'Notes upon a Case of Obsessional Neurosis', p. 234. This example formulates a decisive objection to Certeau's theory whereby every belief presents a 'credit', to the extent that those who 'advance' belief must be uncertain whether the others reciprocate their expectations. The exact opposite happens: the Rat Man does not believe, but still fears that the others will act according to the illusion. Unlike with credit, with belief, something still comes back even when absolutely nothing was paid in advance (compare Certeau, 'What We Do When We Believe', pp. 192–3).

only reality, but, beyond that, also unpleasurable attitudes that do not fit in with their wishes, and they rank their better knowledge below the power of the naive observer, who – as the only solipsist on the terrain – shapes the world 'objectively' according to its illusions. Freud's comment that the 'handing over to [the Deity] of bad and socially harmful instincts was the means by which man freed himself from their domination'[74] seems to suggest a delegation of narcissistic omnipotence to the idiot god who functions as the carrier of the illusions of others.

The fact that it is not magic, but the reverse – the fantasy of 'freedom' (that is, the total ineffectiveness) of thoughts and their depictions – that presents a bit of narcissism can also be shown by way of several therapeutic practices – for example, the psychodrama developed by Jacob Levi Moreno in the 1940s. The paradox of the psychodrama consists in the actual solving of real problems through the enactment of situations in play. Playing can change reality. It is not a precise imagining, remembering or thinking that has this ability, but exclusively the depiction mediated via sensual means. It is not 'philosophy' (understood as a mere conceptual confrontation), but once again 'art' – in this case, acting – that solves real problems. This situation alone might seem grievous – for those who have serious problems are bound to assume that these can only be solved through serious confrontations, and it would take great effort to convince them that the apparent frivolity of a game might have any effect in this respect. And if a fiction has already influenced reality, why does one have to take the embarrassing path onto the stage? Can the matter not be overcome with the help of thought? Like politeness, athletics, knitting, or sucking on sweets as techniques for happiness, as suggested by Alain,[75] the therapeutic techniques of dramatic play developed by Moreno must also reckon with the resistance of the patients, for whom such suppositions might seem beneath them.

Yet precisely this resistance to 'ridiculous' happiness techniques also reveals something about the nature of unhappiness. As in the situation described in Pascal's example, one is dealing with 'arrogant' people here for whom, once again, something is beneath them; the patients prove to be narcissistic, their resistance comes from their self-esteem,

---

74   Freud, 'Obsessive Actions', p. 127.
75   See Alain, *On Happiness*, pp. 119, 10, 106.

and what they do not want to cede is ego-libido. Their disregard for the game arises from this narcissism – as does the exaggerated self-esteem with which they confront their own problem. Believing that games can have no effect also means that real problems can be based only on real causes, and thus that illusions cannot be the cause of real problems. Moreno's approach, on the contrary, rests on the principle that the real problems of his patients are due to illusions, and that these problems can therefore be overcome through the medium of illusion.

The typical game-situations of the psychodrama have to do with actions that patients would like to have carried out once in their life, and which they regret never having had the opportunity to do so: telling a horrible stepfather what they think of him for once, or even beating him up; vindicating oneself in front of the entire family for unjust accusations; or finally living out a sexual fantasy.[76] With the help of other actors, such situations are depicted as scenes in psychodrama and worked out with the guidance of a director using various techniques – role-reversal, introduction of a 'double', 'mirroring' through representative games, and so on.[77]

The played-out situations are precious ones for the patients – they are situations that 'would have changed everything', and whose non-appearance in real life seems to make up the entire cause of the misery of this life. In that the psychodrama creates this precious good for the patients at no great expense, it changes their situation permanently – but not because playing out the 'precious' situation is just as effective and valuable as the situation itself, or because the actors have forgotten the difference for a moment. (The psychodrama also operates with the 'sacred seriousness' of play, and not with a profane seriousness caused by confusing the two.) What the psychodrama works out, instead, is that the situation in question has become such a precious thing only through subsequent illusions. In retrospect, it becomes a solution to everything; everything would be different today if one had acted differently back then. In order to maintain this 'omnipotence' of the precious scene, it is, after all, necessary not to allow oneself depictions of anything subsequent to, and including this scene. One does not even have to imagine that, after playing out the scene, unresolved

---

76 On these examples, see Lewis Yablonsky, *Psychodrama: Resolving Emotional Problems Through Role-playing* (New York: Gardner Press, 1981), pp. 95, 24, 60.

77 Ibid., pp. 116ff.

problems still await. Fixating all desire on the precious scene keeps the actors captivated in a 'prior' in which, without realizing it, they feel entirely comfortable. The wish for the situation that will solve everything is, at the same time, the wish that this scene had never to take place. It is only the fact that it did not happen that presents a solution for everything else.[78]

Playing, on the contrary, leads the actors to the scene and beyond. Its 'cathartic' effect resides in the fact that it turns the supposedly valuable element of this scene into an excretion, robs it of its value owing to the illusion, and allows it to be recognized in its utter banality. The 'wish-fulfilment' achieved through the psychodrama helps the actors let go of their wishes, which such games quite plainly show as fulfilled in their pathetic nature.

Epictetus, the stoical philosopher of happiness, proceeded in the first century of our common era in much the same way as Moreno with his psychodramatic productions. As Alain reports, Epictetus also employed scenic measures against 'unfinished actions':

> Epictetus abounds in harsh examples; this helpful friend puts his arm around our shoulders: 'So you're sad', he says, 'because you haven't been accorded the seat you hoped for in the amphitheatre, and which you believe is rightfully yours. Come then, the amphitheatre is now empty; come and touch this wonderful stone; you can even sit down on it.'[79]

Through the dramatic artificial means of acting out a scene, Epictetus helps the ambitious man arrive at his seat of honour, and thereby cathartically reveals to him the inanity of this wish. Thus, even in philosophy, problems were not always solved 'philosophically', in a conceptual confrontation. As a theory of illusions, this was instead a theory that could say precisely when thinking helps and when one has to turn to artful means.

---

78   The desire for the decisive scene is, to this extent, a 'reflexive' desire – a desire for the desire, and a defence against this scene, in the same way that also the continuing adoration of a beloved by the unhappy lover eventually changes into a defence against the beloved and a mere smug pose of the unhappy person. When desire becomes reflexive, this corresponds with a transformation of object-libido into ego-libido. The Romantic poet prefers his attitude to happiness with the beloved.

79   Alain, *On Happiness*, p. 175.

The fact that such play-acting in fact changes something about patients' problems proves that these problems are not the ones that patients think they are: they are not real problems, but instead imagined ones. For that reason, they cannot be solved through reality, but instead require play; the valuable scene is not only wished for, but is also equally feared; its absence is not the problem, but instead a solution for the rest of life; it does not matter whether the scene has really taken place, but only that a naive observer could have seen it; and the entire problem is not serious, but embarrassingly easy to solve.

The actual humiliation can be found in the fact that the problem, as well as its solution, lies in the hands of the naive observer. Seeking a solution in fulfilment through reality, or from inner contemplation, is an additional measure for evading this humiliating insight and avoiding a solution. The 'gain through illness' of this procedure includes the gain of an unhappiness in place of a solution, and combines these two traits into one character. The ego-libidinous, narcissistic gain of an internal character is the adversary of the external solution through play. Not trusting in play means denying the retroactive imaginary processing through which one has made the problem a problem as such, and claiming the problem as well as the corresponding character as reality. For that reason, the idea of play's lack of effectiveness presents a lingering bit of narcissism.

CULTURES OF NAIVE OBSERVERS

Civilizations Without Discontents

We have posited the agency of the naive observer in order to be able to account for the peculiarity of those procedures that rest on the illusion of the other: happiness through the exchange of apparently petty civilities; feelings of guilt that contradict the subject's knowledge (as well as any rational estimation of the real situation); expressions of everyday magic; performances with 'uncanny' successes; artificial production in the form of magic techniques; therapeutic successes through scenic depictions.

The naive observer is an agency, which, as we have seen, regulates and distributes guilt. For that reason, so-called 'uncivilized' societies are in no way unregulated societies subjected to the mere pleasure of narcissistic individuals (as the so-called 'civilized' have liked to assume, and as can be derived from Freud's assignment of animism to the narcissistic phase of sexual development). Instead, as ethnologists have discovered, in the sex life of such societies there are strict, precisely observed rules.[80] There are thus societies in which rules and a sense of guilt exist without their carriers having access to the psychic agency of a super-ego. They are regulated exclusively through the psychic agency of the naive observer. There are, in other words, *cultures without a conscience.*

This discovery seems remarkable to us because it allows a possible historical explanation for the 'discontents in civilization' noticed by Freud. This discontent would, accordingly, not be a universal feature. It would not emerge with every culture as an irksome side-effect. Should this discontent be associated with the heavy damage to the sexual function through culture, as observed by Freud,[81] and if this damage is typical for cultures that rest on the ideological principle of surveillance through the super-ego, then it seems clear that there are also *cultures with 'outer' observing agencies* that are less damaging to the sexual functions, and thereby cause significantly less discontent. Freud 'historicizes' the damage of the sexual function by assigning it to the epoch of the so-called 'civilized people' when he asserts: 'The sexual life of civilized man is notwithstanding severely impaired; it sometimes gives the impression of being in process of involution as a function, just as our teeth and hair seem to be as organs.'[82]

---

80   See Freud, 'Totem and Taboo', p. 2; 'Civilization and Its Discontents', p. 115.

81   Freud's study, 'Civilization and Its Discontents', as is well known, presents a complete change in the basic assumption about the origins of this discontent. Whereas in the first four sections the cultural damage of the sexual function is thematized as a cause, in section five Freud explains that culture demands 'other sacrifices besides that of sexual satisfaction' (p. 108). The culturally promoted renunciation of drives is 'renunciation of aggression' (ibid., p. 129). With this change, as a result, Eros even appears as an ally of culture (ibid., p. 122); the discontent is thus due solely to renunciation of aggression. Nonetheless, aggression also arises through '*prevention of an erotic satisfaction.*' (See ibid., p. 138). Because the super-ego directs all of the failed drive impulses against the ego (ibid., p. 129), *erotic* privation is also satisfied by the super-ego with the aggression of a sense of guilt. (Otherwise, we would expect that, following denied erotic stimulus, the super-ego harasses the ego *erotically* and not *aggressively.*) This renewed 'permeability' between Eros and aggression once again questions the drive-dualism, as well as the assumed alliance of Eros with culture. This alliance would have brought both into conflict with the super-ego. The discontent would then be one simply of the super-ego, and not a cultural discontent.

82   Ibid., p. 105

This remark must now be read together with the other, according to which sexual life in so-called 'savage', 'uncivilized' societies is organized according to strict rules. According to Freud, there are thus societies, or cultures, that function according to strict rules without damaging the sexual function. A remark by Freud about love in classical antiquity can be considered as evidence that this possibility is conceivable:

> The most striking distinction between the erotic life of antiquity and our own no doubt lies in the fact that the ancients laid the stress upon the instinct itself, whereas we emphasize its object. The ancients glorified the instinct and were prepared on its account to honour even an inferior object; while we despise the instinctual activity in itself, and find excuses for it only in the merits of the object.[83]

In the case described by Freud, one is even dealing with a high culture that apparently acts upon sex in a much less damaging way than current (so-called) high cultures. In order to escape the discontent of civilization, it is not necessary to renounce all refinement, as followers of Rousseau and ecological fundamentalists are prone to assume.[84] A different cultural organization of the psychic observing agencies would be fully adequate. Refinement would thereby consist instead in the ability to 'celebrate the drive' (thanks to a different arrangement of observing agencies). And are those cultures that are capable of this not the most deserving of being called cultured, while those that work towards damaging the sexual function are simply barbaric?

Freud's remark on sexual theory poses the question of the historicity of the organizational forms of psychic observing agencies. It thereby simultaneously brings up the issue of the socially dominant form of illusion found in the theory of ideology: in Mannoni's terms, *there are sexualities of faith and sexualities of superstition.* Cultures that work on the idealization of the object in their sexual life are faith cultures and produce faith sexuality. Only a sexual object that possesses virtues one can refer to self-confidently enables a

---

83   Freud, 'Three Essays', p. 149 (footnote added 1910).

84   In contrast, it was more concerned with reversing anti-cultural stimuli that took place in history. Compare Freud, 'Civilization and Its Discontents', p. 87: '[A] factor of this kind hostile to civilization must already have been at work in the victory of Christendom over the heathen religions'.

subject-position of the faith type. With the help of a respectable object, one can gain prestige – which means taking some of the social respect that is accorded to the object for oneself by virtue of having won over the object.

In contrast, cultures that celebrate the drive are cultures of superstition, and produce a superstitious sexuality. They avoid any reference to an ideal ego. One does not attain any prestige through the drive – even when an entire society considers it godly. One is gripped, overtaken by a drive, as by a superstition. It revokes the subjectivity – to the extent that one has any – at least temporarily. With the respectable object (an object that is recognized as subject), one makes oneself a subject. A drive, on the contrary, turns one into an object.

For the theory of ideology, Freud's remark meant no less than the theory that it is possible to have societies whose ideologies (for example, in the area of sexual life) function without the principle of becoming a subject (subjectivization). Apparently, faith ideologies – which form subjects who are compelled to self-control and ascetic deprivation, and grant disguised pleasure premiums in the form of self-esteem for doing so – are not the only possible ideologies for organizing sexual life and creating the ideological cohesion of societies.[85]

Freud's discovery presents a way of conquering those barriers to knowledge noted above with regard to superstition, which I identified as 'perspectival illusions': those regularly appearing deceptions by virtue of which one's own superstition is overlooked and the superstition of others is always grasped as conviction, or faith. Freud considered it likely, in contrast to such illusions, that faith was not the ideological form organizing love life in antiquity. Whether Freud was right in that remark, and thus accurately described love life in antiquity, is consequently not the initial or only question that must be asked with regard to this passage. Epistemologically, Freud's remark must be assessed as a philosophical thesis, and not as a scientific hypothesis destined for a falsifying process.[86] The truth of this statement alone is not decisive; instead, what is important is what it renders thinkable.

---

85   Freud's remark in 'On the Universal Tendency to Debasement' (p. 188) aims in the same direction, when he states: '[T]he ascetic current in Christianity created psychical values for love which pagan antiquity was never able to confer on it'.

86   On this differentiation, see also Louis Althusser, *Philosophy and the Spontaneous Philosophy of the Scientists* (London/New York: Verso, 1990), pp. 104, 86.

With this remark, Freud broke through the barrier to knowledge regarding superstition, and by opposing the *Schein*, or appearance, evoked by this barrier – as well as his own explicit assumptions – he made conceivable a sexuality of avowal, with a contingent, historical nature, as well as a psychic topography decisive for it (including the agency of the super-ego). On the other hand, a theory that pursues the perspectival illusion, beginning with the assumption that every culture is necessarily an avowal culture and every sexuality a sexuality of avowal – and that, accordingly, the ancients' love life must also be interpreted as the product of a culture of avowal – would become trapped by an epistemological barrier. Even if such a theory were perhaps 'factually' correct with regard to antiquity, it would nonetheless be endlessly far from the truth – since it cannot empirically recognize this 'fact', but instead only *assume* it, in accordance with its own conceptual limitations. In Bachelard's words, it would 'always be wrong, even when right'.

These epistemological remarks appear necessary in order to evaluate Jacques Lacan's critique of Freud's passage. In *The Ethics of Psychoanalysis* (which contains, with regard to the Greek choir, crucial observations for the theory of interpassivity, and also that of superstition), Lacan wrote: 'The whole passage flows forth spontaneously in a way that I call excessive. How does Freud know that we emphasize the object whereas the Ancients put the accent on the instinct?'[87] As a result, Lacan asserts – as would Foucault subsequently[88] – that the elevation of the object, as developed in the medieval practice of courtly love, already had precursors in antiquity:

> It is, of course, of great importance that courtly love, the exaltation of woman, a certain Christian style of love that Freud himself discusses, mark a historical change . . . It is nonetheless true, as I will show you, that in certain authors of antiquity – and interestingly enough in Latin rather than Greek literature – one finds some and perhaps all of the elements that characterize a cult of the idealized object, something which was determinative for what can only be called the sublimated elaboration of a certain relationship. Thus, what Freud expresses over-hastily and probably inversely, concerns a kind of

---

87 Lacan, *Ethics of Psychoanalysis*, p. 98.
88 Foucault, *History of Sexuality*, Vol. 1.

degradation which, when one examines it closely, is directed less at love life than at a certain lost cord, a crisis, in relation to the object.[89]

Freud's theory, according to Lacan, presents the relationship 'over-hastily' and 'probably inversely'. Lacan's own theory thus appears to permit two different conclusions: first, Freud was incorrect histori-cally, and the development went in the other direction. In this case, Freud's theory would be a projection of the relations of the early twen-tieth century onto classical antiquity – of an idealization of the object that is in the process of dissolving. The 'lady of the night', for example, which Freud declared a 'special type of choice of Object made by men',[90] would be more characteristic of the men of the post-Victorian modern era than of the ancient heterosexual Greeks or Romans.

Another possibility is that Freud's error was that he understood something structural as something historical – for example, the ideal present in every wish as an earlier, different variant of this wish. Lacan underpins this interpretation by suggesting that 'the nostalgia expressed in the idea that the Ancients were closer than we are to the instinct' was perhaps no different to 'every dream of a Golden Age or El Dorado'.[91]

In short, the difference claimed by Freud never existed. His clever thoughts were no more than a beautiful dream. Does this Freudian thought itself not bear traces of the wish, per se – the sign of the illu-sion, in Freud's sense?[92] Would it not be necessary to encounter the perspective opened up by Freud's theory – 'Previously sexuality was based on superstition, not on faith' – with reservations similar to those that Mannoni raised in relation to the statement: 'Before, people believed in masks'?

Precisely through this comparison, the difference between Freud's theory and the assumption of a naive belief in masks becomes clear. The assumption of an epoch in which there was naive belief in masks is a product of the perspectival illusion. It views the superstition of the ancestors as their conviction; it thus turns an illusion without owners into an illusion with avowing owners. Freud's theory, on the contrary,

89   Lacan, *Ethics of Psychoanalysis*, p. 99.
90   Sigmund Freud, *A Special Type of Choice of Object Made by Men*, Standard Edition, vol. 11, pp. 163–75.
91   Ibid., p. 99.
92   See Freud, 'Future of an Illusion', pp. 30–1.

does no such thing. His assumption of a differently formed sexuality of antiquity does not imply that the ancient Greeks have a naive, boundless relationship to sexuality. Instead, he credits them with a sexuality that was superstitious (in Mannoni's sense). The term 'closer', which Lacan brings into play (with regard to the instinct) is therefore deceptive. The form that Freud conceived for antiquity is, instead, of the type, 'I know perfectly well, but still', in the sense of 'I know that it is foolish, but what am I supposed to do in the face of a godly instinct?' The type of sexuality that he confers on the love life of the ancients is precisely this distanced dependency on the 'godly instinct', suspended through better knowledge.

In contrast, the assumption that there was a naive belief in masks in earlier epochs denies these epochs all possibility of such a divided, distanced position to their illusion – whereas Freud admits that the ancient Greeks had such a position with regard to their sex lives. Freud's theory makes it possible to think of Greek antiquity as enjoying a relationship to sexuality that is just as animated as that to their gods; yet it does not insinuate that the Greeks have any closeness – either to their instincts or to their religion. It does not imply that the Greeks believed naively in their mythology, or that they followed their instincts directly.

A remark by Nietzsche about ancient theology and the corresponding organization of guilty feelings can be read as a metapsychological explanation for the Freudian diagnosis of an untroubled, blissful love life in the ancient world: 'For the longest period of their history, the Greeks used their gods for no other purpose than to keep "bad conscience" at bay, to be able to enjoy the freedom of their soul: thus, in a sense diametrically opposed to that in which Christianity has made use of its God.'[93] This theology does not cause or even enable people to make any type of guilty self-reproach. What people reproach themselves for in ancient Greece is, mostly,

> 'foolishness', 'lack of judgement', a little 'rush of blood to the head' – the Greeks of the strongest, boldest period have themselves *admitted* as much as the reason for a great deal of what is bad and disastrous – foolishness, *not* sin! . . . But even this rush of blood to the head

---

93 Friedrich Nietzsche, *On the Genealogy of Morals*, Oxford World's Classics, trans. Douglas Smith (New York: OUP, 1998), p. 74.

posed a problem – 'Yes, how is it possible? what might actually cause it in the case of heads such as *ours*, as men of noble origin, of good fortune, we men of good constitution, of the best society, of nobility, of virtue?' For centuries the refined Greek asked himself such questions when confronted with an incomprehensible atrocity and wanton crime with which one of his own had tainted himself. 'A *god* must have beguiled him', he said to himself finally, shaking his head . . . This expedient is *typical* of the Greeks . . . thus the gods at that time served to justify man even to a certain extent in wicked actions, they served as the cause of evil – at that time they did not take upon themselves the execution of punishment, but rather, as is *nobler*, the guilt . . .[94]

Greek theology thus had the function of fundamentally relieving people of their guilt and, to the extent that there is any guilt at all, placing it with the gods. This type of ideology seems necessarily to presuppose a certain psychic topos among its adherents – namely, one that functions without a super-ego. From this, it follows that this ideology cannot exist in the form of a conviction. It is thus practised without reference to an ideal ego. A theology in which the gods are guilty exists in the form of superstition.

Also arising from these ideological and theoretical parameters are the basic contours of a corresponding sexual system. Because guilt was with the gods, because people did not have to become subjects with a conscience capable of guilt, they also did not have to develop a sexuality with a form burdened by conviction or avowal that could only operate with idealized objects. In terms of form, their sexual life could remain just as superstitious as their system of guilt and their gods – something that in German one would call a 'Heidenspaß' (a 'hell of a blast'; literally, a heathens' fun).

The principle of blaming the gods protected people from forming an agency, which (like the super-ego) punishes precisely the renunciation of drives with a sense of guilt. It also protected them from the power of this paradoxical logic, which certainly must be considered the central element of civilization's discontent. After all, the constraint on sexuality commanded by culture is not the sole factor causing the discontent that characteristically appears only in very specific cultures.

---

94 Ibid.

The crucial factor is the feelings of guilt fabricated by the super-ego from the renunciation of drives.[95] Damage to the sexual function, which likewise appears only in certain cultures, does not necessarily result from the sexual constraint present (in one or another form) in all cultures. Instead, sexuality is only damaged in cultures where a super-ego is installed and where, accordingly, both acting on and renouncing drives have unpleasurable results for practitioners. It is not the strictness of the laws, but the way that their psychic representation works that is crucial under 'compulsory sexual morals'. Only avowal sexualities necessarily damage the sexual function; superstitious sexualities, on the contrary – as strict as their rules of procedure may be – do not do so with the same necessity.

The Naive Observer, Taboo Society, and the Field of Immanences

Freud's study 'Totem and Taboo' shows that the illusions of the other – that is, illusions without owners – can present the sole regulative principle for entire cultures. Superstition does not necessarily require a 'superstructure' through the form of avowal, and the agency of the naive observer need not be overruled by conscience or a super-ego. Regardless of how clever or misdirected Freud's theories might be in this text,[96] commentators have hardly noticed that, in it, Freud describes a society that is ideologically regulated exclusively through the form of illusions without owners. The guilt system of these societies, as described by Freud, rests solely on the agency of the naive observer. All transgressions and penalties within such societies depend entirely on the perspective that the naive observer has of things.[97] No

---

95   See Freud, 'Civilization and Its Discontents', p. 134, where Freud identifies the 'sense of guilt' as 'the most important problem in the development of civilization' and notes 'that the price we pay for our advance in civilization is a loss of happiness through the heightening of the sense of guilt'. See also Hans Peter Duerr, Der Mythos vom Zivilisationsprozeß 3: Obszönität und Gewalt, 3rd ed, (Frankfurt: Suhrkamp, 2000), p. 14.

96   A summary of the various anthropological, biological, and also psychoanalytic points of critique regarding this text is given by Peter Gay, Freud: A Life for Our Time (New York: W.W. Norton & Co., 1998 [1988]), pp. 324–34.

97   In this point, taboo society's observational system can be distinguished from the so-called 'village eye' which, as Duerr, Der Mythos vom Zivilisationsprozeß 3, p. 28, has correctly noted, is much closer to that of an omniscient, godly view or the super-ego.

calculations are made about the intentions of the protagonists, and there are no evil deeds – only bad ones.

Making use of Gilles Deleuze's suggested differentiation between 'ethics' and 'morality',[98] one can identify taboo societies as *ethical* societies. At the same time, one could also clarify Deleuze's determination of 'ethical' through two decisive points. First, the 'ethical' is in no way merely a principle of a quasi-narcissistic 'self-preoccupation', in Foucault's sense, but rather a social principle, and can even represent the sole ideological organizing principle of entire societies. Second, through the example of taboo societies, it is possible to interpret in a new light what constitutes 'ethics' – along with the entire area that Deleuze categorizes as the philosophy of immanence. This will be explained in the following. So, what is included in the area of immanence?

First of all, Deleuze separates ethics from morals by differentiating between the conceptual systems of the two orders:

> In this way, Ethics, which is to say, a typology of immanent modes of existence, replaces Morality, which always refers existence to transcendent values. Morality is the judgement of God, the *system of Judgement*. But Ethics overthrows the system of judgement. The opposition of values (Good–Evil) is supplanted by the qualitative difference of modes of existence (good–bad).[99]

Thus, morality, as a theory of *intentions*, is distinguished from ethics, as a theory that deals only with their *effects*. Morality, ignorant of causal laws, creates a theory of what should be. This is opposed to ethics, which is exclusively a theory of what is. Deleuze accordingly reinterprets the biblical 'original scene' as follows: 'It is clear that we have only to misunderstand a law for it to appear to us in the form of a moral "You must." . . . Adam does not understand the rule of the relation of his body with the fruit, so he interprets God's word as a prohibition.'[100]

Eating the apple would not be evil, but simply bad. It would not be a deed indicating reprehensible intentions, but simply one that has bad effects – for example, because the apple is poisoned: 'But because

---

98   See Deleuze, *Spinoza*, pp. 17ff.
99   Ibid., p. 23
100   Ibid.

Adam is ignorant of causes, he thinks that God morally forbids him something, whereas God only reveals the natural consequence of ingesting the fruit.'[101]

Everything that is perceived as evil is, in truth, an 'unfortunate encounter', such as the poisoning.[102] The difference between the domains of morality and ethics, the fields of transcendence and immanence, would thus be one between the 'moral laws of institutions' and the 'eternal truths of nature'[103] – as between, for example, jurisprudence, operating with the concept of 'guilt', and medicine, operating with the concept of 'undesirable effects'.

Yet, according to Freud's 'Totem and Taboo', it is possible to grasp a piece of ethical advice – not to eat a certain apple because of its damaging effects, for example – in a way that does not refer to the difference between jurisprudence and the natural sciences. The terms 'ethics' and 'plane of immanence' are thereby given a new, additional facet. Taboo societies also have dietary rules, similar to those of medicine. Freud writes: 'We have trustworthy stories of how any unwitting violation of one of these prohibitions is in fact automatically punished. An innocent wrong-doer, who may, for instance, have eaten a forbidden animal, falls into a deep depression, anticipates death and then dies in real earnest.'[104]

As it appears, the taboo system satisfies all criteria that Deleuze classifies as belonging on the side of ethics in his differentiation: forbidden food apparently has a poisonous effect. The taboo has effects (after eating, one dies), and it operates without considering intentions (even the innocent, unknowing wrongdoer dies).

Protective measures that have evolved under taboo systems resemble those of medical hygiene down to the smallest details: for example, one should not have sexual intercourse with a certain person or eat from their dishes.[105] Nonetheless, there is a decisive difference

---

101   Ibid., p. 22
102   Ibid. With this choice of terms, Deleuze appears to be referring to the theory developed from the later Althusser of a 'matérialisme de la rencontre'. On this, see Louis Althusser, *Écrits philosophiques et politiques, Tome I* (Paris: Stock/Imec, 1994), translated into English as *Philosophy of the Encounter: Later Writings, 1978–1987* (London/New York: Verso, 2006), pp. 539–80.
103   See Deleuze, *Spinoza*, p. 24.
104   Freud, 'Totem and Taboo', p. 21.
105   Ibid., pp. 39, 53. Compare also the 'délire de toucher', ibid., p. 27.

in the reasoning: one does not refrain from these things because the person concerned is ill, for example, but because they have killed someone or are a relative of someone who has died. The 'hygienic' measure is not based on a chemically traceable substance, but on the other person's history up to that point.

Nonetheless, there is a key difference between the way that taboos work and the way that the laws of chemistry work. The 'innocent wrongdoer' dies from eating the forbidden animal only when he or she becomes aware that what was eaten was the forbidden animal. Whereas only those who violate a taboo, and know that they have done so, die, poisoned persons always sustain injury, regardless of whether they know that they have ingested poison or not. People struck by a bullet shot from a great distance fall down dead regardless of whether they realize that someone has shot at them, whereas those who are bewitched from a great distance die only if they know that a spell has been cast against them. Yet the effects of magic can also surface when someone simply *believes* that they have been bewitched.[106]

Thus, there is a subjective side to taboos, in contrast to natural laws. Both deal only with effects and not intentions. In contrast to the operations of religion, however, the effects of taboos depend on the actor's knowledge rather than on their avowal or intentions. The subjectivity that is active in taboo society and in magical practices is one of knowledge, and not one of enjoying one's own convictions and ability to act. Knowing (or at least believing) that a taboo has been broken, or that magic has occurred, triggers the effects that are expected to result from a certain pattern.[107]

But a second condition seems necessary, in addition to knowing that magic has taken place – namely, knowing that magic is 'nonsense'. Without this moment of contempt, magic would lose its power. An

---

106   See also the comical episode in the essay by Montaigne where a nobleman who believes that he has been bewitched (with an impotence spell) is healed by the magical means of a philosopher who doesn't even believe in magic. Michel de Montaigne, *The Essays of Michel de Montaigne* (London: Allen Lane, 1991), pp. 112, 114.

107   Every type of magic in which someone incurs actual injury must therefore be understood as a magic of the victim and not of the perpetrator. Compare Alain, *On Happiness*, p. 31: 'All of these absurd ideas, even if I don't believe them, take hold deep inside of me . . . For can we not find in the history of any people that there were men who died because they believed themselves cursed? Can we not find that hexes worked very well, as long as the interested party knew about them?'

avowed, professed 'faith' in magic would destroy the magic. It can function only through the knowledge that it is 'simply' a symbolic practice.[108] Better and distanced knowledge underpins magic's power, while naive, immediate avowal destroys it. Transforming distanced knowledge that intensifies the spell into an affirmative attitude able to dissolve it would thus offer a general formula for escaping from magic and compulsion. This approach, which operates ostensibly to the advantage of what is being fought against, seems to form the principle for the technique of so-called 'paradoxical intervention'.[109]

In a theory that judges effects only, and not intentions, not only the effects caused by chemical processes but also those caused by symbolic practices must therefore be included. The object of 'ethics' includes not only a natural-scientific causality, but also symbolic causality. The 'plane of immanence' includes formal, symbolic 'super-ficialities', such as politeness. It is crucial to establish this, because it provides the only possible way to clarify that ethics is more than the sum of the medical or bio-environmentally required preventative measures (which would never be sufficient to hold a society together). Instead, ethics is also the ideological organizing principle of societies that rest on the principle of the naive observer – of societies, that is, that have rules but manage without the principle of avowal and 'subjectivization'. These societies spare themselves the effort of install-ing a psychic representation of their rules in the form of a super-ego that transforms pleasure into manifest displeasure and generates discontent by accumulating ego-libido and feelings of guilt. The immanence plane is a plane of superstition, in Mannoni's sense.

In addition to Freud's description in 'Totem and Taboo', there is a second, more recent draft of such a society: Roland Barthes's depic-tion of Japanese culture in his book *Empire of Signs*. This draft, too, is conceived as a theoretical fiction, like Freud's. Barthes remarks at the beginning: 'I can ... though in no way claiming to represent or to analyze reality itself ... isolate somewhere in the world (*faraway*) a

---

108   The characterization of magic as 'mere' symbolic practice is expressed by practitioners in the use of expressions such as 'it can't hurt to try'.

109   See A. Brandl-Nebehay, B. Rauscher-Gföhler, and J. Kleibel-Arbeithuber, eds, *Systemische Familientherapie. Grundlagen, Methoden und aktuelle Trends* (Vienna: Facultas-Universitäts-Verlag, 1998), pp. 214–20; Camillo Loriedo and Gaspare Vella, *Paradox in the Family System*, trans. Maryanne Olsen (New York: Brunner/Mazel, 1992), pp. 118ff.

certain number of features (a term employed in linguistics), and out of these features deliberately form a system. It is this system which I shall call: Japan.'[110]

One of the features that Barthes emphasizes, which he uses to support his resulting 'deliberate' system-construction, is the peculiarity of Japanese culture with regard to its view of politeness. As Barthes remarks, it differs greatly from the Western position. In Western cultures, Barthes notices a typical reservation with regard to politeness:

> Why, in the West, is politeness regarded with suspicion? Why does courtesy pass for a distance (if not an evasion, in fact) or a hypocrisy? Why is an 'informal' relation (as we so greedily say) more desirable than a coded one?
>
> Occidental impoliteness is based on a certain mythology of the 'person.' Topologically, Western man is reputed to be double, composed of a social, factitious, false 'outside' and of a personal, authentic 'inside' (the site of divine communication). According to this schema, the human 'person' is that site filled by nature (or by divinity, or by guilt), girdled, closed by a social envelope . . . However, as soon as the 'inside' of the person is judged respectable, it is logical to recognize this person more suitably by denying all interest to his worldly envelope: . . . to be impolite is to be true – so speaks (logically enough) our Western morality; . . . but my own person . . . can gain recognition only by rejecting all mediation of the factitious and by affirming the integrity . . . of its 'inside' . . . how simple I am, how affable I am, how frank I am, how much I am *someone* is what Occidental impoliteness says.[111]

Just as I attempted at the beginning of this chapter to show the Enlightenment positions on politeness, Barthes also makes recognizable the hostility against form (*Formfeindlichkeit*) and the motives behind the currently dominant Western concept of politeness. Once again – evoking Freud's depiction of internalization movements in religious history that tend to abolish ritual forms – it becomes clear that the very accumulation of ego-libido on which the cult of one's

---

110   Barthes, *Empire of Signs*, p. 3.
111   Ibid., pp. 63–4.

own person and the desire 'to be someone' are based, destroys the pleasure in forms, and in the end belittles them as mere superficialities.

In opposition to this Western dualistic position, which dismisses the conception of politeness as merely exterior and, on the contrary, wants to claim an integrity of the person that is entirely independent of this exterior, Barthes sets out the Japanese tradition:

> The other politeness, by the scrupulosity of its codes, the distinct graphism of its gestures, and even when it seems to us exaggeratedly respectful . . . because we read it, in our manner, according to a metaphysics of the person – this politeness is a certain exercise of the void (as we might expect within a strong code but one signifying 'nothing') . . . The salutation here can be withdrawn from any humiliation or any vanity, because it literally salutes no one; it is not the sign of a communication – closely watched, condescending and precautionary – between two autarchies, two personal empires (each ruling over its Ego, the little realm of which it holds the 'key'); it is only the feature of a network of forms in which nothing is halted, knotted, profound. *Who is saluting whom?* Only such a question justifies the salutation, inclines it to the bow . . . and gives to a posture which we read as excessive the very reserve of a gesture from which any signified is inconceivably absent. *The Form is Empty*, says – and repeats – a Buddhist aphorism. This is what is expressed through a practice of forms . . . by the politeness of the salutation, the bowing of two bodies which inscribe but do not prostrate themselves.[112]

Whether Barthes's 'system' accurately describes Japanese reality seems to us just as irrelevant as it does to him. What is interesting, however, is that this system is in no way, as Barthes says formed 'deliberately'. Naturally, there is a theoretical predilection – namely, the classical, structuralist position that traces back all apparent sense to the systematic operations of a senseless form.[113] 'Japan' is thus a different name for the pure 'structure', in a structuralist sense.

In Barthes's interpretation, however, this predilection for the

112 Ibid., pp. 68–70.
113 See Ferdinand de Saussure, *Course in General Linguistics* (Peru, IL: Open Court, 1986), pp. 110–11.

senseless mechanisms that regulate the materialization of sense leads to a strange consequence directed against 'deliberateness'. The basic structuralist assumptions not only claim that all sense is due to a senseless mechanism, but also that this is something that must necessarily go unrecognized. Every structure is able to maintain its sovereignty by means of subjects that erroneously consider themselves, and their own intentions, as the origin of sense, rather than recognizing that they are, on the contrary, 'dictated' by the structure. The 'de-centring'[114] of subjects, conditioned by the structure, is thereby a 'de-centring' only when it is erroneously experienced as centring. This means that the failure to see the truth is part of the truth – an imaginary subject is part of the symbolic structure.[115]

For this reason, the conclusions reached by Barthes seem paradoxical and contradictory to his own inclination. For his 'Japan' seems to exist without such an agency of misrecognition. There seems to be only the structure, and no misjudging subjects; signifiers, but no signified.[116] The decentring seems to be obvious without anyone having to maintain the illusion of a centring in opposition to this truth. In contrast, the 'Japanese', as structuralists *avant la lettre*, are apparently even capable of drawing a slight sigh of relief from their decentring – as Barthes's quoted formula of the emptiness of form suggests. The key question with regard to Barthes's text is thus not

---

114   See Barthes's analysis of 'de-centred food', in his *Empire of Signs*, pp. 19ff.

115   See also Jacques-Alain Miller, 'Action de la structure', in *Cahiers pour l'analyse* 9 (1968), p. 95.

116   The idea that the signified could be categorized as part of the Imaginary is an achievement of late Structuralism gained from the theory of Jacques Lacan (see Evans, *Introductory Dictionary of Lacanian Psychoanalysis*, pp. 186–7). For Saussure, on the contrary, the signifier and signified together shaped the 'form' (Saussure, *Course in General Linguistics*, pp. 110ff). The concept of a 'signifier without signified' makes no sense according to Saussure's account, since they can only constitute one another mutually. Although Lacan is correct in pointing out that the understanding of sense contains an imaginary dimension that generates self-assurance and a subject-effect, Saussure's insistence on the non-imaginary, symbolic nature of the signified, which contains a certain realization, is in danger of being lost with Lacan. The signified is, according to Saussure, precisely that which someone who understands a language gains from a signifier when proceeding according to the rules of a language. The signified is thereby not sense: I am able to understand what a word (such as 'interpassivity') is meant to mean, without being able to make sense of it. Spinoza's theory, too, aims at this differentiation, stating that one can have a clear idea of God but not a mental image of him. See Spinoza, 60th letter, in *On the Improvement of the Understanding*, p. 387.

whether Japan is actually the way that Barthes describes it, but whether, based on Barthes's own assumptions, a society *can* even possibly exist that is furnished in the way that he describes.[117]

Even with the objection that the structure 'Japan' finds its misjudging subject precisely in Western culture, this still does not explain why this structure can exist so independently of its subject, or why one can view it entirely in itself, without the necessary refraction of the structurally dictated misjudgement. In Barthes's system, 'Japan' appears as the place where an essence reveals itself as such, free from any distortions caused by its appearance; as the moment when the essence appears, as it were, through open sky, 'à ciel ouvert'; as that moment in which the 'lonely hour of last instance' has suddenly come, against all expectations.

As a result, the solution to this paradoxical problem can only be found in the fact that 'Japan' does not stand next to the 'West' like an 'essence' suddenly surfacing next to its 'appearance', an 'object of cognition' next to its 'real object', or the knowledge of something as a second thing next to it. 'Japan' cannot be that truth the misjudgement of which constitutes Western culture.

Instead, in Barthes's understanding, 'Japan' must identify a different type of ideological formation – another form of organizing social illusion. 'Japan' is thus not the 'truth' of a Western ideology, but instead is itself a form of ideology – although another form, as it were. Barthes himself seems to articulate this conclusion: 'Our ways of speaking are very vicious, for if I say that in that country politeness is a religion, I let it be understood that there is something sacred in it; the expression should be canted so as to suggest that religion there is merely a politeness, or better still, that religion has been replaced by politeness.'[118]

Not only politeness, but also religion can exist in the form of politeness, because in some cultures there is no other ideological form than belief – the ideological form that is so clearly recognizable in

---

117 A question that is similar to the one in reference to 'Japan' by Barthes is posed in relation to the 'Schizo' by Deleuze and Guattari. This also presents a subject without *Subjektwerdung* ('subjectivization') – something decentred without an imaginary centring. See Deleuze and Guattari, *Anti-Oedipus*, pp. 19–20, 349ff. For that reason, here, too, the key problem is not whether schizophrenics are actually like that, but whether – based on the assumptions of the theory – anything at all can exist that is like that.

118 Barthes, *Empire of Signs*, p. 68.

politeness. Religion, too, can take on this form; it would then be no more than a pleasurable formality and 'mere superficiality', without any subjectivization (the main point that I attempted to emphasize in relation to Blaise Pascal and Alain). This theory refers to religions that take the form of ethics, a happiness technique, rather than of morality. Barthes, a structuralist, not only discovered the structural truth behind the form of its necessary misjudgement, but also the possibility of an ideology furnished 'structuralistically' – and of societies that are organized solely through this form of ideology.

Freud's and Barthes's theories have the merit of recognizing the possibility that there are societies organized according to such ideological principles – that is, societies in which the only form of illusion that exists is that of the illusion without owners. This realization is complicated by the fact that this form of illusion generally remains invisible due to a 'perspectival illusion' (see Chapter 2): we do not acknowledge the illusions without owners in our own culture, and consider the illusions without owners in other people's cultures to be those people's own illusions. It is therefore necessary to pay tribute to Freud and Barthes for having recognized the illusion of the other as an effective principle, although confronted with its invisibility, and even to have conceived of societies in which such illusions present the sole ideological principle. They have thereby made it possible to imagine societies that do not underestimate the principle of cultural pleasure, of illusions without owners – unlike current European and North American societies. The massive loss of pleasurable experiences that can be observed in our societies – the lost ludic element in culture noticed by Huizinga, and the massive, culturally conditioned damage to the sexual function noticed by Freud, Reich and Foucault – can consequently appear as avoidable. A culture that is capable of recognizing the form in which its illusions exist, eliminating the need to misjudge the principle of their lust, would also be capable of experiencing its pleasure in ways other than neurotic ones – that is, other than in the form of displeasure. In addition, Barthes's example of Japan, and Nietzsche's and Freud's of ancient Greece, have the advantage of showing that those societies capable of pleasure are not necessarily 'uncivilized', or barbaric – on the contrary, our society, incapable of pleasure, seems quite barbaric in comparison with high cultures that are structured so vastly differently from our own. But the economic conditions that have to exist in order to avoid our all-too-familiar barbarianism, and make conceivable (and, in the long term, even real) other relations, is naturally another question altogether – one that cannot even be touched upon in this context.

Nonetheless, I am confident that further clarification of the discoveries cited here is a useful goal in the various battles raging over the dominant form of social illusion. Breaking the hegemony of avowals would, in effect, topple key ideological pillars of today's seemingly omnipotent neoliberal politics.

Index